Standing on the Shoulders of Giants:

A History of Rugby League in Huddersfield

by
David Gronow
Brian Heywood
Daniel Sheard
Stuart Sheard
David Smith
Rob Smithson
Howard Taylor
David Thorpe

Edited
by
Brian Heywood, Stuart Sheard, David Smith and David Thorpe

Upper Calder Valley Publications
in association with
Huddersfield Rugby League: A Lasting Legacy

THE BIRTHPLACE OF RUGBY LEAGUE

HUDDERSFIELD
RUGBY LEAGUE

A LASTING LEGACY
PRESERVING OUR HERITAGE
FOR THE FUTURE

www.huddersfieldrlheritage.co.uk

First published in 2015
by
Upper Calder Valley Publications
in association with
Huddersfield Rugby League: A Lasting Legacy

ISBN 978/0/9547146/8/0

Printed by
The Amadeus Press, Cleckheaton BD19 4TQ

For Nancy, Keith and David,
esteemed friends and colleagues

This book is dedicated to the memory of three bastions of rugby league in Huddersfield, Nancy Beaumont, Keith Burhouse and David Gronow, all of whom passed away whilst this book was being written. Keith and David died in office as volunteers on the steering group of the *Huddersfield Rugby League: A Lasting Legacy* heritage project, to which they contributed invaluably. Nancy, who was unfailingly helpful to the heritage project, died in office as secretary of and driving force behind the Senior Giants Supporters' Association. More widely, all three have left their own lasting legacies to the health and heritage of rugby league in Huddersfield, and to the game of rugby league.

Keith Burhouse first watched the Huddersfield rugby league club in the 1940s and became a lifelong supporter. In the early 1980s, when the club was struggling to survive, it asked for volunteers to help. The only reply came from Keith. Several times during the next troubled decade, the efforts, skills, resilience and tenacity of Keith and his family stood between the club and extinction.

When better times returned to the club, Keith continued to work behind the scenes as associate director. He also shared with his good friend Sam Morton, duties as volunteer curator of the Rugby League Heritage Centre at Huddersfield's George Hotel, the birthplace of the game. Sadly, the hotel owners went into administration in 2013 and the Heritage Centre had to close. Keith's final contribution to the game was the immense task of moving and temporarily re-housing the many valuable artefacts at The John Smith's Stadium. The collection has subsequently been purchased by the Rugby Football League and is accessible in their Archive at the University of Huddersfield, and in travelling exhibitions.

Later in 2013, the leukaemia from which Keith had recovered in 2008 returned. He fought it with typical quiet courage, but passed away in March 2014, aged 68. A month before he died, Keith was inducted into the Rugby League 'Roll of Honour'. In May 2014 the *Huddersfield Examiner* presented a posthumous 'Special Recognition Community Award' to Keith's wife Carol and his son Martin. These awards are due recognition for this remarkable, kind, modest and unassuming man, who committed himself to the club and the game he loved, and expected and received little in return.

David Gronow was a popular and familiar figure in Huddersfield sporting circles. He was a keen, competitive and astute amateur cricketer for Rastrick, Armitage Bridge and Golcar, and he had rugby league in his blood. Several of David's older relatives played for Huddersfield, most notably his grandfather, Ben Gronow, a Great Britain international forward in Huddersfield's 1914-15 Team of all Talents. David was, for fifteen years, secretary of the Huddersfield RLFC's thriving Players' Association.

Steeped in local rugby league, David meticulously researched and collected an unsurpassed body of information and images, becoming the acknowledged expert about the histories of the Huddersfield club and the local amateur game. Along with his good friend and colleague on the steering group of *Huddersfield Rugby League: A Lasting Legacy*, David Thorpe, he also catalogued thousands of items in the RFL Archive.

David's research has yielded three books about the Huddersfield club, most recently a tribute to the golden years that followed World War II, *Three Fartown Aussies: Hunter, Cooper, Devery*, published in 2012. He has also written many articles for the *Huddersfield Examiner* and, at the time of his death, was still contributing the historical feature to each of the Huddersfield Giants' match day programmes, as he had for many years.

In August 2014, David was watching a Yorkshire county cricket match at Headingley when he died suddenly of a heart attack. He was 70 years old. Among his ongoing projects, he was writing the majority of the chapters for this book. He had already written or contributed significantly to eleven of these. The honour of completing the rest on his behalf has only been possible because of the notes that he had already supplied. In addition, the majority of the images in this book were provided from his collection.

Nancy Beaumont was hooked on rugby league from her first trip to Fartown in 1948. She was co-opted onto the committee of the Huddersfield Supporters' Club in 1954, becoming the first woman appointed to the committee of a professional rugby league club. She became the Supporters' Club treasurer in 1961 and its President in 1967, the first lady President of any rugby league organisation. Among her many duties, she helped to serve refreshments from their Fartown tea hut, organised coaches to away matches, organised player testimonials and, for 26 years, ran the club's lottery, which at its height sold 20,000 tickets per week.

In 1996 Nancy founded the Senior Giants Supporters' Association. Their monthly meetings continue to attract high-quality speakers and 70 to 80 members. In May 2013 Nancy was awarded the club's ultimate honour of life-membership.

In the preparation of this book, Nancy helped to arrange numerous interviews with long-standing supporters and related many of her own memories, several of which are included. Nancy passed away, aged 84, in April 2015, a month before this book was published.

Left to right: David Gronow, Nancy Beaumont and Keith Burhouse

The contributions of Nancy Beaumont, Keith Burhouse and David Gronow to rugby league in Huddersfield are unsurpassed. The hundreds who attended their respective funerals are testimony to the affection and esteem in which they are held, and to the impact their lives had on Huddersfield's sporting community. Those of us following in their footsteps are truly 'standing on the shoulders of giants'.

THE BIRTHPLACE OF RUGBY LEAGUE

HUDDERSFIELD
RUGBY LEAGUE

A LASTING LEGACY
PRESERVING OUR HERITAGE
FOR THE FUTURE

Standing on the Shoulders of Giants:
A History of Rugby League in Huddersfield

Contents

Acknowledgements

Introduction

Acknowledgements

Heritage Lottery Fund Grant

Standing on the Shoulders of Giants: A History of Rugby League in Huddersfield originated from an application to the Heritage Lottery Fund (HLF) to finance the project Huddersfield Rugby League: A Lasting Legacy (HRL: ALL). This project was the brainchild of **Laura Hanson**, then head of Huddersfield Giants in the Community, and of **Dr Rob Light**, the project's first manager. We, the authors, are grateful to them for their ideas.

We express our gratitude to the **HLF** for its support in funding the project, including this book.

HRL: ALL would like to thank those who supported their application in 2012 for the grant that made the project and this book possible: **Professor Tony Collins**, Director, International Centre for Sports History and Culture, De Montfort University, Leicester; **Ken Davy**, Chairman, Huddersfield Giants RLFC; **John R Rawlinson**, Chairman, Huddersfield Local History Society; **Dr Robert Ellis**, Senior Lecturer, Division of History, University of Huddersfield; **Janet Pearson**, Area Manager, Kirklees Culture and Leisure Services; and **Julie Swift**, Junior Club Secretary, St Joseph's Sharks ARLFC.

Larchwood Homes Sponsorship

HRL: ALL would like to thank **Larchwood Homes** for their sponsorship of HRL: ALL, which has enhanced the quality of the project and of this publication.

Advice and Guidance

The authors are privileged to have had the assistance of many individuals who have given their time to share their memories, memorabilia and permitted the use of their photographs. We thank them all, and are particularly grateful to:

James Brammer, Marketing and Media Manager of the Huddersfeld Giants RLFC, who supplied and permitted the use of images

David Calverley, who is responsible for taking many of the modern photographs

Professor Tony Collins, for his advice about the history of the game, and for his support in delivering two lectures about the birth of rugby league and the achievements of Harold Wagstaff

David Thorpe, who allowed the use of his extensive memorabilia collection, and for sharing his expertise about the club's history and of the RFL Archive, where he has contributed many voluntary hours

David Smith and Graham Sykes, who conducted numerous interviews

Freda and Malcolm Heywood, Upper Calder Valley Publications, for their technical advice

Journalists at the *Huddersfield Examiner*, who have been consistently supportive in publicising stories

Staff at the University of Huddersfield, who look after the RFL Archive and have been consistently helpful in allowing access to and locating research materials, and in offering advice

Jane Chesworth, BBC Radio Leeds, for assistance in publicising the achievements of Harold Wagstaff.

General Assistance

HRL: ALL is especially grateful to **Dr Robert Ellis**, **Janette Martin** and **Sarah Bastow** of the **University of Huddersfield** who facilitated the work-placements of students who assisted with the research for this book: Laurence Brammer, Jonathan Morris, Luke Russell, Rob Smithson, Joe Taylor and Adam West, Rob going on to co-write Chapter 14.

We also thank the staff of the following organisations for their help in accessing archives and images:

Huddersfield Local Studies Library	**Kirklees Archive Service**
Huddersfield Giants RLFC	**South Crosland Junior School**
Huddersfield Examiner	**University of Huddersfield**
Imperial War Museum	**West Yorkshire Archive Service**

Original Source Materials

We thank **Kirklees Archive Service** for allowing access to letters written from the front line by Lieutenant Roland Hely Owen (quoted pp).

We thank **Kirklees Archive Service** and the **Duke of Wellington's West Riding Regiment** for permission to reproduce the image of Roland Hely Owen.

We thank **Huddersfield Local Studies Library** for providing access to microfilm of local newspapers, particularly the *Huddersfield Daily Examiner* (*HDE*) from 1914 to 1919, to numerous local history publications, and for providing copying facilities.

We are grateful to **David and Madeleine Gronow, Huddersfield Giants RLFC, St Joseph's ARLFC,** and **Slaithwaite Saracens ARLFC** for supplying numerous high resolution images.

Secondary Source Materials

The books and websites accessed for research are all included in the reference section, but the authors are particularly grateful to the following local authors:

Stanley Chadwick (*Claret and Gold: 1895-1945*; 1945)

David Gronow (*100 Greats: Huddersfield Rugby League Club*; 2008, *Images of Huddersfield Rugby League Club*; 2010, *Three Fartown Aussies; Hunter, Cooper, Devery*, 2012)

Their works provided valuable background, context and additional detail to many stories.

We are particularly grateful to the *Huddersfield Examiner* and its predecessors the *Huddersfield Daily Examiner* and *Huddersfield Weekly Examiner*, for their extensive coverage of rugby league in the district.

Images

The following have allowed us to reproduce illustrations, for which we thank them:

www.allinwrestling.co.uk p78 (Posters)

Tony Allen (www.worldwar1postcards.com) p60

Dennis and Pauline Atkinson p17 (Thewlis collection)

Roger Birch (Images of Todmorden) p32

Peter and Jane Bridgett/www.donmouth.co.uk/women's_football/huddersfield_atalanta p160, 161

BARLA pp147, 152

Keith Burhouse pp122 (Devery), 191, 194

David Calverley pp7 (Stone), 27 (Plaque & Trophy Tour Launch), 35 (Pump Hole), 81 (Plaque), 164 (England Women), 183, 190, 212, 217, 222, 223 (Exhibition), 224 (Fartown)

www.commons.wikimedia.org p181 (barracuda)

Digital Poster Collection (http://digitalpostercollection.com/propaganda/1914-1918-world-war-i) pp54, 55

Shirley Farrand/www.donmouth.co.uk/women's_football/huddersfield_atalanta.html p161

David Gronow pp5, 7 (Gymnasium), 9 (Baines Cards 1 and 2), 11, 12 (Almondbury & Holmfirth), 14, 17 (1890 Team), 22 (Boak), 27 (George Hotel), 31, 33, 35 (Wagstaff), 36, 37 (Kitchin), 38-42, 47, 52, 53 (Proud Are We), 63, 65, 67, 68, 74, 75, 76, 77, 78 (Letter), 79, 81 (Wagstaff), 84 (Fartown), 88, 89, 92, 96 (Markham), 97 (Bowkett), 98, 99 (Final Photographs), 100, 102. 103, 107 (Bawden), 108, 111-113, 116, 117, 119, 120, 124, 125, 127-130, 131 (Cracknell), 132-134, 137, 138, 140-142, 145, 146, 148, 149, 151, 162, 169-171, 172 (Fartown Floodlights), 173, 174, 176-178, 180, 181 (Match Action), 182, 189 (Celebration), 192, 195-198, 205, 207, 208, 211, 214, 224 (New Stadium)

Huddersfield Daily Examiner/Huddersfield Examiner pp75 (Cartoon), 80, 84 (Cartoon), 90, 91, 93-95, 96 (Cartoons), 97 (Cartoon), 99 (Cartoons), 101, 105, 106, 107 (Cartoon), 110 (Reynard), 126, 184

Huddersfield Cricket and Athletic Club/Huddersfield (Giants) RLFC pp43, 53, 115, 159, 189 (Team Photograph), 200, 206, 213, 216, 218, 219, 223 (Sheet Music), 228 (Shirt Amnesty)

Huddersfield (Giants) RLFC Supporters' Club pp122 (Postcard), 157, 226, 227 (1907 Match)

Huddersfield Rugby League: A Lasting Legacy p228 (Trail and Cards)

Keighley Cougars RLFC p181
Kirklees Archive Service pp59
Moorhouse Family p227 (Menu)
Bernie Nunn p201
Liam Ramsden p135 (Ramsden)
Rugby Football League p109
Rugby League Review pp118, 123, 131 (Cartoon)
Slaithwaite Saracens ARLFC pp163, 164, 167 (Slaithwaite)
Sports Illustrated p1, 8
Adam Swift pp165, 166, 167 (St Joseph's)
Sykes Family p139
Sports Inspire Educational Publishing pp21, 22 (Cartoons)
David Thorpe p225
University of Huddersfield Archive pp9 (Baines Card 3), 12 (Baines Cards), Fartown, 44, 110 (Archbell), 172 (Smales)

Interviewees

Interviews with over 200 players, supporters and officials were recorded in researching this book. The authors are grateful to all of them, and to the adults and schoolchildren who conducted the interviews. The names of interviewees whose information is used are listed in the bibliography at the end of the book.

Abbreviations

ASC	Army Service Corps	KSDL	Kirklees Stadium Development Limited
FA	Football Association		
FC	Football Club	NRFU	Northern Rugby Football Union
HAC	Huddersfield Athletic Club	NUFC	Northern Union Football Club
HC & AC	Huddersfield Cricket and Athletic Club	RFL	Rugby Football League
		RFU	Rugby Football Union
HDE	*Huddersfield Daily Examiner*	RLFC	Rugby League Football Club
HWE	*Huddersfield Weekly Examiner*	YMCA	Young Men's Christian Association

Foreword
by
Tony Collins

(Professor of History, International Centre for Sports History and Culture, De Montfort University and Trustee, Rugby League Cares)

A Giant of a Story

Huddersfield has always played a central role in the history of rugby league, on the field, off the field and symbolically. This book tells the complete story of the club over its 150-year history, describing how it has been through every possible change of fortune that a sports team could experience. A pioneering rugby club of the 1860s, one of rugby's greatest-ever teams in the 1910s, struggles with mediocrity, decline in the 1960s, near death in the 1980s, an aborted merger in 2000 and rebirth to be a power in the game once more in the 21st Century.

As befits a sport that prides itself on its community values, the book is also a collective effort, featuring no less than eight contributors, all of whom have dug up fascinating new details about the history of the club.

The book covers pivotal moments that have taken place in Huddersfield, such as the 1895 meeting in the George Hotel that established the Northern Union, and the 1973 meeting that founded BARLA. The amateur game in the town is covered in detail, as are schools and the women's game.

It starts with accounts of 'folk football' in the area during the 1840s before rugby or soccer emerged as separate sports, and explains how Huddersfield Athletic Club was founded in 1864.

By 1885 rugby was so popular in the town that 26 clubs met to establish a district cup, known as the Holliday Cup. 130 years on, the cup is still played for by local community teams.

The Claret and Golds became one of the powerhouses of nineteenth century rugby, winning the Yorkshire Cup in 1890. Being a top club required casting the net for players as far as possible – and that brought Huddersfield up against the Rugby Football Union and its amateur regulations. But worse, the man who alerted the RFU to Huddersfield's transgressions of the amateur code was one of their most prominent members, the Reverend Frank Marshall.

Using interviews with surviving relatives, the book uncovers new details about how George Boak and Jock Forsyth signed for Huddersfield from Cummersdale Hornets in Cumbria in 1893. The pair were fined by magistrates for leaving their jobs to play at Fartown and the club itself was suspended by the RFU for offering them jobs. Coming just weeks after the northern clubs' proposal to allow 'broken time' payments to players had been voted down by the RFU, this signalled the start of the all-out war that would result in the formation of the Northern Union less than two years later.

Two decades later, Huddersfield assembled one of the great sides, which now has three members of the RFL Hall of Fame: Harold Wagstaff, Albert Rosenfeld and Douglas Clark. The story of this 'Team of all Talents' is told in full, as is their subsequent history as participants in World War I.

A second golden age for the club followed World War II when Australian greats Lionel Cooper, Pat Devery and Johnny Hunter lit up Fartown and brought the Challenge Cup and Championship back to the town. But after winning the Championship in 1962, the club gradually fell into a downward spiral. In April 1986 only 303 turned up to watch a match against Keighley.

Huddersfield only survived because of the unbelievable efforts of its fans, and one fan in particular. No-one ever did more for a rugby league club than Keith Burhouse. In his own way, Keith was as important to Huddersfield off the field as Harold Wagstaff or Lionel Cooper had been on it. Likewise, this book would not have been possible without the sterling work of club historian David Gronow. David and Keith both died in 2014.

Such is the level of information in this book that it also makes a significant contribution to the wider social and cultural history of the town. It is laden with wonderful photographs and illustrations, many of which have never been seen before, and deserves to be on the bookshelves not just of Huddersfield supporters but of anyone interested in the history of rugby league.

Standing on the Shoulders of Giants is part of Huddersfield's Heritage Lottery Fund-supported 'A Lasting Legacy' project, which itself is a model for others to follow. With heritage now on the agenda of the RFL, this outstanding book will hopefully be the first of many across the game.

Introduction

In 1676, Isaac Newton wrote: 'If I have seen further it is by standing on the shoulders of Giants.' It seems an appropriate metaphor for the title of this book. Most obviously and literally, it relates to the 'Giants' moniker of the modern-day Huddersfield club. It also relates to the achievements of numerous 'Giants' on which the modern club and game continue to be built.

The first 'Giants' who founded the Huddersfield club in 1864 were quickly followed by the Huth brothers of the 1870s, who took the quality of local rugby to a new level. By 1878 Huddersfield was established at Fartown. Developed by ambitious committeemen into one of the great northern sporting arenas, Fartown remained the club's home for 114 years.

In 1885, club President Charles Holliday inaugurated the Holliday Charity Cup for local clubs, which remains the longest-running amateur rugby league competition in the world.

Harry Lodge was one of several early players who guided the club for many years. Captain in the first season of Northern Union rugby after the 1895 breakaway from the Rugby Football Union (RFU), he later combined administrative duties with decades of features that publicised the club in the local press.

The greatest Giant of them all, the mercurial Harold Wagstaff, broke the mould of how Northern Union rugby was played. Slick, incisive and innovative, he jolted the game from a static, set-piece, forward-dominated game into an altogether more flowing, fluid, attractive spectacle. He was also a social pioneer. Captaining the 1914 Ashes-winning team, he was one of the first working class men to lead an official British party overseas, and did so with diplomatic aplomb. On his return, he captained Huddersfield's Team of all Talents to all four trophies in 1914-15, the pinnacle of the club's many achievements. This team included Albert Rosenfeld, whose all-time record 80 tries in 1913-14 remains a distant benchmark for aspirational modern wingmen. It also included Douglas Clark, Northern Union rugby international, world wrestling champion and war hero, whose extraordinary courage and spirit continues to inspire.

Following in the wake of such Giants was tough, but in the 1930s Len Bowkett led Huddersfield to League and Challenge Cup glories that lifted some of the local gloom from the Great Depression.

A host of heroes arrived after World War II, spearheaded by Australians Johnny Hunter, Lionel Cooper and Pat Devery. Scot Dave Valentine lifted the inaugural Rugby League World Cup in 1954, and master tactician Tommy Smales captained Huddersfield to the League Championship in 1962. Collectively, they inspired a generation of fans who stuck with the club and helped to keep it alive when the collapse of the manufacturing industries, which had employed many of the Fartown supporters, was almost mirrored by the demise of the club.

Foremost among these supporters were Keith Burhouse and his family. Their efforts, and those of others, sustained the club until better times arrived in the form of the McAlpine Stadium and, shortly afterwards, Ken Davy.

Chairman since 1996, Ken Davy is the modern-day Giant whose input has driven the club's progress from the Division 1 Championship in 1997 to the top of the game as the Leaders of Super League in 2013, a triumph inspired by on-field talismen, Danny Brough and Eorl Crabtree.

Representing Huddersfield is a particular honour. The unique decisions of 29 August 1895 at the George Hotel are forever etched into the histories of the town and the sport – the only sport that knows exactly when and where it was born. Seventy eight years after this split of the Northern Union from the RFU – effectively a breakaway of the professionals from the amateurs – there was another breakaway in Huddersfield – of the amateurs from the professionals. In 1973, led by officials from the Huddersfield and District League, the British Amateur Rugby League Association (BARLA) was founded in the town. It assumed responsibility for amateur rugby league from the Rugby Football League (RFL), developed a progressive league structure for amateur clubs, encouraged women's rugby league, and remains one of the most significant developments in the game.

Embellished by much original research, this book provides new perspectives on all of these stories. From the evolution of the earliest games into a regulated sport, through the split of 1895, to the rollercoaster that has taken and returned Huddersfield to the top of the professional game, it is about the broad shoulders of Giants on which the modern game in Huddersfield stands.

Chapter 1

From Mob Football to Rugby Football

The club that is now Huddersfield Giants Rugby League Football Club was formed as the Huddersfield Athletic Club (HAC) in 1864. The origin of the word 'football' in the name of Huddersfield Giants and other modern-day rugby league and rugby union clubs pre-dates the clubs and the laws of both rugby codes by many years.

Various forms of football have been played across Britain for centuries. An edict by King Edward II in 1314 banned football in London and several kings who followed him made similar decrees.

Mob Football

The game that they banned was known as 'mob' or 'folk football'. There were hardly any rules and the aim was to get the ball through the opponents' goal by any means possible. It was mostly played by small groups of men or boys, but on special occasions there were many players on each side, sometimes village versus village, when the goals could be miles apart. Matches often resembled a riot and there were many injuries and some deaths.

The enclosure of land and the growth of the towns drove such games into increasingly inappropriate areas. Much of the farming land around Huddersfield was enclosed between 1720 and 1780, partly so that landowners could rear sheep to supply wool for their mechanised spinning and weaving mills. The Huddersfield district was well suited for wool production, sheep flourishing on the moors, whilst fast-running soft-water streams were ideal for washing their wool. Many people worked in their cottages, spinning and weaving the wool by hand, and rearing animals and growing crops to feed themselves. The enclosure of land, and mechanisation through inventions, such as the spinning jenny, which was first used in

Mob football

Huddersfield in the 1790s, drove these cottage workers out of business and into large mills along the valley floors, or into the town to find employment. Huddersfield grew rapidly, its population increasing by 500% between 1801 and 1871.

There was inevitable unrest, and a powder-keg of discontent exploded in the Luddite Riots of the early 19th century, and again in the Plug Riots of the 'Hungry' 1840s. Through it all mob football continued to be a feature of men's leisure time across West Yorkshire. Writing in the *Hebden Bridge Times* in 1886, a journalist recalled matches in the town from decades earlier, and captured the demographic shift of the game from countryside to town.

> Who among our old Hebden Bridge residents does not remember the lively and fierce football contests of sometimes twenty, thirty, forty or fifty players on a side on the White Horse Croft ... and streets some fifty or sixty years ago? Then there was no quibbling about tries, or mauls, or 'offside' play. A fence at either end was designed as the goal, and each player strove like the apostle Paul, to keep 'the goal in view' ... just imagine the hubbub and confusion!

Census Population Figures for Huddersfield Sub-District, 1801 to 1901

Year	Population
1801	7,268
1811	9,671
1821	13,284
1831	19,035
1841	25,068
1851	30,880
1861	34,877
1871	38,654
1881	42,234
1891	46,098
1901	44,921

Source: Great Britain Historical GIS Project. www.VisionofBritain.org.uk

As towns grew in size, mob football was more frequently played in the streets, becoming notorious for obstructing the highway, damaging property, intimidating non-participants, and at times camouflaging criminal activity. These lawless excesses saw the sport banned on all public roads by the *Highways Act* of 1835. As Richard Sanders wrote in *Beastly Fury: The Strange Birth of British Football*:

> The lives of working people were being slowly hemmed in by fences and hedges, by walls and factory gates, by the harsh morality and pitiless work ethic of the rising middle class and the insatiable demands of the new industrial economy. There was little space for football.

The 1850 Factory Act

It wasn't space, but time, in the form of reduced working hours and a more structured working week, that was the catalyst for the resurgence of football in the industrial north. The sustained campaign for improvements to working hours and conditions was driven by Richard Oastler who, from 1821 to 1840, lived as steward of the Thornhill family estates at Fixby Hall, now the home of Huddersfield Golf Club. With the significant assistance of Todmorden mill owner and MP for Oldham, John Fielden, the Ten Hours Act was passed in 1847.

This Act reduced the inhumane hours worked by women and children in factories, and affected the hours worked by some of their male colleagues who were often part of the same production line. Attempting to offset the loss of production, some mill owners imposed crippling relay shift patterns on the men. These were scuppered to a degree by the 1850 Factory Act. Applying specifically to the textile industries, this Act did not reduce the hours worked, but regulated the working week. Mill owners could no longer enforce unreasonable shift patterns and, crucially for the development of sport, all mills had to close for the week by 2pm on Saturdays.

For the first time, large numbers of men living in close proximity to each other had a few hours of regular, simultaneous free time. The impact on the development of communal leisure activities in Britain's industrial towns and cities was dramatic. The Mayor of Huddersfield, Alderman Wright Mellor, speaking over three decades later at the Huddersfield Cricket and Athletic Club's Annual Athletics Festival in 1884, acknowledged that ...

> ... Until 1850 ... the people had to work so many hours that after they got up early in the morning and worked until late at night they wanted no recreation – only food and rest. The Factory Bill had so altered things ...

Moses Heap, a mill worker, wrote in his diary:

> ...we did not know how to pass our time away. Before it had all been bed and work; now in place of 70 hours a week we had 55½ hours. It became practice, mostly on Saturdays, to play games, especially football and cricket, which had never been done before.

Almost immediately, Huddersfield witnessed increased participation in existing activities, such as cricket, swimming, riding, bowling, quoits and foot-races. The barbaric sports of cock fighting and prize fighting had long since been outlawed, but betting-fuelled secret events were still held on the moors.

Professor John Le Blanc, an enterprising 'Irishman with a long grey beard', sensed a business opportunity and on 3 August 1850 opened the Apollo Gymnasium in Huddersfield. The only public facility of its type in the district, the Gymnasium provided opportunities for general exercise, including the use of gymnastics apparatus, and lessons in fencing and dancing. As an indoor venue, it was particularly popular during the winter months and was used mainly by young men.

Winter sport was not restricted to the Apollo Gymnasium. There was also an increase in the amount of mob football played, ranging from informal kick-abouts to pre-arranged matches. The earliest reference to such a match in the Huddersfield district is between Holmfirth and Hepworth, played near Whinney Bank, Holmfirth, in 1848. The stakes were £5, each side depositing £2 10s. Hepworth took the spoils from a 'well contested' game, each side exhibiting 'the usual amount of contusions, bloody noses, etc.'

Muscular Christianity

Whilst a growing number of Huddersfield men were becoming accustomed to sporting endeavours on Saturdays, other factors were also aligning to promote the growth of sport, and of football in particular.

Most directly, football was becoming integral to life in the public schools, legitimized, at least in part, as one of the more acceptable means by which boys could vent their energy and aggression. If the educational and religious establishment baulked at this crude if practical justification for this barbaric sport, they took succour from perceived highbrow ethical benefits. The rules and moral codes of sport were, it was argued, a means through which boys could practise and learn the rules and moral codes of life. Football was in the vanguard of this crusade of 'Muscular Christianity.'

Different public schools applied different football rules, but all played rudimentary hybrids of what we would recognise as rugby and association football. Crucially, there was common ground, so that compromises about rules could be agreed, allowing football to expand.

Meanwhile, the various rules of the public schools imposed restrictions on conduct so that these games, whilst still quite brutal, were becoming safer to play. The rules also demanded greater application of skill and strategy, engaging much more than pure physicality. It all helped to increase the enjoyment of the players.

Many public schoolboys wished to continue this enjoyment on returning to their home communities. Usually from well-to-do families, these apostles of Muscular Christianity were well positioned to spread the gospel of football. Needing teammates and opponents, they found willing followers among local working men, many of whom learned the basics and also became teachers. As the popularity of football grew, an increasing number learned by watching and emulating.

The formation in 1857 of Sheffield FC, the world's oldest surviving football club, is evidence of the metamorphosis from mob football to organised sport. Football in Huddersfield was less advanced, but an apparent setback to sporting participation in the town would ultimately kick-start organised football.

Birth of the Huddersfield Athletic Club

The setback came in the early 1860s, when Professor John Le Blanc transformed his Apollo Gymnasium into the Gymnasium Theatre. Huddersfield had recently lost one of its three theatres when the Volunteer Rifle Corps requisitioned the town's Riding School hall for a drill hall and armoury. Theatre and Music Hall entertainment was booming – the town's two surviving establishments, the Cambridge Music Hall in Upperhead Row, and the Theatre Royal in Ramsden Street had only recently opened – and the Professor saw a theatre as a more lucrative attraction than a gymnasium.

The young athletes who had frequented the gymnasium were naturally disappointed by the sudden and unexpected loss of their facility and began to plan the formation of an athletics club. Stanley Chadwick, in *Claret and Gold: 1895-1945* records:

> In an advertisement headed "Huddersfield Athletic Club," they invited "gentlemen desirous of becoming members" to attend a preliminary meeting at the Queens Hotel on Wednesday November 16th, 1864.
> The enthusiasm of the promoters ... was fully justified by the "large and influential gathering" present ... after Mr G.O.Crowther had read a letter from one of the honorary secretaries of the Liverpool Athletic Club, containing much valuable advice on the formation of similar clubs, it was unanimously resolved to form the "Huddersfield Athletic Club."

Almost 100 men signed up as members that evening, rising to 150 by 16 December, when a temporary gymnasium was opened in the basement of Kilner and Crosland's warehouse in Back John William Street. Mr FA Pilling was appointed Honorary Secretary, and among those engaged by the committee to instruct and supervise this hive of activity was, ironically, Professor John Le Blanc.

The Huddersfield Athletic Club planned its first major event for the following June, 1865, assisted by event blueprints from local cricket, most specifically from Lascelles Hall Cricket Club. Founded in 1825, Lascelles Hall was the outstanding team in Yorkshire, supplying numerous players to the county XI in the 1860s. In September 1862 Lascelles Hall hosted a well-attended match between 22 Yorkshire Colts and the All England XI, a team of travelling professional mercenaries. In August 1863 the United England XI – a rival to the All England XI – played '22 of Huddersfield', including numerous Lascelles Hall players, at the old Rifle Corps Field, which is now part of Greenhead Park. It was the biggest sporting event seen in the town to that time. A similarly successful match at the Rifle Field in 1864 encouraged big plans for the venue in 1865.

In May 1865 a powerful All England XI, including the country's best batsmen in Richard Carpenter and Thomas Hayward, and its fastest bowler in George Tarrant, returned to play 20 of Huddersfield. The match reached a crescendo of excitement on the third day as, set 103 to win, the All England XI was bowled out for 101.

Five weeks later, on 24 June 1865, the Rifle Field was the venue for the Huddersfield Athletic Club's inaugural Athletic Festival. A grandstand was erected and the price of a seat, two shillings (10p), helped to finance the prizes of a silver medal for the winner of each event and a bronze medal for the runner-up. Some of the events that day were: putting the [24lb] stone; a two-miles walking match; standing and running long jump and high jump; 440 yards flat race; plus 200 yards hurdles; Indian clubs; single vaulting; and boxing. Entry was limited to members of the club and competitors wore 'white knickerbockers, with shirt and stockings' of their own choice.

The festival was a great success. Entry to events was widened to encourage the best athletes from further afield and it grew in stature to become an annual fixture, known colloquially as 'The Ascot of the North.' It declined in popularity after World War I and was discontinued after a poorly-attended Diamond Jubilee Festival on 30 June 1934.

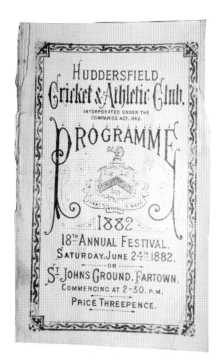

Programme for the HC and AC's
eighteenth Grand Athletic Festival in 1882

Montage of illustrations about the Athletic Festival
at Fartown in 1891 from the *Athletic Journal*

In August 1865, the Rifle Field hosted its third successful event of the summer, the first of Huddersfield's many annual Floral and Horticultural shows.

Football Kicks Off

With its growing membership and successful festival, the Huddersfield Athletic Club was making an impression on the town. By comparison to the excitement of athletics and cricket in the summer, winter activities in the gymnasium must have seemed tame.

Seeking winter time sporting thrills, on Saturday 27 January 1866, 20 members of the Huddersfield Athletic Club and 'a similar number of members of the local Rifle Corps' played a 'football match' on the Rifle Field. The match was drawn, scoreless, and a second was arranged which, after several postponements, was played in late February 1866, this time with 15 players per side.

Future developments at the club strongly suggest that the type of 'football' played in these matches would have resembled rugby union. The Football Association (FA) had been formed and had written its first set of rules in 1863, formalising the split between the association football and what would become rugby football. The formation of the Rugby Football Union (RFU) in 1871 crystallised the divergence of football into two distinct codes. There is no evidence that the FA's rules of 1863 had any bearing on the football played by members of the Huddersfield Athletic Club.

At the Huddersfield Athletic Club's second Annual General Meeting (AGM) in November 1866, Mr A Bradley announced that the club, now comprising 194 members, was to form a football section. Members of the football section began to play amongst themselves at the Rifle Field on 1 December, but received little practical support from the committee and, although the club had over £154 in the bank, no financial support.

They briefly moved from the Rifle Field in October 1867 when Mr Edward Brooke, a vice-president of the club, made a field available to them. He also organised an exhibition match between teams representing Manchester and Leeds, which was played at Fieldhouse, off Leeds Road. A large crowd enjoyed the novel spectacle, some of them closely studying techniques, team formations and tactics that they could aspire to. Other exhibition matches were arranged, including two between Liberals and Conservatives. Inspired by these displays and by the provision of a field on which to practise at the home of one of their players, Percy Learoyd, Huddersfield Athletic Club at last assembled 'a proper team.'

The football section began to run itself as a semi-independent entity, electing Fred Learoyd as Chairman and Mr HB Dransfield as secretary. As the HAC still provided no financial assistance, playing members paid a subscription of 2s 6d to cover running costs and rent of the Rifle Field for matches.

Percy Learoyd and his brother Edwin were prominent players in this fledging team, but it was the outstanding trio of Harry Beardsell, CE Freeman and A Bradley who made the HAC sit up and take notice by earning selection for Yorkshire to play against Lancashire, Bradley as captain. This first-ever representative match was played at Whitehall Road, Leeds, on 28 March 1870. There were 20 players per side, and 'Yorkshire' was selected by representatives from the county's five leading clubs, Huddersfield, Bradford, Hull, Leeds Athletic and Sheffield. Variations in rules within the county were apparent when, according to WHH Hutchinson of Hull, one of his teammates from Sheffield 'grabbed the ball by the laces and hammered his opponent about the head with it', and expressed surprise when he was penalised.

Expressing 'pleasure' at the football section's success, the HAC's 6th AGM on 5 October 1870 promised that, when its funds were more healthy, the football section 'would be provided with a field of their own.' The parent club was now preparing to support its offspring, but the relationship continued to be uneasy. At the AGM of 1871 members expressed concern that the football section's expenditure had increased by £12 although they had only played six matches, opponents as yet being thin on the ground. The annual rent for the Rifle Field was an alarming £23, only slightly offset by a £6 sub-let as grazing land. Football supporters riposted that their section's figures did not reflect its true financial worth, because football was a conduit for attracting members to the HAC. This assertion was borne out in 1872 when, buoyed by an influx of new members, the football section introduced a second team.

Amalgamation with St John's Cricket Club

In 1871 the HAC founded a cricket section which made a £10 profit. In 1875, with the long-term future of cricket in mind, the HAC approached the Hillhouse-based St John's Cricket Club with a proposal that the two clubs should amalgamate.

St John's Cricket Club had been founded in Hillhouse National School on 2 June 1866. They played at Hillhouse until the end of the 1867 season when the club obtained the lease of a field in Fartown, owned by Richard Nutter, landlord of the George Hotel in Huddersfield. The lease permitted cricket and rugby to be played, but the club focused on the summer sport and the cricket ground was opened in April 1868. In 1872 the available land was extended to six acres.

By 1875, when the amalgamation was proposed, St John's Cricket Club had spent over £800 on their Fartown facilities. Many of the club's 160 members were understandably concerned that they would be 'swallowed up' by the 300 members of the HAC. They also had a seemingly insurmountable objection to rugby football being played on their cricket ground, not least because they had hosted a lucrative first-class cricket match in each of the last three seasons. The most recent of these, a prestigious 'North' v 'South' fixture in July 1875, had featured the cream of the country's cricketers. It had also emphasised the excellent quality of the club's pitch which was praised by no less than the brothers WG and GF Grace, both of whom scored heavily as the South batted out for a draw on the third day, making 411 for 5 against a good quality bowling attack

Huddersfield Athletic Club's St John's Gymnasium, opened in 1875

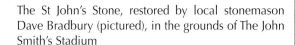

The St John's Stone, restored by local stonemason Dave Bradbury (pictured), in the grounds of The John Smith's Stadium

Fortunately, the cricket club's objection to the boots of rugby footballers trampling their square was addressed by Major RH Graham, agent of the Ramsden Estate that owned adjoining land. He promised that if the amalgamation went ahead, any new lease could include an extension for 'football purposes.'

Despite Major Graham's assurances, the issue was far from certain when the two clubs met for the decisive vote in the Thornhill Arms, Fartown, on 27 November 1875. A show of hands was taken, but was too close to call. Tellers were appointed for a recount, and announced that the resolution for 'a legal amalgamation to form the Huddersfield Cricket and Athletic Club' (HC and AC) had been carried, 55-37.

A bargaining chip of the HAC was its new Gymnasium in St Johns Road, which was formally opened by the Mayor of Huddersfield, Alderman JF Brigg JP, on 29 December 1875. Designed by James Kirk of Huddersfield, it consisted of a large gymnasium hall and sparring and fencing rooms.

Over the centre doorway was a carved stone figure of Hercules. The Gymnasium remained the headquarters of HC and AC until the summer of 1906 when it was sold and the club office transferred to the Pavilion at Fartown. In 1938 the premises were opened as a church. The building was demolished to accommodate the ring road in the 1970s, but Hercules was saved and stored at Fartown. In 2013 the stone was restored by local builder Dave Bradbury, funded by the Heritage Lottery Fund as part of the project 'Huddersfield Rugby League: A Lasting Legacy'. It was positioned in the grounds of The John Smith's Stadium as the centrepiece of a memorial garden for the Huddersfield Giants and Huddersfield Town.

The first meeting of the HC and AC was held in the new Gymnasium on 25 March 1876. A large attendance gathered to approve rules drafted by the committee. They decided that the 12th Annual Athletic Festival was to be held on the 'different but superior' St John's ground, and that the promised adjoining land was to be developed for the 'Football Section'. Meanwhile, the rugby footballers would continue to play at Rifle Fields. Later in the year, the first annual report of the HC and AC showed that a further 126 members had joined, taking total membership to 535.

Although still a junior partner in its own club, Huddersfield was one of the leading lights in Yorkshire rugby football. Along with four other leading Yorkshire clubs, it was about to initiate a concept that had far-reaching consequences for the development of the game.

Chapter 2

T'owd Tin Pot

In 1876, the rugby section of the Huddersfield Cricket and Athletic Club (HC and AC) joined the Bradford, Hull, Leeds and York rugby football clubs in presenting a cup valued at fifty guineas to the Yorkshire County Rugby Football Committee. They proposed that it should be played for in an annual competition. This was the Yorkshire Cup, affectionately known as 'T'owd Tin Pot'. It was to be organised as a knockout competition, based on association football's highly popular and successful FA Cup competition, which had run annually since 1871.

Cup matches had a wider context, formalising comparisons between teams from different places, although Huddersfield quickly found that objective assessment was tempered by the luck of the draw when the powerful Bradford club despatched them from the inaugural competition in the first round. The introduction of this competition had two major impacts. The first – increased interest, larger crowds and resultant financial benefits – was probably anticipated. Less anticipated was the competition's impact on the rules and the spread of the game.

The rules of rugby football had been published on the formation of the RFU in 1871, but there were still differences from place to place in understanding how the game should be played. To be a fair competition, all Yorkshire Cup matches had to be played to the same rules. This accelerated the progress towards commonality. As the rules became more widely understood and adopted, teams from a greater number of places could participate, and the game spread geographically.

The Yorkshire Cup also helped to publicise and raise the profile of rugby football, the local newspapers gradually taking more interest in the progress of their clubs. Huddersfield's local press comprised the *Huddersfield Weekly Chronicle*, founded in 1850 and the *Huddersfield Weekly Examiner*, which was founded in 1852 and was supplemented during the week by the *Huddersfield Daily Examiner (HDE)* from 1871. The timing of the *Education Acts* of 1870 and 1880, after which all children had to go to school at least until the age of ten, also had unintended benefits in publicising sport, as by the early 1880s there were many more adults who could read. At the start of the 1883-84 season, the *HDE* startled its readers by heading one of its columns 'Football Notes.' The column explained:

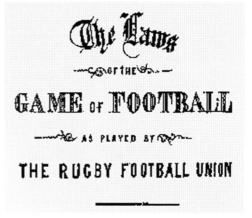

Title page of the first rules of rugby, published by the RFU in 1871

> The popularity of this winter game is now so great, particularly in the North of England, that more attention than has been hitherto accorded to it is felt to be justly its due owing to the interest taken in it by such a wide and ever-increasing circle of readers.

Stanley Chadwick, in *Claret and Gold: 1895-1945* confirms that, locally, 'it marked the beginning of a new type of sporting journalism.' A symbiotic relationship was developing that still exists today, local newspapers helping to develop interest in the sports clubs and sport helping to sell the newspapers.

Collectable Baines Cards, invented by John Baines of Bradford in 1885, were another indication of the burgeoning interest in rugby football.

As rugby football and associated publicity proliferated, it became incumbent on local men to form a team, particularly if a neighbouring town or village had one. The concept of inter-town and inter-village rivalry was already established in the spheres of industry and music before rugby football began to make its mark. The Huddersfield Choral Society, founded in 1836, Skelmanthorpe Band (1843) and Meltham Mills Band (1846) were among the groups that helped to establish the Huddersfield district's fine musical reputation. Meltham Mills Band were the British Open Champions in 1873, and again from 1876 to 1878, becoming the first to win this title in three consecutive years, a feat only achieved by four other brass bands.

Inherently, sport was the most natural and exciting channel for inter-town and inter-village competition. Having a decent, respected team in association football, rugby football or cricket – and preferably all three – became part of town and village identity, contributing to the collective ego and self-worth of its sporting enthusiasts. Shared sporting interests, pride in local teams, and a sense of achievement when they were successful helped many people, mostly men, to feel part of their community. By the mid 1870s, Huddersfield's sporting organisations, and the rugby football section of HC and AC in particular, were poised to take such community-affirming rivalries to a new level.

The Town's Supporting Infrastructure

The rapid developments in rugby football in Huddersfield from the mid 1860s were supported by the town's existing and growing infrastructure. Huddersfield came of age in 1868 when it was granted independent status as a county borough with its own corporation. The corporation inherited transport and communications networks that would be fundamental to developing the town. For the HC and AC, they would be vital to the construction of its ground which, as support grew and entrance fees were charged, would need to be secured by fences and gates, and provide basic safe accommodation, and toilet and catering facilities for large numbers. These networks would also help the club officials to contact players, raise and improve their teams, arrange, travel to and play matches, and to generate and maintain interest and support.

By the 1860s Huddersfield's road network included turnpike routes to Leeds, Halifax, Rochdale, Penistone, Bradford and Manchester, all checked and repaired by a Board of Highway Surveyors. Local horse-bus services began in 1858, and in 1883 Huddersfield became the first local authority to run its own public transport system – tramcars pulled by steam engines. Perhaps the most significant transport development for the growth of local rugby was the opening of Huddersfield Railway Station in 1847, the rail network bringing many more places within one day's return journey.

Communications improved after 1840 when the rudimentary local postal service was supplemented by the national 'Penny Post'. Speed of communications became much faster in 1847 with the introduction of the electric telegraph to sixty places in England and Scotland. These included Huddersfield. In the 1880s and 1890s the latest score from Huddersfield's away matches was regularly wired through and pinned up outside the telegraph office, where crowds of supporters awaited the news. The telegraph office was close to the railway station in John William Street, one of Huddersfield's grand, wide thoroughfares constructed in the 1850s, which remains flanked by many of the town's iconic buildings, including the George Hotel, which was built in 1851.

Control of the large crowds that attended Huddersfield's rugby matches necessitated an ongoing relationship between the club and the local constabulary. Huddersfield's police force had expanded considerably since the appointment of a solitary policeman in the 1820s, as had the work of the County Court, built in 1825. The Huddersfield Royal Infirmary, opened in 1831, was utilised by the club's trainers for the more seriously injured players. The club's bank accounts were with the Huddersfield Banking Company, a public company founded in 1827 after five local banks failed in the early 1800s. The first joint-stock bank in Yorkshire, it eventually merged with the Midland Bank in 1897.

The amalgamation in 1875 of the HAC and the St John's Cricket Club, the opening of the Gymnasium, and the development of the facilities at Fartown, coincided with a much improved water supply to Huddersfield, new reservoirs at Deerhill (1875) and Blackmoorfoot (1876) supplementing the existing piped supply from the reservoirs at Longwood.

Fartown

After three further seasons playing at the Rifle Field, the rugby football section of the HC and AC was finally able to move to Fartown in the autumn of 1878. A number of practice matches took place during September, most prominently the President's XV versus a Captain's XV. Hull were pencilled in as the visitors for the first official fixture on 5 October, but they were unable to raise a team, so after two away games at Bradford and Mirfield, Fartown staged its first fixture on 26 October 1878.

On a heavy pitch saturated by incessant rain during the previous week, visitors York were overwhelmed. Huddersfield christened their new facility with a victory by 2 goals (converted tries), 5 touchdowns (unconverted tries), and two minors (errors by York in their in-goal area, once kicking the ball dead and a touch in goal), to one touchdown. The *HDE* commented:

> Huddersfield played an exceedingly agreeable and exciting game in the presence of a large number of spectators, who took an immense interest in the play.

Huddersfield lined up as follows, with one full back, two three-quarter backs, two half-backs and ten forwards:

HA Hastings

H Huth (capt), Fred Huth

AE Learoyd, F Watkinson

AC Sharpe, GW Bottomley, JH Conacher, JH Walker, JE Bentley, Frank Huth, TH Calvert, E Woodhead, FH Walker, CJ Wheatley

The team's most experienced player was Edwin Learoyd, a stalwart from the 1860s, but the 1870s would retrospectively be referred to as the 'balmy days of the Huths.' Brothers Harry, Fred and Frank Huth, whose father Ernest was one of the founders of the HAC in 1864, had learned the game on the Rifle Field and become lynchpins of the Huddersfield side. All represented Yorkshire against Cheshire in 1878 and Harry became Huddersfield's first international,

Frank, Harry and Fred Huth

The England team that drew with Scotland at Raeburn Place, Edinburgh, in 1879. Harry Huth is seated third from the left.

representing England against Scotland in the first-ever Calcutta Cup match at Raeburn Place, Edinburgh, on 10 March 1879. He was soon followed by forward Ernest Woodhead, who played for England in their victory against Ireland at Landsdowne Road, Dublin, on 30 January 1880.

An Explosion of Local Clubs

The quality of the Huddersfield team was increasingly underpinned by players produced by the growing number of local rugby teams in the Huddersfield district. It seemed that almost every locality was represented by one or more teams, all playing regular matches against the others. A list from the early 1880s included:

Crosland Moor Juniors	Lockwood Crescent
Highfield Rangers	Lockwood Church Choir
Hillhouse Star	Lockwood Rangers
Huddersfield Clarence	Longwood
Huddersfield Hornets	Slaithwaite Hornets
Huddersfield Wanderers	Holmfirth
Leeds Road Clarence	Northumberland Street Rangers

Rugby clubs became part of the activities organised by some of the local churches and chapels and their related Sunday Schools, most of which were built between 1810 and 1860 as religious organisations proliferated alongside industrial expansion. Health, fitness and enjoyment were not, however, the only motivation of the district's religious leaders. Controlling the leisure time activities of their followers would help to keep them on the straight and narrow – and out of the pubs.

Lockwood Church Choir, Longwood Church and Hillhouse Free Wesleyans were among Huddersfield's prominent rugby teams by the 1880s. Hillhouse Methodist Chapel also offered billiards, snooker, darts, tennis and table tennis. Others founded cricket and association football teams.

A number of local schools also took up rugby football, most notably Almondbury Grammar School, whose headmaster, the Reverend Frank Marshall, was on the Huddersfield club's committee, a leading referee and a great advocate of the amateur game.

Playing in the most spartan conditions, numerous clubs flowered briefly, withered and died.

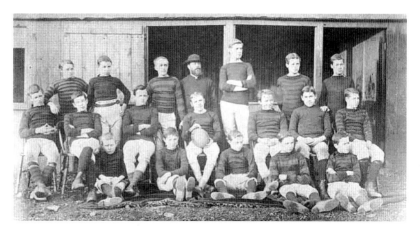

Almondbury Grammar School rugby football team, 1884; in the middle of the back row is the school's bearded headmaster, the Reverend Frank Marshall.

Others were hardier, among them Underbank Rangers, based in Holmfirth, and Lindley, both founded in 1884. Underbank remains the district's oldest surviving amateur club to have a continuous existence.

Left and Right: Baines Cards representing the Underbank Rangers and Holmfirth clubs, the latter depicting two outstanding local players, Joss Hoyle and Harris Bottomley
Centre: Postcard of Holmfirth showing, in the distance, the rugby posts of the Holmfirth club.

The Holliday Cup

Whilst HC and AC was repeatedly denied the success it craved in the Yorkshire Cup, Huddersfield was regularly exposed to the popularity of cup competitions in the 1880s. Fartown was the neutral venue for several Yorkshire Cup semi-finals, and in 1882 a crowd of 10,000 watched the semi-final of the FA Cup between Sheffield Wednesday and Blackburn Rovers, the FA choosing Fartown to promote their sport in what was, at the time, a predominantly rugby-focused town. The first FA Cup semi-final or final staged outside London, it ended 0-0, Blackburn winning 5-1 at Fallowfield in Manchester, before losing the final 1-0 to Old Etonians.

In 1883 local amateur cricket took the plunge with the inauguration of the game's longest running knockout competition, the Heavy Woollen Cup, initially open to teams within a six-mile radius of Batley Town Hall. Almost inevitably, local amateur rugby followed suit.

In September 1885, Charles Holliday, President of the HC and AC, presented a silver trophy, valued at £40, to be contested in a knockout tournament by the junior clubs of the district. This was one of many examples of moral paternalism from Huddersfield's civic and industrial leaders. Charles Holliday, who had inherited the successful Read Holliday chemicals and dyes manufacturing company founded by his father in 1821, intended that the new rugby competition would 'raise the character of the various clubs' and that the proceeds would be donated to local charities.

A meeting of 26 clubs formed a committee to promote 'The Huddersfield and District

Football Challenge Cup.' Of the 26 clubs present, the 16 who participated are included in the tournament progress chart below. The ten who did not participate are:

Flockton	Meltham Mills
Honley	Nortonthorpe
Kirkburton Rovers	Scissett
Lockwood	Shelley
Longwood	Waverley

The first round of this competition, which remains the flagship of the Huddersfield and District Amateur Rugby League, was played on Saturday 19 September 1885. All matches were on neutral grounds, with Fartown hosting a double header, Paddock v Skelmanthorpe followed by St Thomas' v Huddersfield Crescent. The combined gate receipts were about £30, of which £18 13s was taken at Fartown. All matches were won comfortably with the exception of a draw between Paddock and Skelmanthorpe, the latter progressing after a replay at Fartown the following Tuesday afternoon.

The emphatic form of Shepley and Kirkburton established them as early favourites, and both progressed easily to the semi-final, another Fartown double header. A 'large company' watched Kirkburton dispatch Skelmanthorpe 30-14, before a 'relentless' Shepley overwhelmed Huddersfield 'A' – the Fartowners' second team – by 40 points to three.

Fartown was again the venue for the first Holliday Cup Final, played on Saturday 10 October 1885, Shepley emerging as the winners before another large crowd. WH Senior, their captain, was presented with the cup by one of Huddersfield's best players from the 1860s, Harry Beardsell. Gross receipts for the competition were £152 which, after expenses, left about £100 to be presented to local charities.

The Holliday Cup 1885

ROUND 1	ROUND 2	SEMI-FINAL	FINAL	WINNERS
Shepley v Rastrick	Shepley			
	v			
Primrose Hill v Moldgreen	Primrose Hill	Shepley		
		v		
Crosland Moor v Netherton	Crosland Moor	Huddersfield 'A'		
	v			
Huddersfield 'A' v Lindley	Huddersfield 'A'		Shepley	
			v	Shepley
Kirkb'ton v Hillh'se Free Wesl'ns	Kirkburton		Kirkburton	
	v			
St Thomas' v Huddersf'ld Crescent	St Thomas'	Kirkburton		
		v		
St Paul's v Slaithwaite	St Paul's	Skelmanthorpe		
	v			
Paddock v Skelmanthorpe	Skelmanthorpe			

Over its first ten years, before rugby's deep divisions of 1895, the Holliday Cup raised £757 for local charities. Shepley, Paddock and Kirkburton continued to be among the district's most successful teams for several years, with Crosland Moor, Lockwood and Primrose Hill not far behind. Among the excellent players to progress to the HC and AC first team from this thriving local game were Jack Dyson and Wilson Schofield from Skelmanthorpe, the Eagland brothers, Tom and Will, from Slaithwaite and Harry Lodge, an outstanding forward from Kirkburton.

Harry Lodge

Jack Dyson

Harry Lodge continued to play for Kirkburton when not required by Huddersfield, and captained them against Paddock in the 1890 Holliday Cup Final before 10,000 spectators. After two periods of extra time, Paddock emerged victorious from a match heralded as the finest exhibition of rugby football between two district teams seen in Huddersfield.

After retiring, Harry wrote frequent articles for the *HDE*. In one of these he revealed some startling facts about the Huddersfield players' diet during his playing days. Attempting to build their physiques, the club provided large quantities of food on training nights, including about 30lbs of prime roast beef served with vegetables and bread and butter, plus a barrel of oysters, all washed down with bottled stout.

On this robust sustenance, Harry played five times for Yorkshire between 1890 and 1893. In his last match for the county, a victory over the Rest of England by a try to nil at Fartown in February 1893, he was joined by two Fartown colleagues, Will Eagland and Jack Dyson. Following the end of his playing career, Harry served for twenty-one years on the Huddersfield Football Committee, including a year as Chairman.

Success at Last

By 1880 the Huddersfield Rugby Football Club was the town's main winter sports' team. Supporting them was a passion for an increasing number of local men, but the success that they craved – bringing the Yorkshire Cup to Fartown – eluded them.

Their fortunes changed in 1890 when, at last, they reached the final, played at Hanson Lane (later known as Thrum Hall), Halifax, against Wakefield Trinity. Four special trains travelled from Huddersfield but, with the weather set fair, many spectators chose to walk. Anxious for a good vantage point, some set off the night before and slept in the Hanson Lane grounds, which also included the vast outfield of Halifax Cricket Club.

Huddersfield was alive with rugby fervour, and various premises in John William Street arranged for updates to be delivered by telegram during the game, crowds gathering outside the shops to be appraised of the latest score.

A crowd of 20,000 crammed into the sloping Halifax ground, and witnessed a tight, scoreless, forward-dominated game until shortly before half time. Then, in quick succession, Wakefield achieved two 'minors'. Awarded for Huddersfield errors in their in-goal area, both arose from narrowly missed drop goal attempts and counted one point each.

The turning point in the match came early in the second half. Frank Walker intercepted a Wakefield pass, raced clear of their half-backs and slipped a pass to Fred Richmond who touched down under the posts. Brooke slotted the easiest of conversions to complete the 'goal', which counted five points. Huddersfield were now in the ascendancy and their pressure was rewarded when captain Harry Archer appeared to ground the ball during a maul, but the referee surprisingly awarded Huddersfield a minor point.

Baines Card of Huddersfield captain Harry Archer

Wakefield came close when a kick at goal by their full back

Harry Stafford hit the post, and from the ensuing five-yard scrum Will Eagland kicked the ball dead, conceding a minor point. This was the last of the scoring as Huddersfield held out to land the club's first trophy.

The news clattered into Huddersfield's electric telegraph office and was posted in windows along John William Street. Church bells rang out across the town and a crowd of 4000 gathered outside the railway station in St George' Square to greet their returning heroes. They had a long wait as the team travelled from Halifax by wagonette. Just after 7pm they reached the Infirmary at the top of New North Road, cup prominently displayed. There, the crowd unfastened the four horses and began to pull the wagonette themselves. At Fitzwilliam Street, the Huddersfield Brass Band marched to the head of the procession and played the traditional anthem for successful sports teams, *See the Conquering Hero Comes*.

At last, the procession reached St George's Square. Stopping outside the George Hotel, which was illuminated by Chinese lanterns, the team was cheered loud and long, and Harry Archer was chaired into the hotel for the official reception. Joseph Crosland, the President of the Football Section of the HC and AC, addressed the crowd from the windows of the hotel, with Archer summoned to the balcony on numerous occasions.

Afterwards there was an adjournment for tea, followed by a slow, torchlight procession of two waggonettes carrying the team and committee, accompanied by a large crowd, through the main streets of the town. Eventually they reached the home of Joseph Crosland in Park Drive where there was a firework display in front of the house. The cup was then filled with champagne and each member of the team had his sip, followed by congratulatory speeches by the Reverend Frank Marshall and others.

Communal morale continued to feast on this sporting success. Poems appeared in the local press, a tram was illuminated with the words 'Hurrah for the Claret and Gold', and local composer Robert Field wrote a spirited song of the same title that celebrated every section of the club and many individuals by name. A fortnight after the Yorkshire Cup Final, on 18 April 1890, *Hurrah for the Claret and Gold* was performed for the first time by Henry Wright during the Theatre Royal's Easter pantomime, *Blue Beard*, which was adapted to accommodate it. The song became a Huddersfield Music Hall favourite, and Robert Field was persuaded to write a follow-up for the 1890 Christmas pantomime season. Unfortunately, his second number, *They Haven't Met Their Equals Yet*, was soon historically inaccurate. It would be twenty years before Huddersfield's next Yorkshire Cup triumph.

Huddersfield v Wakefield Trinity
Yorkshire Cup Final
at Hanson Lane (Thrum Hall), Halifax, 5 April 1890

Huddersfield	**6**	**Wakefield Trinity**	**3**
Goals: 1 (5pts);		Minors: 3 (3pts)	
Richmond touchdown			
and Brooke conversion)			
Minors: 1 (1pt)			

Huddersfield
WH Eagland; J Dyson, F Richmond, ALBrooke; J Kaye, H Archer (captain); F Walker, W Lorriman, J Shaw, G Mitchell, O France, T Eagland, JW Thewlis, P Jackson, J Schofield

Wakefield Trinity
H Stafford; H Fallas (captain), JH Fotherby, M Varley; H Dawson, JH Thompson; P Booth, W Binks, R Dawson, J Latham, H Whiteley, A Garforth, J Jones, A Thompson, J Gomersall

Referee: Mr Holmes (Midland Counties)   Attendance: 20,000

Hurrah for the Claret and Gold

by

Robert Field

The followers of Football in Huddersfield are proud,
Our team the Yorkshire Challenge Cup has won;
We've tried our very utmost to win that good old Cup,
For years we've in the finals been out-done;
And now we are successful to each member praise is due,
For the gallant way he's fought for Huddersfield;
Let all stick to the colours of the Claret and the Gold,
And the Championship of Yorkshire never yield.

Chorus:
Then Hurrah for the Claret and Gold,
Hurrah for the Claret and Gold,
The champions of the day,
Long may each member play
'Neath the colours of the Claret and Gold.

The men behind our scrimmage are champions every one,
Acknowledged by the public and the press;
Such men as Brooke and Dyson are marvels all will own,
Such scorers as no other clubs possess;
With Richmond in the centre then we never fear defeat,
And if by accident they miss the ball,
There's Eagland just behind them who will quickly clear his lines,
For Will is just as safe as any wall.

Repeat Chorus

Our gallant captain Archer, and also smiling Kaye,
At half-back always play a dashing game;
As leader of our forwards Tom Eagland is well known,
And those who work the scrimmage I will name,
There's Schofield and Frank Walker, Thewlis, Shaw and Oscar France,
Paul Jackson, Mitchell, Lorriman, all told;
A champion set of forwards and we hope they long will play,
'Neath the colours of the Claret and the Gold.

Repeat Chorus

Hurrah! for J.P. Crosland, a gentleman we know,
Who has our football interest at heart;
Hurrah! for our committee, amongst those gentlemen,
Will Hirst and Harrop take an active part;
Our umpire Lupton Littlewood deserves a word of praise,
His efforts for our team ne'er seem to tire;
And also one more character, the trainer of our team,
Well known when on the field as Doctor Squire.

Repeat Chorus

Huddersfield had few, if any, unsung heroes in 1890.

Huddersfield's 1890 Yorkshire Cup-winning team

Back row (standing):   J Dyson, G Harrop (hon secretary), WH Eagland, L Littlewood (umpire), FH Richmond, JH Shaw, W Hirst (hon secretary), JW Thewlis, TH Eagland, JP Crosland (President);

Middle row (seated):   G Mitchell, P Jackson, H Archer (captain), O France, J Schofield;

Front row (on ground):   J Kaye, P Walker, W Lorriman, AL Brooke

Top: John W Thewlis and the front and back of his 1890 Yorkshire Cup-winners' medal.
Bottom: A silver engraved fob watch awarded by the club to the players in the 1890 Yorkshire Cup-winning team, and the Huddersfield cap awarded to John after his seven seasons with the club.

17

The townsfolk's spontaneous joy and pride at their club's Yorkshire Cup success showed the extent to which rugby football, and the club itself had become integral to local community life. From its humble beginnings as an offshoot of the HAC in the 1860s, the rugby section had progressed to become Huddersfield's foremost sporting team, representing the town with honour way beyond local boundaries. It had become one the focuses of the community, a conduit for demonstrating and developing community spirit, a feeling of togetherness and a sense of belonging. The club's weekly fortunes on the pitch impacted, to a degree, on the morale of the town.

The cup success attracted many new supporters. Encouraged and emboldened, the club planned ground improvements costing £5000, financed by the issue of 5000 shares at £1 each. Quickly over-subscribed, the share issue paid for levelling the cricket ground, the construction of a cycling track around it, and improved rugby facilities. The latter prevented any home matches in the first nine weeks of the 1891-92 rugby football season.

The delay was worth it. Fartown re-opened on 31 October 1892 to gasps from many of the 10,000 spectators. Huddersfield had a stadium as grand as any in the north. To cap the day, Cardiff were defeated 14-7. Two days later Blackheath, the second visitors of this celebratory weekend, lowered Huddersfield's colours in a 'rare exhibition of the science of rugby', but much of the attention still focused on the ground, the *HDE* commenting:

> Certainly the Huddersfield club have something to be proud of and the sight when the crowd assembled was worth seeing.
> It was a grand idea to convert the old tennis courts into the terraces for the accommodation of the popular people, and the fifteen tiers of spectators looked well and happy. Facing them is a handsome and extensive stand which, in a few days will be covered, and with all the ends and sides of the ground utilised for the crowds, it is expected that over 20,000 people will be provided for, and everyone in a position to see.

A month after this opening, Fartown hosted the Roses Match. A crowd of 23,250 and receipts of £843 13s 3d set new records for sport in the town and confirmed Fartown as a regular venue for big matches. These would include three Challenge Cup finals (1908 and the two replayed finals of 1911), three Championship finals (1907, 1936 and 1979) and the third Test Match between Great Britain and Australia in 1937.

In the more immediate future, the Huddersfield club's mushrooming status and expanded facilities brought pressures and expectations that success on the field would be sustained. These pressures would lead the club into direct conflict with the RFU, and to the forefront of the greatest crisis in the history of the game.

Chapter 3

Birth of the Northern Union

Huddersfield's Yorkshire Cup win of 1890 and the subsequent grand developments at Fartown brought new pressures and expectations. A focus of local attention, their matches attracted large crowds and gate receipts. There was a strong temptation to break the sanctity of the RFU's cardinal amateur rules by attracting and retaining the best players through payments and other enticements such as goods, a job and accommodation. Rumours abounded about the rewards offered and received by players at the north's bigger clubs. In the early 1890s there was almost a feeling that 'everyone was at it.'

In August 1893 Huddersfield signed the best two three-quarter backs in Cumberland, George Boak and John 'Jock' Forsyth from Carlisle-based club, Cummersdale Hornets. The fallout from these transactions would change the history of rugby in the town.

Amateurs and Professionals

The first team sport to accommodate professionalism was cricket. The summer sport had inherited a tradition of professionals from its earliest days when players were among the beneficiaries from betting-fuelled single-wicket matches.

As northern club cricket developed, professionals played alongside working class amateurs and were fêted for their skills. This contrasted with the professionals' second-class status in county cricket, where the amateurs were revered for their high social class as gentlemen who could afford to play for nothing. By implication, the amateurs were playing for the sake of the game and were therefore moral sportsmen who did not need to 'win at all costs'. Professionals needed the money – in itself a public display of lower social class – their 'poorer breeding' and financial dependence implying an increased likelihood of unsportsmanlike conduct. Cricket conveniently ignored the conduct of some amateurs, most notably WG Grace, who received large payments of 'expenses' and was not averse to bending the rules. Such 'shamateurism' reflected the hypocrisies of the rigid Victorian class system, but by turning a blind eye cricket stumbled along a pragmatic route that accommodated diversity – every man from north to south, aristocratic gentleman to working-class factory worker, amateur or professional – could play, and in the same matches.

By contrast, professionalism was banned in both association and rugby football until the mid-1880s, when the FA faced a growing crisis about payments and other enticements to players, usually driven by a craving for success in the FA Cup and in the increasing number of provincial cup competitions. Most of the offending clubs were in the game's northern hotbed of industrial Lancashire. Fortunately for the FA, its secretary and helmsman was Charles Alcock who had initiated the FA Cup, played in its first final, and fully appreciated what it meant to win it. In 1885, under his astute leadership, the FA bowed to the inevitable and allowed payments to players.

The RFU's Amateur Ethos

Of the three major team sports, only rugby now disallowed payments to players. In 1886, partly in reaction to the FA's decision, the upper-class gentlemen amateurs of the RFU formalised a ban on payments to players in RFU rules.

The RFU's amateur ethos – fair play and participating for the sake of the game – had been indoctrinated through the ideal that underpinned sporting morality in the public schools, 'Muscular Christianity'. Enshrining amateurism in the RFU's rules was an extension of this code. It kept rugby, at least in the eyes of its ruling elite, unsullied, and morally and socially superior to association football.

Regardless of their ability, rugby players who were not financially independent had to earn a living outside the game. In the south, where the game was primarily played by upper class gentlemen in front of mainly small crowds, this was not an issue. In the industrial northern towns of Yorkshire, Lancashire and Cumberland the amateur ideal was economically unsustainable. Rugby's Yorkshire Cup had the same effect as the FA Cup. Seduced by the allure of cup glory, clubs increasingly used enticements to attract and retain players, mirroring their Lancashire counterparts in the association game.

Huddersfield was not the only rugby club in the north attracting huge crowds. At Headingley in 1891, 27,654 watched the 3rd round Yorkshire Cup tie between Leeds and Halifax, bigger than the crowd for the FA Cup Final that year. As rugby's popularity and affluence increased, so did the tension between what clubs could afford to do and what they were allowed to do. No doubt many payments and other enticements went undetected, a good number were unproven, but for those who were caught, the punishments were harsh.

In 1889 one of Wakefield Trinity's best and longest-serving players, Teddy Bartram, was banned for life for receiving payments. In the same year Heckmondwike, whose players included England international and future captain Dickie Lockwood, were found guilty of paying and finding work for some of their players and banned from playing for three months,.

In July 1890 the Yorkshire RFU blocked the move of Albert Storer to Otley because he was to be a professional and groundsman in the club's cricket division. Similarly, Yorkshire wicketkeeper Sandy Bairstow was banned from playing rugby for Keighley because he was also Keighley's cricket professional and groundsman. Such bans were tacit admissions that the Yorkshire RFU could not police whether payments for rugby were hidden in cricket salaries.

In 1891 the Yorkshire RFU, pressurised by its leading clubs, inaugurated a league, the Yorkshire Senior Competition. They were attempting to copy the success of the Football League, which had been founded in 1888. Huddersfield committeeman, the Reverend Frank Marshall, accurately regarded the new league as 'a step towards professionalism'.

Marshall, headmaster of Almondbury Grammar School since 1878, was an acknowledged authority on the game and had absolute belief in the amateur ideal. The Yorkshire Senior Competition intensified rivalries between clubs. The pressure to sign and retain the best players increased, as did suspicions and accusations of professionalism. The Reverend Marshall, Huddersfield's representative on the Yorkshire County Committee, pursued the accused with fanatical zeal. Charges were brought against several clubs, notoriously Bradford and Elland in 1892, the latter implicating two Huddersfield players. It resembled a witch hunt, with Marshall as self-appointed witch-finder general. In his view, clubs 'had to be compelled by the stringency of rules' because of their 'evident disinclination to be tied by the spirit of honour.'

Broken Time Pay

The leading northern clubs were largely defensive when professionalism was discussed – most if not all were guilty – but they were more aggressive in their support of bona fide 'broken time' payments, which the RFU also disallowed. Broken time pay was the repayment of wages lost if a player had to leave his place of work early to play. In an era when mines and factories were open until 1 or 2pm on Saturday afternoons, broken time payments were common recompense in club cricket and in association football, particularly for players in away teams. An overwhelming majority in the north believed such payments were just, and should be applied to rugby footballers too.

The volatile economy added fuel to the arguments for broken time pay. By 1893 the country had slipped into recession. Pay had been cut, jobs lost, and industrial unrest had become violent in several northern rugby towns. In St Helens miners set fire to the Pilkington Glass Factory after the Pilkington family sacked miners in their coal pits. There was a five-month lock-out at the Oldham cotton mills. Troops charged striking mine workers in Bradford's Town Hall Square. More troops were required to disperse a picket line outside a coal mine at Featherstone. The miners resisted and two of the pickets were shot dead. After violence from striking dock workers in Hull, the government positioned gunboats on the Humber.

Against this backdrop of unrest, on 5 June 1893, the Yorkshire RFU's AGM passed a unanimous decision. At the national RFU's AGM on 20 September, the county's President, James Millar, was to propose modification of the laws, permitting remuneration for players' bona fide loss of time as 'the only means of resisting professionalism'.

A special train was chartered to Kings Cross to maximise votes in favour and the Westminster Hotel was packed as Millar urged the RFU to recognise the unfairness of their sport to working class men. They were playing at a financial loss they could ill-afford, before thousands of spectators who were paying to watch them. Most of the Lancashire clubs were in support, but a majority of the speakers in the impassioned debate were intransigent in opposing the motion, arguing that broken time pay would be the first step towards full professionalism. There was little empathy or sympathy for working class players in the north. The motion was defeated by 282 votes to 136. Millar felt particularly betrayed by the Reverend Frank Marshall who broke ranks with his Yorkshire colleagues by speaking and voting for the status quo.

James Millar and the Reverend Frank Marshall

The meeting then passed even more stringent regulations in favour of amateurism. Any player or club accused of professionalism would be regarded as guilty until proven innocent, contrary to the country's accepted burden of proof. In prioritising the Corinthian amateur ideal over the economic reality of working-class players, the message was clear. If a man could not afford to play rugby he should not play. A schism in rugby's ranks loomed. For clubs that relied on working class players, a breakaway union was one solution. The other was to pay their broken time – and the rest – and not get caught!

Satirical cartoons from *The Yorkshireman* reflected and perpetuated the ridicule heaped on the
Reverend Frank Marshall.
The first depicts Marshall and Yorkshire RFU President James Millar outside the gates of Almondbury
Grammar School, where Marshall was headmaster. The writing on the gatepost proclaims:
'ALMONDBURY GRAMMAR SCHOOL FOR YOUTHS OF INDEPENDENT MEANS ONLY'.
The cartoon was captioned:

Marshall: Oh, fie, go away naughty boy, I don't play with boys who can't afford to take a
holiday for football any day they like!

Miller: Yes, that's just you to a T; you'd make it so that no lad whose father wasn't a
millionaire could play at all in a really good team. For my part I see no reason why
the men who make the money shouldn't have a share in the spending of it.

The second cartoon caricatures Reverend Frank Marshall as Mrs Partington, who was famous for
trying to sweep back the tide of the Atlantic.

Boak and Forsyth: Huddersfield Accused

The club hoping most fervently not to be caught was Huddersfield, which was under suspicion
for illegally enticing and paying George Boak and John 'Jock' Forsyth, two of the best players
from Cumberland. Bill Boak, George's grandson recalls: 'George
was a three-quarter, so as you would expect, he had a turn of speed,
and he was quite a renowned local sprinter over 100 yards.'

Boak and Forsyth had arrived in Huddersfield on 8 August 1893,
walked straight into accommodation and within two days had jobs
at Read, Holliday and Sons chemical works. They also began to
train with the Huddersfield club, of which Mr Holliday, owner of the
chemical works, was President. It was Holliday who proposed them
as members of the rugby club on 15 August. Had the formal approval
of broken time at the Yorkshire AGM in June lulled Huddersfield
into complacency?

George Boak

The Reverend Marshall, who suspected subterfuge and understood the workings of the RFU, pleaded with his fellow Huddersfield committee men to formally secure the transfers of Boak and Forsyth from Cummersdale Hornets as soon as possible, and certainly before they played any matches. In Marshall's opinion, it was 'the step that would have guarded and protected the club'. Sadly, Marshall had long since been alienated for his views about professionalism. As far back as 1889, a Special Meeting of the Huddersfield committee had asked him to stop prosecuting cases of alleged professionalism. Most on the committee neither liked nor trusted him, but the price for ridiculing and ignoring his advice about 'the hazardous nature of the course the Committee were adopting' on this occasion would be a heavy one.

On 2 September Boak and Forsyth made their Huddersfield debuts in the first match of the season against Salford. On the same day Huddersfield contacted Cummersdale Hornets, but the players had taken the field before permission for their transfer was received, an error that invited scrutiny from the RFU.

Three days later, 5 September, Huddersfield received a hostile reply from Mr Jordan, Honorary Secretary of Cummersdale Hornets:

> The circumstances under which Forsyth and Boak left Cummersdale are such that my committee have been obliged to refer the matter to the Cumberland Rugby Union, hence we are unable to grant the transfer request. In any case your application arrived too late seeing that the players referred to were actually taking part in a match on the very day of the application.

On 9 September Cummersdale wrote to the Cumberland County RFU, stating that Forsyth and Boak and been 'induced to leave' their club.

Meanwhile, on 4 September, Marshall had questioned an ex-Huddersfield committeeman William Hardy, whom he suspected of 'engineering' the migration of Forsyth and Boak through inducements. 'His reply confirmed me in my suspicions and I resigned immediately from the committee.' With Marshall now a free agent and unlikely to keep his own counsel, Huddersfield's prospects looked bleak.

One can imagine Marshall's emotional state at this time. The Boak/Forsyth issue was still to be adjudicated and had just precipitated his resignation from the Huddersfield club. Against his wishes, the Yorkshire RFU was about to propose in favour of broken time pay at the RFU's AGM in London on 20 September. Marshall was always going to oppose broken time in London, but in speaking with particular passion against it and as a member of the county committee proposing it, he made arguably the most influential contribution to the debate. Would he have spoken quite so earnestly and effectively but for the Boak/Forsyth issue?

For Huddersfield, the RFU's AGM was a disaster. Defeat for the proposal on broken time pay, and the passing of even more punitive laws on amateurism, reversing the burden of proof were bad enough. Then, to their horror, the Cumberland County RFU notified the national body that they were bringing a charge of professionalism against Huddersfield. The first club in the dock under the new principle of guilty until proven innocent was Huddersfield.

Boak and Forsyth in the Dock

Huddersfield's problems briefly took a back seat. On 30 September at Carlisle Police Court, Cummersdale Print Works charged Boak and Forsyth with leaving their employment without giving due notice.

Forsyth, who was 26 years old, was a skilled machine printer earning £1 a week. Boak, aged 22, was a 'back tender' (machine assistant) earning just 10s per week. Their employer claimed that twenty pieces of cloth had been ruined trying to get Forsyth's machine to operate and that a production line of machines had ground to a halt for a week because 'no one was acquainted with the thread of his work'.

Neither man appeared in court. Both were found guilty and ordered to pay costs of 10s, with fines of £3 against Forsyth and £1 against Boak.

Bill Boak has some sympathy with his grandfather:

> He was earning the princely sum of 10 shillings per week at Cummersdale, so really he had a tremendous incentive to move to Huddersfield or anywhere else that would pay him more money ... he would certainly be much better off in Yorkshire and I don't really blame him for what he did. After all, he'd had to leave his family behind and the incentive must have been there.

Huddersfield in the Dock

Attention now switched to the RFU enquiry, on which the *Bradford Observer* commented:

> The case of the two Cumberland men has been under consideration ever since they migrated, and was bound to form the subject of examination sooner or later. The gravity of the matter only becomes apparent when one supposes the event of Huddersfield being convicted of professionalism ... The enquiry into the Huddersfield transfers should take place at Carlisle tomorrow, but the accused club, with rather doubtful policy, objects to the venue.
>
> It seems to us that as "Huddersfield court the fullest enquiry" they should throw no obstacles in the way of the same taking place without delay ... Anyhow, Forsyth and Boak appear to have been played by Huddersfield in ignorance of their manner of leave-taking at Carlisle, because no club would voluntary take a risk of that kind upon itself ... Huddersfield are no worse than their neighbours, but this enquiry looks rather more serious than the usual thing, and that for several reasons. The Rugby Union is on the 'qui vive' now that it has received the mandate from the country at large to hunt up cases of professionalism, real or imaginary. Another thing which causes matters to look rather ominous is that somebody appears to know something special about the Huddersfield case.

Forsyth and Boak had indeed been regulars in the Huddersfield team to that point in the season. The 'somebody' who had inside information about their case was, of course, Frank Marshall, who was asked to appear before the enquiry as an 'independent' witness.

The enquiry, on 13 October 1893, was switched from Carlisle to Preston at Huddersfield's request. The Yorkshire and Cumberland county authorities were refused representation on the investigating RFU sub-committee, which sat in private from 4pm to 11pm and heard evidence from many witnesses. The Huddersfield case was presented by the club's joint honorary secretaries Harry Beardsell and William Hirst.

Their explanation for Huddersfield's delay in applying to Cummersdale for the transfers was that 'the football season had not then commenced', and 'Cummersdale Hornets was not at that time a member of the English Rugby Union'. It didn't succeed, but was merely a prelude to the main event; how did Boak and Forsyth come to sign for Huddersfield at all, and, specifically, were they offered inducements?

Beardsell, Hirst and their witnesses then embarked on a convoluted tale which began with a youth called Armstrong who hailed from Langholme, four miles from Carlisle.

Armstrong, who was employed in a hardware shop in Huddersfield, claimed to have known Jock Forsyth for five or six years and had seen him play football. Around Easter 1893, whilst waiting for a train at Carlisle, Armstrong had allegedly bumped into Forsyth, who had told him he was 'tired of being in such a quiet, out-of-the-way place as Cummersdale'. He had asked

Armstrong to let him know if he heard of any employment which might suit him, and that 'he had a friend who would also like to leave'. The implication was that the initial approach had come from the players via Armstrong.

A second chance meeting had occurred in Manchester, between William Forsyth, Jock Forsyth's uncle, and Huddersfield RFC's ex-committeeman, William Hardy. They had discussed rugby football and Hardy was invited to visit Forsyth in Cummersdale that summer. He travelled up there in July but was recalled to Huddersfield early and so planned to return to Cumberland in August. By then, Armstrong had written to Jock Forsyth to tell him that a Huddersfield chemical works, Read, Holliday and Sons, was taking on extra hands. Armstrong had, meanwhile, met Hardy in Huddersfield and, learning that he was travelling to Carlisle to visit William Forsyth by excursion train on Saturday 5 August, bought two return tickets for Jock Forsyth and George Boak.

On Sunday 6 August, Hardy watched Forsyth and Boak run at an athletics meeting in Kendal, and he was seen in their company several times over the next couple of days, before returning with them to Huddersfield on Tuesday 8 August.

The Huddersfield club freely admitted all of Hardy's and Armstrong's actions. Their defence was that Hardy had resigned from both their committee and as a member of the club several months earlier, that they had no knowledge of the players until after they arrived in the town, and that there was no evidence to prove otherwise.

This unlikely claim became even more incredible when the Reverend Marshall gave his evidence. Marshall was asked to explain why he had resigned from the Huddersfield committee, and the following is a précis of his letter to the Huddersfield committee detailing his reasons.

Marshall's suspicions were first aroused when he saw Forsyth and Boak at a cricket match at Fartown on Saturday 12 August, 'being taken round in company with prominent members of the football section and … openly introduced as new players who would strengthen the football team'. The 'prominent members' were the Huddersfield three-quarter back, Jack Dyson, a committeeman, Leonard, and Hardy.

Later in August, at the club's St John's Gymnasium headquarters, Marshall 'learnt sufficient to cause me to suspect that matters were not altogether right as regards Forsyth and Boak'. This was confirmed by a conversation with Hardy on 4 September.

> I could not be a party to the methods adopted by the Committee. Their plan was to assume ignorance – to know nothing officially … The club may not be guilty (legally), but I am so convinced that the removal of the men from Cummersdale has been brought about by means that are contrary to the spirit of the laws of the Rugby Union … that I will have nothing to do with the club officially. I decline to make myself 'particeps criminis'.

Marshall also supplied evidence that Hardy had attended a committee meeting during the summer and had recently sat in committee seats in the stand during matches at Fartown.

In Huddersfield it was known that during September Marshall had also been to Carlisle and arranged for two Cummersdale men to visit Huddersfield to confirm Hardy's identity. Hardy had refused to see them. Intriguingly, these witnesses were then followed through Huddersfield, and later through Leeds by two men, one of whom was Jack Dyson. It is not known whether this piece of information was presented to the enquiry.

Unsurprisingly, Huddersfield was found guilty of breaking the rules on professionalism by enticing players through payments and offers of work. The enquiry cited that: Armstrong was barely acquainted with Forsyth and did not even know Boak; neither were Hardy and William Forsyth previously acquainted, making Hardy's invitation to holiday with Forsyth unlikely; Forsyth and Boak were unlikely to move just for a change of scenery; and Hardy seemed prone to an improbable number of chance meetings.

All of this, plus the advance train tickets and pre-arranged jobs at the company owned by the club President pointed to a plot hatched by the club, which Marshall's evidence only confirmed.

The findings of the sub-committee were reported to the RFU Committee on 26 October at a meeting at the Craven Hotel in the Strand, London. After a seven-hour discussion, Forsyth and Boak were suspended permanently.

Only the sentence for the club remained. Expulsion from the union was seriously considered. Many feared that Saturday 11 November 1893 would see the last match at Fartown.

The crucial meeting was held in London on the evening of Tuesday 14 November. Hundreds assembled by the electric telegraph office in John William Street to await the news, which was wired at 10.30pm. Huddersfield had been suspended until the end of 1893, a total of eight matches. They had also to pay the costs of the enquiry, originally fixed at £50 but later reduced to £33. The sentence was harsh, but was also a long-term reprieve. Minutes show that the committee's initial intention had indeed been to expel Huddersfield from the RFU.

The Birth of Rugby League

The Rugby Union continued its campaign against professionalism. Other clubs – Broughton Rangers, Rochdale, Swinton and Tyldesley were investigated and Leigh, Salford and Wigan, like Huddersfield, were banned. Tensions between the RFU's amateur elite and the working-class northern clubs reached breaking point.

The amateur ideal had proved impossible to police effectively or fairly. The gap between sporting ideal and economic reality had become a chasm. Opinion had polarised: amateur v professional; south v north; upper class gentleman v working class factory worker. Yet, even with the game about to split asunder, the RFU remained dogmatic and uncompromising. Any prospect of professionalism besmirching the game was to be crushed by the ruthless persecution of suspected 'pros' and their clubs.

Seething at the injustice, the principal Yorkshire and Lancashire clubs met at Huddersfield's George Hotel towards the end of 1894. They declared that the views of the Rugby Union towards professionalism 'are not a reasonable and just interpretation and cannot be accepted by us'. This meeting, according to a local contemporary, 'practically settled the question'.

Even so, lengthy deliberations over the next few months suggest that, had the RFU acceded over broken time pay, the northern clubs would have continued their league competitions under the RFU banner. The RFU's refusal to compromise made a breakaway inevitable. On Thursday 29 August 1895 at the George Hotel, Huddersfield, representatives from twenty-one clubs reconsidered the issues. After three hours they resolved, by 20 votes to one, to resign from the RFU, to 'form a Northern Rugby Football Union and … push forward without delay … on … the payment for … "broken time" only'. Broken time pay was set at 6 shillings per day.

The 21 clubs at the meeting were: Batley, Bradford, Brighouse Rangers, Dewsbury, Halifax, Huddersfield, Hull, Hunslet, Leeds, Liversedge, Manningham and Wakefield Trinity (Yorkshire): Broughton Rangers, Leigh, Oldham, Rochdale Hornets, St Helens, Tyldesley, Warrington, Widnes and Wigan (Lancashire and Cheshire). Dewsbury, which voted against, remained within the RFU for a further six years, but Stockport and Runcorn brought the Northern Union's number to 22.

These clubs were quickly cut adrift by the RFU which ruled that no matches would be allowed between 'clubs belonging to our union' and 'any club … of the Northern Union'.

The Rugby Football Union did eventually allow players to be paid – in 1995, one hundred years after the game split in two and saw the birth of rugby league, which was the name adopted by the Northern RFU in 1922.

Top Left: The plaque on the George Hotel, commemorating its place in rugby league history, was unveiled in October 2012 as part of the pre-tournament Trophy Tour launch of the 2013 Rugby League World Cup.

Top Right: The George Hotel in the 1890s

Below: Centrepiece of the launch event was a performance by Year 6 children from Scholes Junior and Infant School based on the final scene of Mick Martin's play about the birth of rugby league, *Broken Time*. The scene reproduces the famous meeting of 1895 in the hotel's Charter Suite, at the end of which the vote was taken to break away from the RFU and to set up the Northern Union.

The Holliday Cup

The formation of the Northern Rugby Union looked likely to affect the Holliday Cup. How could an amateur rugby union competition continue among clubs likely to follow the lead of the town's senior club into the Northern Union and its allowance of broken time pay? Huddersfield's district representative on the Yorkshire Union, the newly-elected Mr J Berry, commented:

It is probably the last time that the Holliday Cup will be offered for competition, as the committee who manage it are of the opinion that the object for which it had been instituted has been attained.

Mr Berry's opinion proved to be totally wrong. As the local amateur clubs switched virtually en masse to Northern Union, the Holliday Cup became a Northern Union competition. The competition's long and distinguished history remains unbroken, bar the wartime years of 1914-18 and some of 1939-45. In April 1994 the old trophy was replaced after 109 years as its continued use and cleaning was gradually wearing away the engraving. At the request of the Huddersfield and District League Committee, a replacement trophy was provided by Holliday Dyes and Chemicals Ltd, the family successors, a few takeovers and amalgamations removed, from the Read Holliday company that supplied the original trophy.

Boak Family Memories

What of the chief protagonists in the Boak/Forsyth saga?

The Huddersfield club produced for its members a 'Committee's Report of Cumberland v Huddersfield on a Charge of Professionalism'. It concluded:

> Unfortunately the result of the judgement affects your Club very materially, not only in its status, but also from a pecuniary point of view. The loss will be large, but no doubt your Club will be able to partly recoup itself after the period of suspension … It is a matter of extreme regret that the status of the Club … should at this period in its history, when gaining ground rapidly, have a stain upon its character by reason of this unfortunate suspension.

The verdict hardened Huddersfield's view of the RFU and made their involvement in any breakaway union more certain. Geographically central to the founder clubs of the Northern Union, the Huddersfield venue for the birth of the Union also suggests that the club was particularly committed and their support guaranteed.

In 1896, within a year of the birth of the Northern Union, the Reverend Frank Marshall resigned his headmaster's position at Almondbury to become Rector of Mileham in Norfolk. He died on 19 April 1906, aged 58.

An undated newspaper cutting suggests that Jock Forsyth and George Boak were indeed enticed to Huddersfield, stating that Forsyth would probably start on 30 shillings per week with Boak on 25 shillings, with future increases dependent on how they suited the team. These wages improve on their earnings in Cummersdale by 50% for Forsyth and by 150% for Boak, certainly enough to persuade them to move.

If the two players returned to Carlisle after they were banned from playing on 26 October, they would at least have had finance to tide them over a few weeks. They may even have continued to work at Read, Holliday and Sons for a time.

Nothing is known of Jock Forsyth after 1893, but, George Boak's descendants, interviewed in 2012, have revealed much about the rest of George's story.

Bill Boak, George's grandson, was asked what impact it would have had on the family when George moved to Huddersfield:

> I think it would obviously put a strain on the family. He left a wife in her early twenties with three children. He had two girls up to 1893 - one was born in 1893 - I guess he must have felt pretty lonely, especially after the unfavourable publicity of the move.

The 1901 census shows George Boak back in Carlisle, where Carlisle RUFC was the only Cumberland club still playing rugby union, the rest having switched to the Northern Union code. There is evidence that Boak played Northern Union. Ironically, a few years after his 'permanent' ban by the RFU, he was one of the few players given permission to return from Northern Union to play rugby union. It seems logical, given their ban from rugby union, and their age, that Forsyth also played Northern Union at some point. Perhaps both players were able to earn remuneration from rugby after all. Bill Boak commented:

> I don't know how he felt after things had settled down and he'd come back to Carlisle but I imagine that he'd be extremely disappointed to lose the prospect of a decent wage and perhaps a more congenial sort of job.

George became a successful publican, first at the Royal Oak in Caldewgate, near the biscuit works in Carlisle. In 1905 he moved across the city with his wife and family to run the Spinners Arms, a building which is still standing in Milbourne Street. Bill Boak recalls:

> He must have still been pretty athletic, because I remember Mum saying that he would think nothing, if somebody was getting rowdy or stroppy, of jumping over the bar and kicking them out ... he still had the athleticism. Although he only appeared to be quite a small man he still had the physique to turf somebody out.
>
> I knew George's wife (my grandmother) Isabella, who was called Bella. I knew her well, very well. She still lived in the pub, the Spinners Arms, which ceased to be a pub in 1916 when the Control Board nationalised pubs in this area and in parts of Scotland. That was because drunkenness amongst the workers was affecting production in the munitions factory at Gretna, which was the largest in the country. The government turned the pubs into temperance houses.
>
> Bella carried on living there and I think she tried to run it as a non-liquor pub for food and soft drinks and that sort of thing. After all, she had to make a bit of money somehow. When George died, she had had twelve children, ten of whom survived. She was a kind old soul. Everybody liked her.

George Boak drowned in the River Eden in 1914. He was 43 years of age.

George Boak's Athletic Legacy

Bill Boak tells us that George's athleticism lives on through his descendants:

> George has over 100 descendants and I'm delighted to say that his sporting prowess – his sporting ability – has been passed down four generations.

Sport was certainly a serious business in the family. Bill Boak's mother told him about George once admonishing his son, Sam …

> … for going swimming in the morning of a day when he was going to run in a boys' race. The feeling at the time ... was that swimming and athletics – running – just didn't mix, that swimming was bad for running, and running was the family sport, not swimming.

Echoing George's move to Huddersfield, in 1923 Sam was invited to play as centre forward for Castleford and Allerton United FC. The package to move from Carlisle included accommodation and a job at Allerton Bywater Colliery. Unlike George's move 30 years earlier, such enticements were, of course, entirely within the rules.

In the 1950s, George's grandson, Bill, represented England in several international cross-country events, and was good enough to record victories over both Jim Peters and Huddersfield's Derek Ibbotson in 1953. Ibbotson went on the win bronze in the 5000 metres at the 1956 Melbourne Olympics and to set the world record for the mile in 1957.

Almost a century after George's death, his athletic legacy continued; in 2012 George's great-great children, Robert and Gillian, were due to run in the New York Marathon which was cancelled in the wake of Hurricane Sandy. 'I don't know whether the athleticism will continue through future generations,' said Bill, 'but it would be nice to think so.'

The notorious Boak and Forsyth case did not actually force the formation of the Northern Union. But as the most high profile and contemporary case when broken time pay was rejected by the RFU in 1893, the point of no return, it was arguably the most influential.

Chapter 4

Settling into the Northern Union

It is appropriate that Huddersfield, a town with a proud radical heritage, should be the birthplace of the Northern Union. The image of northern working class sportsmen sticking up two metaphorical fingers to the upper class, predominantly southern aristocrats of the Rugby Football Union (RFU) sits comfortably alongside Luddite riots, and the town's political conscientious objectors of World War I who identified more closely with international working class comrades than with Britain's political and military elite.

Following the famous meeting at the George Hotel, the RFU immediately banned its clubs from playing matches against Northern Union clubs. Rugby Union players who participated in a Northern Union match would also be banned.

The first Northern Union matches were played on Saturday 7 September 1895, just nine days after the split. Huddersfield were not among the 20 competing clubs on the opening day, and had to wait until 14 September to take the field, when Wakefield Trinity visited Fartown.

Captained by Harry Lodge, beginning the last season of his fine career, Huddersfield sported a new strip of claret shirts with white collars and the borough coat of arms on the left breast, blue shorts and claret socks. Huddersfield won 10-0 with two second half 'goals' (converted tries) but it was a rare success in a season of 'disappointment and disaster.' Of 42 matches, they won only ten, losing 27 and drawing five to finish third from bottom in the Northern Union League.

Northern Union rugby was one of two far-reaching changes at the Huddersfield club that season. On 31 August 1895, two days after the famous meeting at the George Hotel, the Fartowners formed an 'Association Section.' Erecting goalposts in front of the rugby posts, this team also played its home matches at Fartown, usually prior to the second team rugby matches on Saturday afternoons. In 1902 they moved to a pitch at Marsh, returning briefly to Fartown in 1904-05.

Still formalising its rules, in October 1895 the Northern Union voted to allow 'bona fide broken time' pay, limited to six shillings (30p) per day, but banned any other form of payment to players. Halifax and Wakefield proposed reducing the number of players from 15 to 13 per side to make the game more open and exciting, but this was defeated by 18 votes to nine, Huddersfield voting against. Progress towards a more attractive spectacle was gradual, beginning in 1897 when line-outs were abolished, and points-scoring altered so that a try counted three, with conversions and penalty goals two.

The RFU, meanwhile, reinforced its inflexibility by imposing a ban on the Huddersfield Police Force. This ridiculous decision followed a charity rugby union match between the local constabulary and the 'Old Fossils' to raise funds for a horse ambulance. Because the match was at Fartown, the RFU declared that the policemen were professionals and refused to allow them to practise on the Paddock rugby union ground for the return match.

In 1896-97, to reduce the excessive number of fixtures while retaining local rivalries, the fledgling Northern Union split into two separate county-based leagues – the Yorkshire Senior Competition and the Lancashire Senior Competition. This also left room for a new knockout cup competition – the Challenge Cup. The first round draw was made at the George Hotel, Huddersfield, on 3 September 1896, pairing Huddersfield with Swinton in a tie that the locals lost 12-4. The closest Huddersfield came to honours was hosting the semi-final between Warrington and eventual winners, Batley.

The Huddersfield team of 1896-97
Back: W Stubbings, A Boothroyd, J Conley, J Moxon, M Sutcliffe (Capt), TE Dickinson,
T Dickinson, J Debney, A Bennett (trainer)
Middle: H Taylor, HH Wood, F Bath, PM France, JW Bradley, A Wilson, J Clifford
Front: WH Smith, F Lorriman, JF Taylor

Partly attracted by the excitement of league and cup matches, and partly fearful of losing players to clubs that could recompense lost, broken time earnings, a growing number of clubs in the industrial north switched codes to the Northern Union. An increasing number of rugby union clubs found themselves bereft of local opponents and also switched, so that the Northern Union grew exponentially. New names appeared on the Huddersfield fixture list, the Yorkshire section for 1896-97 including Bramley, Castleford, Heckmondwike, Holbeck, and Leeds Parish Church. By 1898 the Northern Union had 59 member clubs.

Membership of the Yorkshire Rugby Football Union (YRFU) plummeted from 150 clubs in 1895 to 14 by 1907. National RFU membership collapsed from 481 clubs in 1895 to 244 by 1903, nearly all of the lost clubs joining the Northern Union.

The leading Northern Union clubs were flourishing financially. Huddersfield Cricket and Athletic Club (HC and AC) turned a deficit of £96 in 1895-96 to profits of £420 in 1896-97 and £1525 in 1897-98, aided by a then record Fartown crowd of 14,500 which paid receipts of £202 for the visit of Brighouse Rangers on Boxing Day 1897. Public enthusiasm, captured by the context of the Northern Union's league and cup matches, was reflected and encouraged by increasingly sophisticated analysis and reporting in the press.

In 1898, buoyed by its success, the Northern Union allowed professionalism for players, providing that they had other employment and had worked the last three working days before they played. The bona fide employment clause was viewed as bringing a moral dimension to professionalism, as espoused by Huddersfield's joint secretary Harry Beardsell in 1899:

> ... playing of the game for the sake of remuneration only should not be the sole aim of life.

Professionalism proved to be a mixed blessing for the sport. Whilst the leading clubs from the larger conurbations could now attract the best players, smaller ones struggled. Liversedge, the smallest of the Yorkshire Senior Competition clubs who founded the Northern Union in 1895, could no longer compete with the best after 1898. Nearly all Northern Union clubs

Todmorden's rugby ground – The Holme – in 1899, screened from the eyes of non-paying spectators by canvas erected on match days. On the boundary of the country's most vibrant football hotbeds – rugby in West Yorkshire and association in North East Lancashire – fierce annual competition for use of this ground from clubs of both football codes pushed up the rent. Todmorden changed from rugby union to Northern Union in 1897, but disbanded owing to financial problems in 1903. The club reformed in 1911, disbanded in 1914, reformed in 1925 and disbanded in 1931.

initially tried to follow the professional model, but the smaller ones had to work very hard to raise the money. The memberships of the Yorkshire Senior Competition's feeder divisions were in constant flux as clubs were formed whilst others went bankrupt or faded out of existence, some re-forming later.

The unrelenting need to balance the books whilst paying, at the very least, broken time and transport expenses, in addition to training the players and preparing the pitch, made huge demands of volunteers. Many pitches were improvised on parks and recreation grounds, requiring immense effort to screen and secure them to prevent spectators from watching without paying the entrance fees that were the lifeblood of the club. In some districts, increasing competition from association football for pitches put desirable land at a premium, so that profiteering landlords could demand large annual rents. Unsurprisingly many clubs over-reached themselves in finance and manpower. A high-profile casualty was Brighouse Rangers, which folded in 1906, forced to sell the club's assets to pay arrears in rent. Most of the surviving clubs eventually agreed not to pay their players anything. Today there are fewer than 50 professional and semi-professional rugby league clubs and many more amateur rugby league clubs.

The large crowds brought behavioural issues at Fartown and other venues. In 1896 a group of youths threw ashes at the players during a match at Fartown, and later in the year one of the same group threw an open pocket knife onto the pitch. After Huddersfield's match at Castleford in January 1900, the referee needed a police escort as protection from 'a hooting, yelling, and cursing crowd of rowdies.' There were similar wild scenes from incensed Huddersfield supporters in 1903. Fartown was closed for three weeks after the Salford players were molested as they left the pitch, and an ambush was prepared for the referee who 'had to escape by a back entrance.'

Huddersfield's stalwarts players in these early days of the Northern Union included wing-forward Milford Sutcliffe, who made his debut aged 16 in 1894 and was captain for seven seasons, taking over from Harry Lodge in 1896. He represented Yorkshire at rugby union and Northern Union, and went on to be Chairman and a life member of the Fartown club.

In 1900 Milford Sutcliffe was joined in the Huddersfield team by Billy Kitchin, a Cumberland wing three-quarter who played at Fartown for eleven seasons. The adoption of professionalism attracted many rugby union players from the mining villages of south Wales to the Northern Union. Huddersfield had five in their ranks by the end of the 1897-98 season, but the best of these early migrants was Llewellyn Deere, a three-quarter back from Mountain Ash, near Merthyr Tydfil, who signed in 1900. Another recruit was Arthur Larard, a native of Hull who had fought in the Boer War and won two caps for the South African rugby union team, scoring their first-ever international try in 1896.

Milford Sutcliffe

Kitchen, Deere and Larard were influential in a long-term improvement in the Huddersfield team, but their impact was far from immediate. In 1901-02 the NRFU adopted a 'first division' of clubs from both sides of the Pennines, with the remaining clubs from the Yorkshire and Lancashire senior competitions in parallel second divisions. Huddersfield only avoided relegation because, for 1902-03, the top division was expanded from 14 to 18 clubs, now with one second division. After two further seasons of strife, Huddersfield were relegated in bottom place in 1903-04. The blame for the club's descent 'into the abyss of second-class football' was laid squarely, if not entirely fairly, on the sizeable Welsh contingent

Loss of fixtures against the biggest clubs and demotion to second class status had proved terminal for several clubs, three of which – Holbeck, Manningham and Stockport – had switched codes to the association game in 1903 and were lost to the Northern Union forever.

Jolted by these major setbacks, the Northern Union reverted to one division in 1905-06. This announcement came just in time for Huddersfield. Dismayed by Second Division rugby football, dismal performances and poor crowds, the HC and AC called a special meeting of the general committee for 13 February 1905. The rugby football committee was invited to resign en bloc. It was suggested that the club should follow the example of Manningham – which had reformed as Bradford City FC and was now playing with some success in Football League Division 2 – by abandoning the Northern Union code and establishing a professional association football club. The Huddersfield and District Association League, founded in 1898, had accelerated the growth of the association game, which was rapidly approaching the popularity of Northern Union rugby in the locality.

The proposal that the NRFU should return to a single division, and with it the prospect of more lucrative fixtures against leading clubs such as Bradford, Halifax, Salford and Wigan, bought the rugby section some time. Four months later on 2 June 1905, the AGM of the HC and AC discontinued the Fartown association section owing to poor support – it too was losing money. Stanley Chadwick, writing in *Claret and Gold: 1895-1945* asserts:

> The abandonment of Association football at Fartown ... led to the formation of a local company to run a first class football team, and the establishment of the Huddersfield Town club ... at Leeds Road.

Huddersfield Town FC was founded in 1908. The association game was so strong in Huddersfield and district that Huddersfield Town was accepted into the Football League in 1910. The club's continuous existence in the Football League since 1910, including its spectacular rise to become the most successful in the country in the 1920s, suggests that decisions taken at the HC and AC meetings of 13 February and 2 June 1905 were pivotal to professional sport in Huddersfield.

Soon after the termination of Fartown's association team, the NRFU passed a resolution that no clubs would be 'admitted or allowed to continue' unless their football commitment was 'entirely devoted to the Northern Union game.' Chairman of the NRFU was Huddersfield's John Clifford.

It would be 60 years before the game would attempt a two-division structure again. In 1905 the NRFU took further steps to stem the haemorrhage of clubs, allowing open professionalism and introducing the Yorkshire and Lancashire Cups. These innovations were followed in 1906 by long-mooted attempts to make the game faster and more exciting – the play-the-ball to restart play after a tackle, and the reduction of teams from 15 to 13 players.

Three years earlier, the NRFU AGM of 1903 had voted 54-24 in favour of a 12-aside game, five votes short of the 75% majority needed to effect the change. Huddersfield voted against the reduction, but nevertheless participated in one of the game's 12-aside trial matches, winning their 'friendly' 1903 Boxing Day fixture against Brighouse 11-3.

Fartown hosted another unusual fixture twelve months later. Following a smallpox outbreak in Dewsbury, two clubs, Bramley and Rochdale Hornets cancelled their home matches against Dewsbury to avoid the risk of infection spreading to their towns. Bramley were fined £7 by an unsympathetic NRFU and, failing to heed the warning, Rochdale were fined £20. The NRFU threatened that any further clubs failing to fulfil their fixtures with Dewsbury would incur 'substantial damages.'

After meeting local health officials, Huddersfield proceeded with their match against Dewsbury on 10 December 1904, but only members were admitted to the ground, guaranteeing that no Dewsbury supporters could see the game. Mounted police ensured that the gates remained locked, although some supporters obtained a distant view of the match from higher land around the ground.

In 1905-06 the Northern Union proceeded with the one division structure that had quite possibly saved the Northern Union section at Fartown, but the new 31-team league looked cumbersome. Clubs could not possibly play all the others home and away, so positions were decided by percentage points achieved from those possible. The system did, however, allow clubs to play more matches against near rivals, whilst seeing exactly where they stood in the game's hierarchy. Cumbersome or not, it worked.

Despite their recent tribulations Huddersfield, as one of the aristocrats of rugby union in the North, had enormous potential. Fartown was a prestigious, well-appointed ground that hosted county and major club matches. Scores of local amateur teams reflected the passion for the game. Crowd support would boom if a successful, attractive team could be assembled. Despite the club's near 'total eclipse' in 1905, Huddersfield was about start assembling arguably the greatest club side the English game has seen.

Chapter 5

The Team of All Talents

In the summer of 1905, Llewellyn Deere returned to Wales to persuade the principality's latest rugby star, 22-year-old Jim Davies, to join Huddersfield. Harry Lodge also travelled down to present Davies with 140 sovereigns, generously donated by three wealthy supporters, as his signing-on fee.

Success was long overdue, and here was the first inkling of the glories to come. An athletic, quick-thinking stand-off half, Davies was a class above any Huddersfield player to that time.

Just over a year later, on Saturday 10 November 1906, a paragraph in a local newspaper heralded the debut of an even greater player, a youngster whom Huddersfield had recently signed from local amateur club, Underbank Rangers.

> A trial will be given to H. Wagstaff, a promising youngster who has been assisting the Underbank club in the Bradford and District League. Wagstaff is only fifteen years of age.

Harold Wagstaff was born on 19 May 1891 at Underbank, Holmfirth, a Pennine village a few miles west of Huddersfield. His father Andrew moved from Underbank to work in the Rochdale mills in the 1870s and married fellow mill-hand, Hannah Rhodes. Harold's older siblings, Ann, Eliza and Arthur were born in Rochdale before the family returned to Underbank around 1881. Harold and his two other brothers, Young and Norman, were Yorkshiremen.

Harold's father was employed in the mills for much of his life, but was a railway labourer at the time of Harold's birth. Harold's mother died in 1904 when he was 12 years old.

Rugby was the game to play in Holmfirth, fuelled by the intense and enduring excitement generated by Underbank Rangers Rugby Football Club. Founded in 1885, Underbank is by some distance the oldest surviving amateur rugby league club in the Huddersfield area.

Harold and his mates were rugby-mad. As young boys they used an old yeast bag stuffed with rags for a ball and by the age of thirteen, in 1904, he was playing for Pump Hole Rangers. This was a team formed by Harold and his mates, who gathered at the village pump in Holmfirth and, playing Northern Union rules, competed against other lads' teams from the locality. Their matches, usually played in farmers' fields without goals or pitch markings, were sometimes terminated when they were evicted.

Pump Hole

Harold was the outstanding talent in this spartan Northern Union nursery and, shortly before his fifteenth birthday in 1906, he achieved his ambition, making his debut for Underbank Rangers. Playing at centre, he was an instant success, scoring two tries.

Underbank Rangers had left the Huddersfield and District League and joined the Western Division of the Bradford and District League in 1905-06, where the opoosition included

Harold Wagstaff

teams such as Rastrick, Marsden, Slaithwaite Juniors, Salterhebble, Brighouse St James, Thrum Hall, and the reserve teams of the professional clubs at Huddersfield and Halifax.

John Clifford, who signed Harold Wagstaff for Huddersfield, was a former captain of Huddersfield in the 1880s. The Huddersfield representative at the George Hotel meeting of 1895, he was elected President of the Northern Union in 1902. He was joint-manager of the first two touring teams to Australasia in 1910 and 1914, the latter captained by Harold Wagstaff.

Despite his tender years, Harold was a prolific scorer and it was no surprise when George Dickenson, a referee who was a former Halifax captain and Yorkshire forward, approached him to join the Halifax club. On learning his age the Halifax Committee declined to sign him and Huddersfield's John Clifford appeared on his doorstep with an offer to join the Claret and Gold.

On 2 November 1906, just six months after his Underbank debut, Harold signed for Huddersfield for five gold sovereigns. Eight days later on 10 November, aged 15 years 175 days, he made his first team debut at Barley Mow, Bramley, scoring a try as Huddersfield won 28-11. Only Bramley's Harold Edmondson, 15 years and 81 days old when he appeared against Bradford Northern in 1919, has played senior rugby league at a younger age.

Writing in the *Sports Post* of 16 February 1935, Harold recalled his debut, pitting his young sub-11 stones frame against the veteran Yorkshire County centre, the 13 stones-plus Albert Hambrecht:

> The first time I went to tackle Hambrecht … I can feel the bump now when I think of it. If ever a youngster felt that he had been under a steamroller, I did.

From his first appearances, Harold showed glimpses of the greatness to come. His debut came in the season when the Northern Union reduced the number of players per team from 15 to 13, an attempt to increase the game's speed, openness and excitement. This was ideal for Harold. The hundreds of hours playing small-sided games with his mates had honed his skills, and his spatial and tactical awareness. Creating and exploiting space was second-nature to him. His positioning, support play, handling, running with the ball and timing of the pass were devastating and revolutionary, accelerating the evolution of Northern Union rugby from a forwards, set-piece dominated sport to an open, running game.

He made his Yorkshire debut aged 17 years and 151 days on 17 October 1908 in a 30-0 victory over Cumberland at Fartown, and played well enough to retain his place against Lancashire at Salford two weeks later.

Caricature of Harold Wagstaff

Percy Holroyd

Much interest in the 1908-09 season focused on the first Australian touring team to Britain. Harold and Huddersfield half-back Percy Holroyd made their international debuts in the first Test Match at Fartown on 2 January 1909, Holroyd securing the try that gave England a 14-9 victory. At 17 years and 228 days, Harold became, and remains, the youngest international of all time.

Billy Kitchin, who captained Huddersfield to their first trophy under Northern Union rules, the 1909 Yorkshire Cup, went on the serve on the club's committee for many years.

For a world-class sportsman, Harold's health was surprisingly fragile and his career began to be punctuated by periods of injury and illness. A grazed knee in the opening fixture of the 1909-10 season against Bramley seemed inconsequential until, two matches later, it turned septic. Harold became gravely ill with blood poisoning, then diphtheria, necessitating recuperation at Seacroft Isolation Hospital, Leeds.

The illness caused him to miss Huddersfield's first major Northern Union trophy, the defeat of Batley by 21 points to nil in the Yorkshire Cup Final in November 1909. Harold was back in training in January 1910, but a leg injury then put him out of action until March.

Fartown, packed for the local derby against Halifax in 1909

Building the Team around Wagstaff

Fully recovered for the 1910-11 campaign, Harold resumed his exceptional progress as the team's creative inspiration. Towards the end of the season, shortly before his 20th birthday, he was appointed captain of Huddersfield's large and growing pool of outstanding talent, showing the impact he had made as a player and a team man. He held the position, except for one season, until he retired in 1925.

Huddersfield's established stars were Jim Davies, the Welsh half back from Swansea, and the versatile Cumbrian WF 'Billy' Kitchin who could play on the wing or at centre. Percy

Holroyd and Arthur Swinden, both recruited from local rugby, were experienced and respected performers, and a young full back/centre from Morecambe, Jack Bartholomew, the future uncle of comedian Eric Morecambe, showed great promise.

Jim Davies

During September 1908 Huddersfield had recruited reliable full back and goal-kicker Major Holland, spotted during a workshop tournament at Fartown, and Edgar Wrigley, a member of the New Zealand 'All Golds' brought over by Albert Baskerville in 1907. Wrigley was the first of many colonial players to sign for Huddersfield, and was followed by Paddy Walsh, who toured with the 1908-09 Australians, playing all three Test Matches against England. Wrigley and Jim Davies were, according to that shrewd judge of the game, Harry Lodge, 'the two experts who fully developed the football genius' of Harold Wagstaff. 'Harold could not have been in the heads and hands of two more able tutors.'

On Christmas Day 1909 Tommy Grey, a superb scrum half signed for Huddersfield from Halifax and on 8 January 1910 John Willie Higson, who had won four cup medals with Hunslet in 1907-08, made his debut in the Fartown pack.

Billy Kitchin

Huddersfield adorned this nucleus with some world-class gems such as eighteen year-old Cumbrian, Douglas Clark, registered in April 1909. A formidable character, he became a county and Test player, a Great Britain tourist in 1914 and 1920, and in later years a world champion wrestler.

Arthur Swinden

Another key signing was Albert Aaron Rosenfeld. Born into a Jewish family on 28 July 1885, Albert began his working life as an apprentice tailor under his father, who had escaped persecution by emigrating from Poland to Australia in the 1880s. He began playing rugby union at the age of 15 in the eastern suburbs of Sydney, virtually unaware that another form of the game – Northern Union – existed on the other side of the world. For seven years he played for Eastern Sydney Borough, but when the Northern Union rugby revolution took hold in New South Wales in 1907, Rosenfeld turned to the new type of rugby football.

Major Holland

The catalyst was the arrival, in August 1907, of the rebel New Zealand touring team, Baskerville's 'All Golds', en route to England, where they were to play the teams of the Northern Union. Docking at Sydney, they played three matches against New South Wales under rugby union laws, because no formal Northern Union rugby rule book was available. A crowd of 22,000 watched the first match at the Royal Agricultural Ground on 17 August, but the New South Wales players had effectively banned themselves from ever playing rugby union again. These included Albert Rosenfeld.

Edgar Wrigley

The ban kick-started the Northern Union game in New South

Douglas Clark

Wales, and the New Zealand 'All Golds" return journey included a three-match series in Sydney, the first Test Matches in the Southern Hemisphere. Rosenfeld appeared in all three, scoring a try in the first Test on 9 May 1908, which New Zealand won 11-10.

A nine-team competition was established in New South Wales. Joining the Eastern Suburbs club, Rosenfeld played in Australia's historic first round of rugby league club matches on Easter Monday (20 April) 1908, when he was stand-off in a 32-16 win over Newtown at Wentworth Park.

Easts were runners-up that season, losing the Premiership final to Souths on 29 August, but 23 year-old Rosenfeld and five of his team-mates missed the encounter. On 15 August they had left Sydney on HMS *Macedonia*, bound for England with the first Australian tourists, the 1908-09 'Kangaroos'.

Rosenfeld was not in the original tour squad and was only added after an outcry over his omission. One report noted Rosenfeld ought to be chosen because he is a clever five-eighth, understands (Dally) Messenger's play, is good in attack and defence, has the physique necessary for a long tour, is fond of hard work, is a non-smoker and total abstainer, and because of his loyalty to the League. In fact, Rosenfeld suffered his share of injuries, played in only fifteen games, scored five tries and appeared in only one Test Match, the second at St James' Park, Newcastle.

John Willie Higson

One of his best games was at Goodison Park, Everton, in November, when the Australians beat a strong Northern Union XIII 10-9. Playing at left wing three-quarter, his pace and power caused constant problems. It was a portent of things to come.

Most significantly for Huddersfield, during the trip Albert fell in love with a young woman from the town, Ethel Barrand, a local mill-manager's daughter, and intended to marry her. On 22 February 1909, two days after the Australian's met Huddersfield at Fartown, the *Huddersfield Daily Examiner* (*HDE*) announced:

> The committee of the Huddersfield Club on Saturday added to the bewildering variety of nationalities represented in their players by securing the signatures of two of the Australian Northern Union players.

> The Fartown team, despite its general excellence, has shown the want of a wing three-quarter and another good forward ... these have now been secured in Albert Rosenfeld and Patrick (Paddy) Walsh respectively.

Albert Rosenfield

Rosenfeld returned home with the Australians, playing a couple of games against the Rest of New South Wales, before re-joining Easts. In June he represented New South Wales in two victories over New Zealand, scoring four tries and a goal in a 26-21 triumph and following that with a try and a goal in a 27-20 win.

In August 1909 Albert returned to Ethel and to begin his career at Fartown. Emigration spelled the end of his international career, apart from two matches for a Colonial XIII against the 1910 Australian tourists. Albert impressed against his compatriots in a 31-15 win at Headingley in September and a 22-40 defeat at Wigan in December, when he scored his first hat-trick on English soil.

Barely 5ft 6in tall and weighing 12 stone, Albert was a powerful, elusive runner, particularly adept at the short kick and re-gather at speed. Described by the *HDE* as 'the wary, nippery, slippery little Australian', Huddersfield saw him from the start as a specialist winger.

He opened his account with two tries from the right wing on his Fartown debut against Broughton Rangers on 11 September 1909. Most of his other games during that first season were at centre owing to the illness of Wagstaff, but he nevertheless scored 22 tries from 35 appearances. Returning to the right wing, Albert ran in 35 tries in 1910-11, but the best was to come.

The fast-developing team acquired another exceptional local talent when, in December 1909, a month after the Yorkshire Cup victory over Batley, Stanley Moorhouse, made his debut at Dewsbury.

Stanley had played in the local Hillhouse Council (Primary) School team at the age of nine, later graduating through Hillhouse Congregational Intermediates and on to the Huddersfield 'A' team. Although he played stand-off on his debut, he soon moved to the centre before establishing himself on the left wing, where his partnership with Wagstaff became feared throughout the Northern Union. A keystone of Huddersfield's run of success, they scored tries as freely

Stanley Moorhouse

as Rosenfeld on the opposite wing, accumulating 68 tries between them in 1911-12.

Moorhouse enjoyed the big occasion and scored a try in his first cup final on 25 November 1911, a 22-10 win over Hull KR at Wakefield that secured the Yorkshire Cup. The following Saturday he ran in a hat-trick of tries as Huddersfield beat the touring Australians 21-7 before a Fartown crowd of 17,066. Another piece of the great Huddersfield jigsaw was in place.

Wagstaff paid the following tribute to Moorhouse in the *Sports Post,* March 1935:

> Moorhouse would have been a great wing-man in any team … he had a big match temperament and I could always depend on him. More than that I could tell to a few inches whether he would score, and it was very seldom indeed that he let me down when I gave him a pass. He had a kick-through of his own that was just as effective as that developed by Rosenfeld, though it was an entirely different kind. Moorhouse going at top speed could kick in his stride – the ball just left his hands for his feet and shot away in front: but there was no slackening of Stanley's speed. He could kick-through on the ground for himself or he could kick across for his forwards, and when he kicked across for his forwards it was rare indeed that he did not find them there waiting for the move.

Moorhouse played five times for Yorkshire and twice for England. Against Wales at Plymouth in 1913 he scored an England record four tries in the match. A century on, he shares this record with Jim Leytham, Peter Norburn, Keith Fielding, Stuart Wright, Martin Offiah, Sam Tomkins, Tony Clubb, Josh Charnley and Ryan Hall.

In 1910-11 Ben Gronow became the latest world-class addition to the squad, signed from his home town club in the rugby union hotbed of Bridgend, where he was born into a family of six brothers and two sisters on 3 March 1887. Ben progressed from street rugby along the well-worn path to Bridgend Harlequins and on to senior football with Bridgend at the tender age of sixteen. In 1908-09 he was given the captaincy and went on to make the first of sixteen appearances for Glamorgan County. The following year he represented Wales in their four rugby union internationals, scoring a debut try in a 49-14 win over France at Swansea on New Year's Day 1910.

Ben Gronow

Two weeks later Ben earned his place in rugby union history by kicking off the first ever international staged at Twickenham. Although England beat Wales 11-6, he enjoyed victories over Scotland (14-10) at Cardiff and Ireland (19-3) in Dublin.

Some of Ben's immense power can be attributed to his trade as a stonemason. Over six feet tall and wearing size 10 boots, he had huge hands and elongated arms that enabled him to fire out long passes and force opponents to go just where he wanted them and no further! It was no surprise when the 22-year-old goal-kicking forward attracted the attention of professional clubs. The first approach came from the Ebbw Vale Northern Union Club, but it was Huddersfield who obtained his signature for a fee of £120.

Ironically his debut for Huddersfield, at Fartown, on 3 September 1910, was against Ebbw Vale. By the end of the season he had made 31 appearances, including an 8-2 defeat to Wakefield Trinity in the Yorkshire Cup Final, and won the first of his 12 Welsh Northern Union/Rugby League caps, spanning 1910 to 1923.

Gronow and Douglas Clark were two of the finest forwards in the world and the most feared and respected pair in the Northern Union. They were at the heart of an improving pack that would disrupt the opposition and supply the possession for Huddersfield's array of talented centres, half-backs and wingmen. The pack was further bolstered in December 1911 by the signing of Halifax forward Fred Longstaff, another international in the making.

Locally published postcard of the rapidly improving Huddersfield squad

1911-12: The Team approaches its Peak

By 1911-12 this great Huddersfield team was approaching its peak. Opposing teams were assured of a non-stop barrage of attacking rugby.

In November the Yorkshire Cup was regained with a 22-10 win over Hull KR. Huddersfield were beaten 2-0 by Oldham in the third round of the Challenge Cup, but the season ended in a flourish as the Yorkshire League and the League Leaders' crowns were secured with four wins more than any other team. The Championship play-off final saw the mighty Wigan defeated 13-5 at Thrum Hall.

Winning three trophies out of four was a magnificent team effort, but it was Albert Rosenfeld who consistently grabbed the headlines. Partnered by New Zealander Edgar Wrigley, Rosenfeld was now firmly established as the perfect running machine at the end of an inspired back line, the cutting edge of a team that set and maintained standards rarely if ever seen in the game. Wakefield Trinity felt their full force when Rosenfeld ran in a personal best eight tries against them on Boxing Day 1911. In total the Rosenfeld/Wrigley wing combination accounted for 388 of Huddersfield's 1196 points, with Rosenfeld scoring an incredible 78 tries, smashing the previous Northern Union record of 49 tries in a season, set in 1908-09 by Wigan's England winger Joe Miller and Halifax's Welsh international Billy Williams.

It was the turn of left winger Stanley Moorhouse to take the plaudits in 1912-13, as the Fartowners again landed three trophies, only the Yorkshire Cup eluding them. The highlight was the club's first appearance in the Challenge Cup Final against Warrington at Headingley on 26 April. In a tight match Moorhouse scored all of Huddersfield's points with a hat-trick of tries in a 9-5 victory. Seven days later he added another try as the Fartowners demolished Wigan 29-2 in the Championship Play-off Final at Wakefield.

Johnny Rogers

Meanwhile, the engine room of the team was further strengthened by several signings. In November 1912, Australian Tommy Gleeson arrived from the Glebe club in Sydney as a new centre partner for Rosenfeld. Gleeson only just scraped into the country as, three months later, protests from New South Wales resulted in a ban on overseas players in the British game which was effective for fourteen years.

For the start of the 1913-14 season Jack Chilcott and Aaron Lee added their considerable weight to the Huddersfield pack, feeding possession to a new scrum half, diminutive Johnny Rogers.

Born in Abergwynd in October 1892, Rogers later lived in Tondu, about three miles north of Bridgend, home of Ben Gronow, whose influence on his career was profound.

Gronow's benefit brochure of 1924 relates:

> While at Bridgend, Gronow, not satisfied with Saturday matches, played on Wednesdays also. It was in one of these latter games that he first came across Johnny Rogers, then a midget of fourteen, and was generally struck by his play. Shortly afterwards, when dressing for a match at Bridgend, he was told that one of their wing three-quarters could not play. Happening to look out of the window he saw Johnny amongst the small crowd of enthusiasts who were waiting to watch the team go down to the field. Ben sent for Johnny and asked him if he would fill the vacant place. Johnny nearly collapsed with astonishment, but when he recovered jumped at the chance. The next difficulty was to find clothes and boots small enough. One wag threw Johnny a pair of boots belonging to the nineteen-stone man, Griffiths. Eventually suitable raiment was unearthed, and though the fourteen-year old was all but lost to sight on the field, he played so well that he was afterwards selected as first reserve among the backs. He had to wait some weeks ere his chance came. Then he deputised for one of the halves and to such purpose that the man for whom he played understudy never got back, and Rogers commenced on an uninterrupted partnership with Clem Lewis (winner of eleven Welsh caps and a great stand-off) which continued, first with Bridgend and then with Cardiff, until he came to Huddersfield.

Rogers moved from Bridgend to Cardiff in 1911-12, making 35 first team appearances. Aged 20, he signed and made his debut for Huddersfield on 1 March 1913, scoring three tries and kicking a goal in a 73-5 home win against Bramley. He was completely mystified by the differences between rugby union and northern union, but glimpses of his 'puzzling swerve', devastating acceleration over the first few yards and trademark dashes through a startled defence confirmed that, at £100, Huddersfield had a rare bargain. Within a year he had earned the first of his three Northern Union Welsh caps, and Lions' tours of Australasia were to follow.

Harold Wagstaff, wrote about Rogers in the *Sports Post,* March 1935:

Often I have marvelled at the way in which Johnny Rogers, the fastest of attacking scrum halves the rugby game has known, worked when he was in our side. Rogers was always placed correctly at the scrum and there was the start for his brilliantly fast action, the like of which we may never see again.

Rogers was wonderfully quick into his stride and his dash often took him through the defence and up to the full back before the defence knew what had happened. His speed off the mark was phenomenal: but do not forget that he always gave himself a chance because he wasted no time in getting hold of that ball when his forwards heeled it.

In 1913-14 Rogers replaced Tommy Grey, Huddersfield's incumbent half back, and opened the season by kicking nine goals in a 54-5 win at York. He ended the season with 20 tries and 27 goals from 41 appearances. Rogers' first medal arrived with a 19-3 win over Bradford Northern in the Yorkshire Cup final in November. The Yorkshire League title followed in the spring. A club-record 119-2 win over junior side Swinton Park in the first round of the Challenge Cup featured twenty-seven tries, seven by Rosenfeld, and eighteen goals from the boot of Major Holland, but Huddersfield were unable to successfully defend the trophy.

On 30 March 2014, exactly a century after Albert Rosenfeld's 80th try of the 1913-14 season, Huddersfield Giants celebrated his achievement with a Heritage Celebration Game.

Interest switched to the League Championship and Rosenfeld's try tally. In 1912-13 he had scored a mere 56, but throughout 1913-14 he cut loose in a manner that has never been equalled before or since. At Bradford's Birch Lane Ground on 30 March 1914 he ran in his 80th and final try of the season, a rugby league record that is likely to stand forever – the closest tally, apart from his own previous best of 78, is by Brian Bevan who scored 72 in 1952-53.

League Leaders for the third consecutive season, the Fartowners met second-placed Salford in the Play-off Final at Headingley. The notoriously defensive Lancastrians had conceded only 140 points all season, over 100 fewer than any other club, and kept Huddersfield's play-makers and wingers Rosenfeld and Moorhouse in check to grind out a 5-3 victory.

1914 Lions' Tour of Australasia

Nevertheless, eight trophies in three seasons marked Huddersfield as the game's major force, recognised by the selection of six players for the 1914 British Northern Union tour of Australia and New Zealand. Among the pack were Douglas Clark, Fred Longstaff and Jack Chilcott. Injury prevented Ben Gronow from bringing Huddersfield's forward contingent to four. The backs featured Stanley Moorhouse, Johnny Rogers and Harold Wagstaff, who had already captained England, and now added captaincy of the Lions to his growing list of honours.

Giving a good account of themselves, Wagstaff, Clark and Chilcott played in all three Test Matches against Australia and the others in one each.

The 1914 Northern Rugby Football Union Touring Team to Australasia. Huddersfield contributed six players, plus the Tour Manager to this second NU side to tour Australasia.
4th Row from front: Stanley Moorhouse (far left), John Chilcott (third from left)
3rd Row from front: Fred Longstaff (third from left),
Harold Wagstaff (captain, fourth from left), Douglas Clark (far right)
2nd Row-seated: Johnny Rogers (second from left), John Clifford, Tour Manager (third from left)

Moorhouse scored two tries on his Test debut as the Northern Union beat Australia 23-5 at the Royal Agricultural Ground, Sydney on 27 June. Australia levelled the series two days later, leaving the third and final Test Match at the Sydney Cricket Ground on 4 July 1914 as the decider. Against the Lions' wishes, the entire series had been played within a week. Deprived of half-a-dozen injured first choice players, they were now the underdogs. As kick-off approached, tour manager John Clifford addressed the players:

> You are playing in a game of football this afternoon, but more than that, you are playing for Right versus Wrong. You will win because you have to win. Don't forget that message from home; England expects every one of you to do his duty.

The Lions led 9-3 at half-time, but debilitating injuries to Frank Williams, Douglas Clark and Billy Hall reduced the team to ten men within minutes of the re-start. Substitutes were still half a century away and Clark, who had broken a thumb and dislocated his collar bone, twice returned to the fray, desperate not to let his team mates down, before leaving the field for a final time in tears. When Stuart Prosser was briefly sidelined late in the game the Lions were reduced to nine men.

Against these seemingly impossible odds, Harold Wagstaff's leadership qualities were never more needed or more apparent. Aggressive, skilful and shrewd, the captain virtually made up the numerical difference on this own – simply the finest match of his magnificent career. In a second half that, with injury time, lasted fifty-four minutes, the Lions amazingly added a further try and held on to win 14-6.

Australia v British Northern Union
Third Test Match
at the Sydney Cricket Ground
4 July 1914

Australia 6	British Northern Union 14
Tries: SP Deane	Tries: WA Davies
W Messenger	A Johnson
	Goals: AE Wood (4)

Australia
AH Hallatt (Souths);
D Frawley (Easts), SP Deane (Norths) capt, R Tidyman (Easts), W Messenger (Easts);
C Fraser (Balmain), A Halloway (Easts);
C Sullivan (Norths), WA Cann (Souths), F Burge (Glebe), EJ Courtney (Wests),
SC Pearce (Easts), RR Craig (Balmain).

British Northern Union
AE Wood (Oldham);
F Williams (Halifax), W Hall (Oldham), H Wagstaff (Huddersfield) capt, WA Davies (Leeds);
WS Prosser (Halifax), F Smith (Hunslet);
D Holland (Oldham), AP Coldrick (Wigan), R Ramsdale (Wigan), A Johnson (Widnes),
J Chilcott (Huddersfield), D Clark (Huddersfield).

Referee: T McMahon (NSW)   Attendance: 34,420

In the entire history of rugby league this match stands pre-eminent among the epic victories against the odds. The Australian sporting press dubbed it 'The Rorke's Drift Test', comparing the rearguard resistance of Wagstaff and his teammates to that of the 150 British and colonial troops who defended the trading post garrison in Natal Province, South Africa, against an intense assault by 3000 to 4000 Zulu warriors of King Cetshwayo's army in 1897. Eleven Victoria Crosses were awarded to the soldiers of the garrison, along with a number of other decorations and honours. No Victoria Crosses were won by the 1914 tourists, but the principle of spirit, determination and endeavour to triumph against overwhelming odds is the same.

On 1 August 1914 the Lions won their only Test in New Zealand 16-13, Moorhouse adding two more tries from the left wing to round off a triumphant trip. Both 'series' had been won and Harold Wagstaff returned home with 'the Ashes'. He had proved to be a magnificent leader, his inspirational example on the field matched by his diplomacy off it. One of the first working class men to lead an official national party, sporting or otherwise, to a foreign country, Harold had once again blazed a trail for others to follow.

Even as the tourists packed their bags in Auckland, back home the dreaded shadow which had loomed over Europe for many months became a reality. The tourists returned to a country at war. Amidst uncertainty about food supplies and public transport, and a growing clamour for young, fit men to volunteer for the forces, the celebration dinner for the returning tourists was cancelled.

1914-15: The Team of All Talents

The 1914-15 season began amid a furore about whether football – association, northern union or rugby union – should continue. The Northern Union season proceeded with a majority of clubs close to full strength, largely because the war was 'expected to be over by Christmas.'

Huddersfield's international tourists arrived home on Saturday 26 September 1914 to a team that had made an inconsistent start to the season. Two wins, two draws and one defeat from their opening five matches was hardly championship form. Although Clark was still injured and the ever-combative Longstaff was suspended following an 'incident in the last match of the tour,' on 3 October Wagstaff, Moorhouse, Rogers and Chilcott took their places in the team which beat Batley 10-5.

A shock 18-8 defeat at lowly Barrow the following Saturday showed that, even with their Lions stars back, Huddersfield could take nothing for granted. Perhaps it was the wake-up call they needed. During the rest of the season – 24 October 1914 to 6 May 1915 – Huddersfield played 37 matches, winning 35 and drawing two. The first trophy, the Yorkshire Cup arrived in November with a 31-0 destruction of Hull at Headingley.

Huddersfield v Hull
Yorkshire Cup Final
at Headingley, Leeds
28 November 1914

Huddersfield	31	Hull	0

Tries: H Wagstaff (2)
         H Banks
         S Moorhouse
         J Rogers
         A Rosenfeld
         G Todd

Goals: M Holland (5)

Huddersfield
Major Holland;
George Todd, Albert Rosenfeld, Harold Wagstaff, Stanley Moorhouse;
Johnny Rogers, Bob Habron;
John Wille Higson, Douglas Clark, Ben Gronow, Fred Longstaff, Arthur Swinden, Herbert Banks.

Hull
E Rogers;
AJ Francis, W Batten, J Harrison, J Devereux;
S Deane, T Milner;
T Herridge, W Holder, J Hammill, SJ Darmody, P Oldham, R Taylor.

Referee: JF May (St Helens)   Attendance: 12,000   Receipts: £422

Action shots, believed to be from Huddersfield's 18-0 victory at Keighley
in the opening match of the season on 5 September 1914.
The bottom picture appears to capture a Huddersfield forward in an unorthodox challenge for
the ball.

There was a 'Major' shift in the team for the trip to Bramley on 5 December. Major Holland was troubled by a groin strain and Ben Gronow took over his goal-kicking duties. Hitherto, Gronow had kicked 20 goals in four seasons at Huddersfield. At Bramley he kicked eight from eight attempts in a 34-7 win and the following Saturday kicked a further nine in a 60-7 victory over Bradford Northern. These powerful, consistent and accurate strikes moved Gronow from replacement to incumbent in a fortnight. He cemented his position with eleven goals in a 79-0 rout of Bramley in January and ten more as the defeat at Barrow was avenged 59-5 in April. Despite taking on the role 15 matches into the season, Gronow's prolific right boot eclipsed Major Holland's club record, kicking 140 goals in the season. Gronow's tally of 292 points was a league record, passing the 280 points scored by Salford's Jim Lomas in 1906-07.

Huddersfield's Challenge Cup campaign began with an attritional afternoon at Leigh, the Fartowners scraping through 3-0. After that it was plain sailing to the final. Widnes resisted inducements to transfer their second round tie to Fartown, but were beaten 29-3 on their own ground. Salford were despatched 33-0 in the quarter-final, and Huddersfield's 27-2 victory over title contenders Wigan in the semi-final was arguably their most impressive result of the season.

Huddersfield were Challenge Cup finalists and, for the fourth consecutive season, League Leaders. Of 34 league matches, they were unbeaten in the 24 that also counted towards the Yorkshire League, clinching the county title. But the margin between great teams and merely very good ones is small, defined by how they cope with the pressure matches at the season's climax. Brushing aside Rochdale Hornets 33-2 in the League Championship Semi-final, Huddersfield faced Leeds for the title.

The Fartowners looked confident from the kick-off, scoring two tries in the opening ten minutes. They stretched an 18-2 half-time lead to 35-2 by the final whistle, setting a new League Championship Final record score and winning margin. Ben Gronow's seven goals and 20 points were also new records for the occasion, and Harold Wagstaff became the first skipper to captain his side to three Championship Final wins.

Huddersfield v Leeds
League Championship Final
at Belle Vue, Wakefield, Saturday 24 April 1915

Huddersfield	35	Leeds	2
Tries: B Gronow (2)		Goals: D Lewis	
D Clark			
F Longstaff			
S Moorhouse			
J Rogers			
H Wagstaff			
Goals: B Gronow (7)			

Huddersfield
Major Holland;
Albert Rosenfeld, Tommy Gleeson, Harold Wagstaff, Stanley Moorhouse;
Bert Ganley, Johnny Rogers;
Herbert Banks, Douglas Clark, Ben Gronow, John Willie Higson, Aaron Lee, Fred Longstaff.

Leeds
D Lewis;
WH Davies, WA Davies, JD Campbell, A Jenkinson;
I Jones, J Sanders;
J Chilcott, F Carter, G Rees, F Webster, W Ward, F Godward.

Referee: JF May (St Helens)   Attendance: 14,000   Receipts: £750

Standing between Huddersfield and the season's fourth trophy, the Challenge Cup, was a St Helens team handicapped by a dressing room dispute that was only resolved minutes prior to kick-off. The Saints' players had been paid ten shillings for each match during their cup run, and expected a bonus for appearing in the final. When the club Chairman, Tom Phillips, told them there would be no bonus, only a passionate pre-match speech by captain Tom Barton persuaded them to take to the field. Within minutes Tommy Gleeson collected a perfectly-timed pass and, with Rosenfeld lurking with intent at his side, he dummied the defence and doubled inside to score.

Saints' forwards came back strongly, but their attacks broke down in the threequarters at crucial times. In complete contrast, Huddersfield's backs were in top form. When Wagstaff swept majestically onto a pass that looked suspiciously forward from Gronow to score, Gronow converted and Saints' defensive resistance was all but shattered. The Fartowners crossed for three more tries to take a 21-0 half-time lead. A strong, dour second-half rally by the Saints' pack held the Fartowners at bay for about 20 minutes but, as tiredness set in, the Huddersfield backs again took the initiative. Wagstaff created a huge gap to send Moorhouse in, then Gronow crossed for a try which he duly converted. Rogers added Huddersfield's ninth try with a clever burst from midfield before, in the final minutes, Saints' forward Daniels, crashed over for a consolation that Barton failed to convert.

Wagstaff collected the club's fourth trophy of the season from Mr JH Smith, Chairman of the Northern Rugby Football Union after a 37-3 win, the biggest in Cup Final history until Leeds beat London Broncos 52-16 in 1999.

Huddersfield v St Helens
Challenge Cup Final
at Watersheddings, Oldham, Saturday 1 May 1915

Huddersfield	37	St Helens	3
Tries:	T Gleeson (2)	Tries: S Daniels	
	H Wagstaff (2)		
	B Gronow		
	M Holland		
	S Moorhouse		
	J Rogers		
	A Rosenfeld		
Goals:	B Gronow (5)		

Huddersfield

Major Holland;

Albert Rosenfeld, Tommy Gleeson, Harold Wagstaff, Stanley Moorhouse;

Johnny Rogers, Bert Ganley;

Herbert Banks, Douglas Clark, Ben Gronow, John Willie Higson, Aaron Lee, Fred Longstaff.

St Helens

H Roberts;

T Barton, J Flanagan, T White, H Greenall;

F Trenwith, M Creevey;

S Daniels, T Durkin, G Farrimond, W Myers, W Jackson, J Shallcross.

Referee R Robinson (Bradford)   Attendance: 8,000   Receipts: £472

Thus 'All Four Cups' were won. Huddersfield's 'Team of All Talents' had guaranteed their place in history, emulating Hunslet's feat of 1907-08. One player able to directly compare the two teams was forward John Willie Higson. Signed from Hunslet in 1909, he remains the only player to play in two teams that won all four cups in the same season.

Over four seasons, no team has ever matched Huddersfield's record from 1911-12 to 1914-15 – twelve trophies, and a playing record in league matches of:

Played 136; Won 115; Drawn 7; Lost 14

Huddersfield NURFC Match Results 1914-15

Date		Opponents	Venue	Points		Result
				For	**Against**	
Sep	Sat 5	Keighley*	away	18	0	W
	Mon 7	WARRINGTON	HOME	12	13	L
	Sat 12	Bradford*	away	5	5	D
	Sat 19	HALIFAX*	HOME	15	8	W
	Sat 26	York*	away	7	7	D
Oct	Sat 3	BATLEY*	HOME	10	5	W
	Sat 10	Barrow	away	8	18	L
	Sat 24	Dewsbury*	away	16	4	W
Nov	Sat 21	Batley*	away	17	2	W
Dec	Thurs 3	Halifax*	away	17	12	W
	Sat 5	Bramley*	away	34	7	W
	Wed 9	HULL KINGSTON ROVERS*	HOME	52	11	W
	Sat 12	BRADFORD*	HOME	60	7	W
	Sat 19	Wigan	away	18	0	W
	Fri 25	HULL*	HOME	20	10	W
	Sat 26	Wakefield Trinity*	away	44	4	W
Jan	Fri 1	Warrington	away	26	10	W
	Sat 2	LEEDS*	HOME	27	10	W
	Sat 9	OLDHAM	HOME	23	3	W
	Sat 16	Hunslet*	away	21	5	W
	Sat 23	WIGAN	HOME	7	6	W
	Wed 27	HUNSLET*	HOME	25	5	W
	Sat 30	BRAMLEY*	HOME	79	0	W
Feb	Sat 6	Hull*	away	11	8	W
	Wed 10	SALFORD	HOME	38	2	W
	Sat 13	KEIGHLEY*	HOME	37	0	W
	Sat 20	Leeds*	away	5	5	D
Mar	Sat 6	Hull Kingston Rovers*	away	15	15	D
	Wed 17	DEWSBURY*	HOME	37	5	W
	Sat 20	Oldham	away	28	8	W
	Wed 24	WAKEFIELD TRINITY*	HOME	57	18	W
Apr	Sat 3	Salford	away	10	6	W
	Mon 5	BARROW	HOME	59	5	W
	Tues 6	YORK*	HOME	30	11	W
	Sat 17	ROCHDALE (Semi-Final)	HOME	33	2	W
	Sat 24	Leeds (Final)	Wakef'd	35	2	W
Yorkshire Cup Matches						
Oct	Sat 17	York	away	24	13	W
Nov	Thurs 5	Halifax	away	10	2	W
	Sat 14	HUNSLET (Semi-Final)	HOME	64	3	W
	Sat 28	Hull (Final)	Leeds	31	0	W
Challenge Cup Matches						
Feb	Sat 27	Leigh	away	3	0	W
Mar	Sat 13	Widnes	away	29	3	W
	Sat 27	SALFORD	HOME	33	0	W
Apr	Sat 10	WIGAN (Semi-Final)	Hunslet	27	2	W
May	Sat 1	St Helens (Final)	Oldham	37	3	W

* match counted towards both Championship and Yorkshire League competitions

Northern Rugby Football Union Final Table
1914-15

Position	Team	Pld	W	D	L	Points		Pts	%age pts gained
						For	Against		
1	Huddersfield	34	28	4	2	888	235	60	88.24
2	Wigan	32	25	1	6	679	206	51	79.69
3	Leeds	34	24	3	7	486	207	51	75.02
4	Rochdale Hornets	34	24	2	8	306	194	50	73.53
5	Hull	36	24	1	11	705	301	49	68.06
6	Broughton Rangers	30	18	1	11	308	289	37	61.66
7	St Helens	32	19	0	13	368	342	38	59.37
8	Halifax	34	18	3	13	342	268	39	57.36
9	Oldham	34	17	4	13	375	301	38	55.89
10	Wakefield Trinity	32	17	1	14	309	340	35	54.69
11	Hull Kingston Rovers	34	17	2	15	374	324	36	52.94
12	Widnes	32	14	3	15	291	292	31	48.44
13	Warrington	32	14	3	15	242	323	31	48.44
14	Batley	34	15	1	18	229	288	31	45.59
15	Leigh	31	14	0	17	252	185	28	45.16
16	Swinton	30	13	1	16	171	240	27	45.00
17	Dewsbury	32	12	2	18	310	353	26	40.62
18	Hunslet	32	12	0	20	298	356	24	37.50
19	Bradford Northern	32	11	1	20	249	464	23	35.93
20	Bramley	32	11	1	20	143	474	23	35.93
21	Salford	30	8	4	18	134	313	20	33.33
22	Barrow	32	10	1	21	288	363	21	32.81
23	York	32	9	2	21	261	422	20	31.25
24	Keighley	30	6	2	22	120	542	14	29.37
25	Runcorn	27	0	1	26	84	590	1	1.85

Huddersfield's Leading Points-scorers 1914-15

Tries		Goals	
A Rosenfeld	56	B Gronow	136
S Moorhouse	47	M Holland	46
H Wagstaff	35		
G Todd	32		
T Gleeson	27		
J Rogers	25		
WH Ganley	18		

Huddersfield's Team of all Talents, 1914-15
From left to right:
Standing: A Bennett (Trainer), A Lee, JW Higson, H Banks, E Jones, E Heyes, F Longstaff, D Clark, A Swinden, H Bennett (Asst Trainer)
Seated: R Habron, M Holland, S Moorhouse, H Wagstaff (Capt), T Gleeson, G Todd, B Gronow
Front: Yorkshire League Cup, WH Ganley, Northern League Cup, A Rosenfeld, Northern Challenge Cup, J Rogers, Yorkshire Challenge Cup

It is easier to celebrate and recognise the achievements of this wonderful team a century on than it was at the time. By May 1915, the unprecedented industrial war overshadowed everything. As military commanders struggled to devise attack strategies against weaponry that could cut men down from concealed, distant emplacements, convoys of wounded soldiers were becoming a common sight at Huddersfield Railway Station, the latest from ill-conceived attacks at the Battle of Neuve Chapelle.

Two days after the Challenge Cup Final, the *HDE* attempted to strike a balance between the team's achievements and the war, the tendrils of which were creeping ever further into every aspect of daily life.

Whilst not wishing 'to belittle the remarkable performance that the team has achieved', the *HDE* was clear that:

Captain Harold Wagstaff and trainer Arthur Bennett with all four cups

the reporting over the triumph of the Huddersfield NU Football Team ... must necessarily be more subdued than it would have been in other circumstances ...

... they deserve particularly well of all who are proud to see Huddersfield stand high, whether it be in athletics, in music and in song, or in the weightier matters of manufacture, education, and intellectual, moral and political import.

... we feel that we are entitled to go a step further and ask if, in the crisis of the nation's fate, the fine fellows who have brought such an honour upon the athletic life of the town are going to let their achievements end there when so much greater honour is within their grasp. The physical vigour, and fitness, the regard for discipline, and especially for self-discipline, and the high emulation which have carried them successfully through the lower struggle are the very qualities which the higher and vastly more important struggle against the foes of Britain and of civilisation so pressingly demands. What a glorious coping-stone for a fine season's work would be the enlistment of the men who have brought honour to Huddersfield … to set the example to large numbers of football men in the minor clubs, and of football followers, also, by offering their strength and courage to help to defeat the Huns!

The *HDE* had read the situation accurately. There would be no more professional sport until the war was over.

"Proud are we, proud are we."

(COPYRIGHT)

Tune—" Proud I am, proud of a cablegram from Uncle Sam."

IN the World of Football, Rugby Football
    There's a Team of great renown
And multitudes all journey to a place they call Fartown,
  For it's there behold, the Claret and the Gold
    Keep you spell-bound all the while
    As one and all they juggle with the ball
  In a manner that would make you smile ;
  And their perfect style of play is on every tongue to-day.

CHORUS

    Proud are we, proud are we,
  Proud of our Football Team you'll all agree ;
  We've a real half-back and a splendid pack
  Brilliant three-quarters and a great full-back ;
  Then shout hurrah, for every one's a star
    In the Northern Union line,
  We're the Champions to-day and every one will say
    That we shall be for a long long time.

Well you know our " Waggie," good old " Waggie,"
  He's our Captain, tried and true :   [do.
While Douglas Clarke is on the mark if there's some work to
  Then behind the scrum', our Johnny makes things hum,
    In the twinkling of an eye
    He'll dash away and open out the play
  Then Todd is sure to score a try ;
  And when Gronow plants the ball, ten to one he kicks a
    Chorus.—Proud are we.   [goal.

                G. W. CHAPPELL.

Song written to celebrate the Team of all Talents

In 2014 the Huddersfield Giants celebrated the centenary of the Team of all Talents with two heritage shirts. The away shirt (right, modelled by Jason Chan) depicted the 1914-15 team. The home shirt, claret with narrow, gold horizontal hoops was a replica of the 1914-15 shirt. A bonanza for the club's commercial department, they were the fastest-selling shirts in the club's history.

Chapter 6

World War I

By the end of the 1914-15 season it was all too clear that the war was not going to be over quickly. The flow of volunteers into the forces increased the pressures and tensions on families, businesses and services as people adapted to the growing emotional stress and austerity. In July 1915 a Government poster ominously announced 'It is better to go than to be pushed.' Conscription was in the air.

A month after the end of the 1914-15 season, the Northern Union voted to suspend competitions for the duration of the war with the exception of under-eighteen and schoolboy games. Along with the Football League, it banned payments to players at its Annual General Meeting in the summer of 1915.

The game continued, but on a much reduced regional basis, organised by the Yorkshire and Lancashire County Committees. Many Northern Union players would also find opportunities to play rugby, usually the Rugby Union code, during their military service.

Volunteers, Conscripts and Professional Sport

At the beginning of the war Britain had a professional well-trained army, but it was tiny compared to the other main countries involved in the conflict, all of which had conscripted troops. The regular army consisted of less than 250,000 men and almost half of these were stationed across the British Empire. These regular soldiers could be boosted by the Territorial Forces and various reservists, over 90% of whom immediately consented to serve overseas, but it was clear that, despite the power of the Royal Navy, Britain's land forces were wholly inadequate to fight a European war.

Lord Kitchener, the War Minister, whose features soon stared imposingly from the most famous of the recruitment posters, predicted that the war would last for years, not months, and that the country would need an army of millions.

Prime Minister Asquith ruled out conscription at this stage so a major recruitment campaign began to encourage men to volunteer for military service. Reinforced by strong public pressure on men to join up, the campaign erupted into a national clamour for sports and other forms of entertainment to be suspended, so that they would not deter men from enlisting.

Directly in the path of these vitriolic outpourings were association and rugby football clubs. The start of their seasons had coincided with the start of the war, and their players and supporters were overwhelmingly men of military age. It was an uncomfortable time for the professional clubs, Huddersfield NURFC and Huddersfield Town FC, particularly after the amateurs of the Huddersfield Old Boys RUFC abandoned their season in August 1914. The Old Boys' captain and Yorkshire County star, Roland Hely Owen, an army officer, wrote a stinging letter to the Old Boys' secretary.

Will they never come?

REPRINTED FROM
"THE WEEKLY DISPATCH"

This was going to be our great year. Well, so it will be if we send as many onto the field of battle as we send on to the field of play.

The Old Boys' secretary forwarded this letter to *The Weekly Dispatch* which printed a composite picture of a wounded soldier standing over a fallen comrade, and a large crowd watching a football match in the background. The War Office adapted it, adding the caption 'Will they never come?' It became one of the most successful recruitment posters of the war.

The national debate about whether sports should continue was reflected in the *HDE* which printed many letters condemning local sports clubs that continued to fulfil their usual engagements. The continuing activities of Huddersfield Town FC and Huddersfield Northern Union Rugby FC were subjected to the most caustic arguments about potential detrimental impacts on recruitment. After heavy losses at the Battle of Mons, on 23 August 1914, one of the football correspondents commented:

> Footballers are always of necessity the most physically fit of our population. The Blackheath club have taken the lead in the matter, and have cancelled all their fixtures, and other Rugby Union clubs have followed suit. Will the Northern Union and the English [Football] League follow this patriotic example?

Francis H Knaggs, a local ophthalmic surgeon who subsequently died in 1917 from illness and injury sustained on military service, concurred:

> It is an appalling thought, when this country's very existence is at stake, that our young men should be spending their time training for sports, when they should be training for the defence of the motherland and their own homes ... there is a time for everything, and ... the present is not one for playing games before thousands of spectators, who should be more usefully employed in their country's cause.

In similar vein a former resident of Honley, Walter Knott, wrote after the German navy had bombed Hartlepool, Whitby and Scarborough:

> When we heard of the raid on the East Coast we were all glad – of course sorry for the women and children, but we all wished the shells could have dropped on some football field with a game in progress. Are Yorkshiremen waiting till the Germans get their guns mounted on Castle Hill or the Standedge before they wake up or has their blood turned to water?

Thomas P Crosland, who had been Conservative MP for Huddersfield 1892-95, added:

> I think you and your readers will agree with me that a football match held at Fartown, and witnessed by some thousands of young fellows, who ought to be at the front, would be a disgrace to the fair name of Huddersfield.

This moral battering continued until a letter from Arthur Hardisty highlighted the hypocrisy of singling out professional football for criticism.

> Is it to be understood that in keeping with ... suggested cancellation of all football

engagements, the same stricture should be applied to cricket, lawn tennis, golf, bowling, theatres, music halls, picture houses, motoring; to, in fact, any and every form of amusement or pleasure? I put this question because if the stricture is applied to one it should be applied to all. Perhaps … we should draw on all the blinds, and sit in sackcloth and ashes while our gallant soldiers are fighting for their King and country …

… Then supposing football matches were cancelled, what reason is there to suppose that this would lead to those "thousands of young fellows, who ought to be at the front" actually going to the front? I must also point out that the average football match – whether it be at Fartown or at Leeds Road, is attended by thousands of men who, for many and various reasons, cannot serve their country at the front.

Rightly or wrongly, many football players – as also cricketers, golfers etc. – play as professionals … The cancellation of matches would therefore lead to considerable shortage in means of sustenance, not to mention the loss to ground staff, caterers, tradesmen etc.

… I certainly do not think it 'would be dangerous to the fair name of Huddersfield' if the matches are played at Fartown as usual, as far as circumstances will permit.

Another correspondent, 'Spectator', pointed out that injury could be devastating for professional sportsmen.

In industrial spheres the promise of re-instatement has been made to recruits, but this is not altogether practicable in the case of men whose living depends on their physical fitness and soundness of limb. Even a slight wound might debar them from attaining their former skill with the ball. Hence, the obvious unfairness of comparing footballers with other professions or employments.

Even the Chief Constable of Bradford valued sport as a distraction in his city where, as in Huddersfield, many woollen industry workers were enjoying increased disposable income.

… unless they have attractive football matches on Saturday afternoons to attend there is certain to be a deplorable increase in drunkenness.

In reality, cancelling the season was more straightforward in the strictly amateur game of Rugby Union than it was in the professional ranks of association football and the Northern Union, where the clubs were large economic concerns, dependent on paying spectators, and the players depended on the game for their living.

However, the impact on local amateur clubs in these codes was immediate and drastic. Northern Union clubs, Almondbury and Marsden Villa, ceased to compete before the end of August 1914. Almondbury attributed their demise to the collapse in local trade and Marsden, on the geographical edge of their league, cited unsustainable transport costs. On 24 September, the Huddersfield and District Northern Rugby Union announced:

Owing to the great European War, and the consequent resignation (for the present season) of several clubs … through players being either in the Territorials or having joined Kitchener's Army, it has very reluctantly been found necessary to suspend the Intermediate League for 1914-15.

The context of this debate was a widespread belief that thousands of unpatriotic, cowardly 'slackers' were evading the call to arms. This belief was fuelled by many sections of the press and political rabble-rousers such as Horatio Bottomley. Much less understood at the time was the extraordinary success of Kitchener's call to arms. He had asked for an initial 100,000 volunteers but in fact 175,000 men volunteered in a single week ending 5 September and a staggering 750,000 had come forward by the end of September 1914. Volunteers continued to come forward at a rate of about 125,000 per month until June 1915 when the rate fell somewhat. As a result the army had more men than it could train and equip.

Caught in the recruitment crossfire, the Football Association (FA) and the Northern Union were actually struggling from the loss of players and spectators who did enlist.

As early as October 1914 concern was mounting about attendances at Northern Union games which had fallen by about 50% on the previous season. On 20 October, a special meeting of clubs to address this problem voted by a clear majority to reduce players' wages and referees' fees by 25%. All clubs were ordered to report players' wages and the savings made as a result of the cuts. Almost immediately players from the leading clubs, including Huddersfield, opposed this proposed cut in their incomes. The Northern Union committee was intransigent and, as a consequence, players at Huddersfield, Halifax, Oldham, Rochdale and Wigan went on strike on Saturday 7 November. A few days later players' representatives elected a four man deputation, one of whom was Harold Wagstaff, to meet with Northern Union officials. Events moved quickly. Referees threatened to strike and 14 clubs complained about interference in their business affairs. After meeting the players' deputation on 17 November, the Northern Union rescinded the enforced wage cuts.

Support for the War Effort

For all the criticism, it is estimated that across the country about 100,000 of the first 700,000 volunteers came from supporters and players of the various football codes, boosted by the footballers' battalions, deliberately created to encourage supporters to serve alongside their sporting heroes, and by regular recruitment propaganda at matches. There were several such initiatives at Leeds Road and Fartown as Huddersfield's two professional clubs trod the narrow line of continuing their activities whilst being seen to support the war effort. On 14 November 1914, before a Fartown crowd swollen by numerous wounded soldiers, there were several recruitment speeches on behalf of the Royal Engineers at half time, and a further meeting after the match, when GL Paton of the Parliamentary Recruiting Committee commented:

> … the West Riding of Yorkshire stands at the bottom so far as numbers per head of population joining the ranks of recruits ... that is a stain upon their patriotism ... Those men with their wounds are far more eloquent than … I am capable of. Huddersfield have won the game by a margin of 61 points, and I appeal for at least that number of recruits. We must score against the Huns as well as Huddersfield have scored against Hunslet.

The President of the Huddersfield club responded to this criticism and more general criticism by pointing out that the club had recently contributed £100 to the War Relief Fund. An earlier report in the *HDE* on 26 August 1914 had also sought to deflect similar criticisms:

> There has been a good deal of comment in local football circles as to the action of the Fartown club in not handing over the proceeds of the practice matches to the local war relief fund. In fairness to the club officials it should be widely known that long before the war was commenced an application was made to the Northern Union authorities for permission to hand over the proceeds of practice matches to the funds of the District League. The permission was obtained and the original intention was carried out. It has always been the desire of the club committee to make a grant to the local war relief fund, and at a meeting held last night – the first since the war began – the magnificent sum of £100 was voted for the purpose. The splendid spirit shown by the club officials should allay any adverse criticism that may have been directed against it.

The national debate about the continuation of sport reached a crescendo in February 1915 when Prime Minister Asquith received a protest from 'many ministers of religion and the mayors of numerous boroughs, condemning professional football and the playing of cup finals during the present crisis.' Asquith told Parliament that, following negotiations between the War

Office and the FA, international matches had been abandoned but that the FA 'did not see their way to stop the playing of cup ties.'

Professional wartime sport had, it transpired, a valuable ally in Lord Derby, who was heavily involved in the Government's recruitment campaign and in October 1915 became 'Director of Recruiting.' Lord Derby was a leading figure in horse racing, as well as a patron of the Northern Union. He provided a boost for all sports in March 1915, when horse racing was threatened by controversy about the cost of feed:

> Please understand if racing is stopped, you are going to stop all – races, football, cricket, and all the theatres. I say, 'No, do not stop them.' As far as the troops in the field are concerned, they like to hear the results of football and cricket … Sport of all kinds is absolutely engrained in every single Englishman. All our similes are taken from sport, and the ideal of a soldier is taken, surely, from sport. The best you can say of a soldier is that he has played the game right well.

At a more parochial level a letter from Private J Roebuck of Lockwood, expressing pleasure that 'Town … had beaten Barnsley' was one of several in the *HDE* unknowingly supporting Lord Derby's view. The keen interest of many troops in the sports' reports and results from home helped to defuse the arguments about the continuation of sport. The *HDE* eventually committed itself on the issue in its editorial of 22 April 1915.

> Those who have taken such a strong line against recreation during the period of the war have overlooked two important facts – the need of the workers for relaxation and the interest of the soldiers themselves in the various competitions.

It was against this backdrop of controversy that Huddersfield's 'Team of All Talents' swept the board, winning all four cups.

The lower than average levels of recruitment in the West Riding during the winter of 1914-15 had little to do with sport. The war had produced plenty of work and overtime for workers in West Riding textile mills, many of which were quickly adapted to the production of khaki. For large numbers of the local workforce there was an economic imperative to stay at home. Politically, Huddersfield was a specific case. Its long tradition of radicalism and dissent surfaced in strong anti-war sentiments espoused at regular peace meetings. A significant socialist minority identified more closely with international working class comrades than with the national military.

In the early months of the war, the national pattern of enlisting differed significantly between professional and white-collar workers, and those in manual work. As the *Athletic News* pointed out, many working class footballers could 'not afford to throw their wives and families on the fickle charities of the public by enlisting.' Nevertheless, Tony Collins suggests that just over 1400 amateur and professional Northern Union players had enlisted by April 1915.

The professional sports teams and players from Huddersfield and the West Riding were also regularly involved in fundraising for war charities. With cricket's County Championship suspended from 1915 to 1918, Huddersfield's England Test Match cricketers Wilfred Rhodes, George Hirst, Percy Holmes, Schofield Haigh and Alonzo Drake played as weekend league professionals and were in popular demand to play in midweek charity matches, where fundraising was routinely combined with recruitment appeals and accompanying propaganda. All five played at Lascelles Hall in September 1917 when GH Hirst's XI played W Rhodes' XI for the benefit of Lepton War Hospital. Similar matches were played at Fartown, and the local stars also travelled to play in charity matches on club grounds across industrial Yorkshire and Lancashire. In August 1915, Batley Cricket Club hosted a match between a Local Tradesmen's XI and GH Hirst's XI which featured the usual array of professional cricketers, plus Huddersfield's Northern Union stars, Harold Wagstaff and Johnny Rogers. The local cricket stars featured in one of the biggest charity cricket events of the war, a 'carnival of cricket' at Bradford Park Avenue in August 1918, which opened with a match between Yorkshire and 'An England XI.'

Regular wartime collections were made during rugby matches at Fartown. In September 1916 Leeds Road hosted the 'Huddersfield Military Police Sports' which attracted a crowd of 4000 and raised several hundred pounds for local war relief funds. Participation was restricted to soldiers and munitions workers, but there were 480 entries from as far afield as Derby County Athletics Club and Lincoln.

Various groups also assisted soldiers recovering from injuries, who enjoyed regular visits to Huddersfield's theatres and cinemas, and concerts by local musicians at the hospital. They took part in trips to countryside beauty spots, and sports and refreshments afternoons at the Huddersfield and Outlane Golf Clubs. In July 1917 and July 1918, crowds of 6000, including large numbers of wounded soldiers, attended memorable War Hospital Sports afternoons at Fartown. The latter event raised £661, described by hospital Chaplain, the Reverend Herbert Gwyer, as 'beyond the most sanguine hopes of the promoters.'

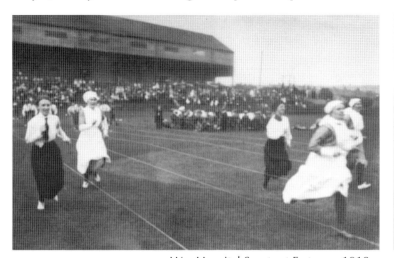 

War Hospital Sports at Fartown, 1918

Northern Union Rugby and Huddersfield Rugby Players 1915-1918

By the summer of 1915, the loss of players, supporters and financial income made professional rugby in its established format unsustainable. It also looked increasingly inappropriate.

In June 1915 the Northern Union suspended competitions with the exception of under-eighteen and schoolboy games. Payments to players were banned, but rugby continued to be played on a regional 'friendly' basis under the supervision of the Yorkshire and Lancashire County Committees. Newspapers published unofficial league tables and the registration rules were relaxed to allow players to turn out for clubs near their military base or place of work.

Some of Huddersfield's stars guested for other clubs, and the Huddersfield team often included players from other clubs. With no income from rugby, many Huddersfield players had to find alternative sources of income. Some of them picked up occasional funds from other sports. Half back Johnny Rogers won £15 prize money in a 70 yards handicap at a Salford Football Ground athletics contest in January 1917. In July 1918 forward Arthur Swinden used his strength and fitness to knock out Oxford boxer Chris Lake at an evening of bouts on Colne Road. Harold Wagstaff found more regular income by qualifying as a motor driver and working as a deliveryman for a local grocer. Others had already signed up for the forces, including Fred Longstaff who joined the 16th Battalion of the West Yorkshire Regiment – the Pals Battalion from his native Bradford.

With no players to pay, the Fartown club slashed admission prices by 50% for the 1915-16 season. The available players gave their services for expenses only, which sustained the club for fans and players alike. The team changed week-on-week, determined partly by who was home on leave. Of the Northern Union's established professional teams, only four were unable to compete in the 1915-16 season, but three other teams – St Helens Recreation, Featherstone Rovers and the re-formed Brighouse Rangers – were promoted to replace them.

The players competed with surprising intensity, and old grudges resurfaced when Huddersfield's visit to Bramley in November 1915 descended into brutality, the *HDE* reporting that:

> … players in turn became something worse than the savages who wrecked Louvain. How it was Ward [the Bramley half back] survived to finish the match was a surprise to some. The man who takes a running kick at an opponent just in front of the referee must consider himself fortunate to be allowed to continue.… the suburban Leeds club [should] … enforce upon its playing members the necessity of playing football as a sport.

Such animosity was not limited to the Huddersfield-Bramley rivalry. In March 1917 the *Yorkshire Post* reported that games were 'fought in a much rougher and keener spirit than in normal competition days.'

Wartime analogies appeared in numerous Huddersfield match reports in the *HDE*. Their win at bogey ground Salford in 1916 was described as rare as 'successful offences by the Hun Kiel Canal Fleet.'

Conscription

In January 1916 the Military Service Act brought an end to voluntary recruitment and introduced conscription for unmarried men aged between 18 and 41. Clubs could not now be accused of deterring men from volunteering. This accentuated the advantage for clubs which had more of their players in reserved occupations, both in the quality of their team and in raising a team at all.

Military Service Tribunals (MSTs) were formed by local councils to hear applications for exemption from conscription into the forces. Famously associated with cases involving conscientious objectors, most of their work dealt with applications for exemption based on business or domestic grounds.

"And what work are you doing of National Importance?"
"Why, I'm rearin' eight children an' helping to make airyplanes!"

In March 1916, the Huddersfield MST considered the case of Harold Wagstaff. The MSTs, particularly their pro-war Military Representatives, were notoriously hostile to appellants. Wagstaff appeared to have drawn the short straw, as the Military Representative on his tribunal was Arthur Crosland, who had achieved local notoriety for his intolerance of appellants.

With 'about 90% of local industries ... involved in war work of some kind', the Huddersfield MST faced particular problems and frequently compromised by authorising temporary exemptions to allow employers to make alternative arrangements for the loss of employees.

Wagstaff was one of two 24-year-old married employees appearing at the behest of a firm of wholesale fruit and vegetable merchants. The first to be considered was the firm's salesman and head bookkeeper. Military Representative, Arthur Crosland, dismissively suggested: 'I should give him the concession we are giving to all the married men', which was a two-months temporary exemption. Wagstaff was next. He had learned to drive during the autumn of 1915, probably to boost his income after the Northern Union banned all payments to players. Crosland, himself a prominent amateur sportsman and administrator, was suddenly and uncharacteristically friendly. He found …

> … it was a strong point in favour of Wagstaff that he had qualified himself in motor driving in order to get in the motor transport section.

Wagstaff denied that this was why he had learned to drive. He did, however, quickly point out that he: (a) had attested his willingness to serve when called upon under the Derby Scheme; (b) did not know that he was in a certified trade; and (c) was there because his employer and not he had appealed. Wagstaff was nobody's fool, and the diplomatic skills that had served him so well on the 1914 tour of Australasia were again evident as he and Crosland shadow-boxed around their personal reputations, Crosland anxious not to be cast as the ogre who sent Wagstaff to war, and Wagstaff equally anxious to avoid the suggestion that he was a 'shirker' or a coward. The result was unique among local recorded MST hearings, the Military Representative presenting the case for the appellant and the appellant suggesting that he had no objection to fighting for his country.

Like his company colleague, Wagstaff was eventually granted two months' exemption with leave to appeal. Later in the summer Wagstaff joined the Army Service Corps Motor Transport Unit and in 1917 was posted to the Middle East. For Wagstaff, who had a lifelong vulnerability to illness, this was far from ideal. As one local trooper put it, the region had two seasons, 'dust and dysentery' and 'mud and malaria'; Wagstaff was ill for part of his wartime service.

In September 1916 the *HDE* listed 17 Huddersfield players who had joined the forces. In addition, 'practically every reserve team player' had gone. Full backs Major Holland and Edward Illingworth were in reserved occupations and Arthur Swinden remained from the forwards, but elsewhere Huddersfield made up their numbers with 'any Northern Union or Rugby Union player … who has ability and is living in the district and wanting a game.' These included guest players, and local amateurs, although, with the local amateur league in abeyance, they were short of match practice and fitness.

The club limped on into 1916-17, despite a loss of £455, partly explained by a fall in membership from 1295 to 788 and, in common with sports clubs across the district, free membership given to men serving in the forces. The Northern Rugby Football Union proceeded with the 1916-17 season 'as a means of relaxation for munition and other workers.' It further endeared itself by presenting to the nation a motor ambulance worth £600. There were to be 'no fixtures which would involve long railway journeys', but fulfilling any fixtures became an increasing struggle for Huddersfield.

On 23 September Huddersfield were still looking for players ten minutes before kick-off at Batley. Following a predictable 16-7 defeat supporters were asked to …

… charitably remember that a full hard week's work – in some cases long hours of exhausting overtime – does not conduce to fast movements on a football field …when personal inclination must often turn to rest rather than vigorous football. The pace of football today is a war-time pace, and, in justice to our munition players everywhere, don't let us overlook this fact.

Seeking further solace after a fifth straight defeat, the *HDE* commented:

> We have seen the days when Huddersfield could win, like sportsmen, and it was even more pleasing to see that they could take their gruel, and it was a stiff dose, with a smiling face and unflagging spirit ... I am sure every Huddersfield man on the ground would be delighted with the way the wearers of the claret and gold accepted such an unprecedented situation.

Reinforced by a few rugby-playing guards stationed on the east coast, Huddersfield finally won at the sixth time of asking in October 1916, 28-2 at York. November's match at Bramley started late owing to war-related delays on the railway, where the transportation of troops and munitions took priority. Later in the month, on 25 November, what became known as 'the Northern Union fiasco' showed a game on its knees.

> The players were "all mixed up" so that many clubs had foreign help, three games were abandoned because of the weather, in one match only fifty three minutes' play took place, in another the players "went in" because of the rain – an unheard of thing in serious football – and refused to come out again; whilst still another match involving Bramley and Hunslet ended in a free fight.

Huddersfield's match at Hull KR started 15 minutes late and ended 22 minutes early as it was 'too dark to continue.' The Northern Union's response to the escalating problem of late starts was to reduce the duration of matches in each half from mid-November 1916. Seven days later Huddersfield's return match against York kicked off with only 19 players on the park, of whom York had eight. Compounding the problems, Christmas brought a 50% increase in passenger rail fares and a reduced service. As players were scattered all over the country, in munitions, mining, engineering and other work, clubs incurred heavy travelling expenses every week and the increased fares were a further blow to financial viability.

With matches lacking the context of league and cup competitions and the quality of play diminished, interest and crowd numbers inevitably dwindled. Even without players to pay, the Huddersfield club could no longer meet its expenses. Mainly on financial grounds, the club temporarily abandoned rugby after the 1916-17 season. The deteriorating balance sheet was a greater threat to the club's long-term future than suspending operations for the duration of the war. The Northern Union committee expressed its disappointment but reassured the club that they would be welcomed back once peace returned.

That summer the Northern Union agreed that matches would be 12-a-side for the rest of the war, and set up a relief fund to tide clubs over. This did not prevent other clubs falling by the wayside.

One beneficiary of the rugby club suspending operations was Huddersfield Town, which had a free run in capturing the affections, interest and loyalty of the town's sports' fans for the rest of the war, helping them to establish the ambitions and foundations that took the club to the top of the English game with three consecutive Division 1 titles in the 1920s.

Relations with Rugby Union

Ever since the breakaway of the Northern Union in 1895, the RFU had a rule to ban for life any rugby union player found guilty of playing Northern Union rugby, or even playing with someone who had played Northern Union rugby. This rule applied whether or not any payment had changed hands. The pressures of war would, however, bring about a significant exemption to this rule, albeit only a temporary one and in limited circumstances.

The first major rugby union charity match to be played in the north was between the 'North of England Military Team' and an Australian and New Zealand (Anzac) representative side at Headingley in April 1916. When the North was first announced it was made up exclusively of officers and rugby union players. However, in a second announcement two weeks before the match, the North team included Huddersfield's Northern Union stars Harold Wagstaff, Ben Gronow and Douglas Clark, plus Willie Davies, the captain of Leeds. Huddersfield's Tommy Gleeson, best man at Wagstaff's wedding in January 1915, played for the Antipodeans alongside Oldham's Viv Farnsworth, and Hull's Syd Deane and Jimmy Devereux.

The *Yorkshire Post* explained that:

> … the teams will play under Rugby Union rules, but they will do so as soldiers of the King; questions of amateur or professional principles do not come into view at all.

The *HDE* commented:

> The war has wrought many changes in our national life, but probably none more striking than the bringing together of Rugby Union and Northern Union football players on common ground. Who, two seasons ago, would have dared to suggest such a match as that to be played at Leeds this weekend? Any Rugby Union player would have been forbidden to take part in a match in which "professionals" were to participate. Indeed if he played on a Northern Union ground he was tainted! And now Harold Wagstaff, Douglas Clark, Ben Gronow, and others are to play shoulder to shoulder with Rugby Union men! What a beneficial effect it might have on the great national game if the conditions could continue after the war. But according to a well-known critic the thing is impossible!

> … entry into the army wipes out all differences … so far as football is concerned.

North of England Military Team v the Anzacs at Headingley, April 1916, a high profile coming together of Northern Union and rugby union players on the same pitch. Played to rugby union rules, line-outs such as this were one of the differences to which the Northern Union players had to adapt.

Of the Huddersfield players ...

> ... Gronow settled down as though he had played nothing but Rugby Union football, and Clark soon settled down to his new surroundings … Had Wagstaff settled down like his club mates the North would probably have done even better. The Huddersfield captain made some good bursts but he was at a loss what to do when tackled ...

Wagstaff had only ever seen one rugby union match, but adapted to his role by half time and, intercepting an Anzac pass, ran half the length of the pitch to score what proved to be the match-winning try. A Douglas Clark try, two conversions by Gronow, and a Tommy Gleeson try for the Anzacs, took the Huddersfield points tally to 13 of the 24 scored in the match, the North winning 13-11.

This remarkable coming together of rugby union and Northern Union football players on common ground was twice repeated in May 1916 when the North of England Military Team, including seven Northern Union players, beat the Tees & Hartlepool Garrison, and then a Welsh side, chosen by Welsh RFU secretary Walter Rees, at Liverpool FC's Anfield Ground.

On 4 October 1916 the RFU reluctantly passed a resolution that:

> Northern Union players can only play with Rugby Union players in bona-fide naval and military teams. Rugby Union teams can play against naval and military teams in which there are Northern Union players ... These rulings only obtain during the war.

This belated legitimisation of the new situation encouraged further recruitment of Northern Union players to military teams. Major RV Stanley, the Oxford University representative on the RFU committee and commanding officer of the Army Service Corps Unit at Grove Park, was particularly active, pulling some high-ranking strings to recruit several Northern Union players for army training at the Grove Park depot. During 1916-17 the backbone of the Army Service Corps (Motor Transport) rugby union XV was Wagstaff and his Huddersfield team mates Albert Rosenfeld, Ben Gronow and Douglas Clark, along with Oldham's Frank Holbrooke and Rochdale's Joe Corsi and international Ernest Jones. They were the best team not only in the forces, but probably in the country, their seven Northern Union stars surpassed in numbers but not in quality by the nine that were assembled at the Devonport Royal Navy depot. The Devonport team pushed the boundaries even further, playing matches under Northern Union rules as well as Rugby Union rules, and playing against some Northern Union sides.

In their 26 matches, the Army Service Corps won 25 and lost just one, scoring 1110 points and conceding 41. Harold Wagstaff was the team's shining light, twice registering five tries, and on one occasion supplying his wingman with no fewer than thirteen tries. Strict military etiquette was expected in communication between officers and men on the team, even during the matches. Thus Harold Wagstaff was expected to address his winger, Lieutenant Nixon, as 'Sir' whilst the Lieutenant would refer to his centre as 'Wagstaff'.

In 1917 the ASC team disbanded to various theatres of war. Clark and Gronow went to the Western Front, Wagstaff went to Egypt and Rosenfeld was posted to Mesopotamia (Iraq) under the name of Rosenfield, to conceal his Jewish heritage and faith as protection against racial and religious prejudice should he be captured. Among 'Rosenfield's' non-military achievements in Mesopotamia, he won the regimental cup for the 110 yards dash.

Once the war ended the RFU reverted to its strict rule prohibiting any links with Northern Union rules and players. This continued, in relation to contact with professional Rugby League until 1995, when, coinciding with the centenary of the Northern Union break away, the RFU finally declared their game 'open' and thus removed restrictions on payments to players.

The Army Service Corps Rugby Union XV 1916-17
The Huddersfield Northern Union players are Douglas Clark (back right), Ben Gronow (third from the right, middle row) and Harold Wagstaff (second from the right, front row).

The Experience of War

Little is known about the specific experiences of most Northern Union players and supporters during the war, but there is no reason to think it was any different to that of the other millions of combatants. This shocking experience is captured by the poet of the ordinary soldiers, Woodbine Willie (Geoffrey Anketell Studdert Kennedy) in the following poem:

The Spirit
by
Woodbine Willie

When there ain't no gal to kiss you,
And the postman seems to miss you,
And the fags have skipped an issue,
Carry on.

When ye've got an empty belly,
And the bulley's rotten smelly,
And you're shivering like a jelly,
Carry on.

When the Boche has done your chum in,
And the sergeant's done the rum in,
And there ain't no rations comin',
Carry on.

When the world is red and reeking,
And the shrapnel shells are shrieking,
And your blood is slowly leaking,
Carry on.

When the broken battered trenches,
Are like the bloody butchers' benches,
And the air is thick with stenches,
Carry on.

Carry on,
Though your pals are pale and wan,
And the hope of life is gone,
Carry on.

For to do more than you can,
Is to be a British man,
Not a rotten 'also ran,'
Carry on.

One of the first Huddersfield players to join the forces was forward Fred Longstaff, who joined the Pals regiment of his native Bradford in 1916. At zero hour on 1 July 1916, the first day of the Battle of the Somme, 2000 Bradford Pals went over the top to attack the village of Serre. Within an hour 1770 of them had been injured or killed. Fred survived this carnage, and on 9 July his battalion took charge of part of the front on the Leipzig Salient. On 15 July the Germans charged, led by bombers and a new weapon, liquid flame throwers. Fred scrambled onto his fire step into searing flame that shot across the ground. Seriously wounded, he was transferred to a nearby field hospital. He died from his wounds on 22 July 1916 and is buried at Blighty Valley Cemetery, Authile Wood.

Fred Longstaff is one of four Huddersfield players known to have perished. Edward Haigh, a nineteen-year-old clerk at Huddersfield Railway Station, and a forward in the second team was killed in Flanders on 1 June 1915. He is commemorated on the Menin Gate at Ypres. A third fatality was Private Joe Taylor from Milnsbridge, who went to the western front with the second line (2/5th) Huddersfield Battalion of the Duke of Wellington's West Riding Regiment on 17 January 1917. He was killed in an attack on the village of Puisieux just over a month later on 28 February. Joe was a 'well-known athlete, having won numerous prizes for running and walking', and played as a wing-threequarter for the Huddersfield'A' team. Former second team player John Hirst, who had emigrated to Canada and was serving in a Canadian battalion, was killed in January 1918. He had also played amateur rugby for Underbank and cricket for Scholes.

Huddersfield's lost fewer players than some Northern Union clubs. Leeds lost 15 of 51 players who enlisted whilst Hull lost 12 players. As no official figures were compiled for the total number of Northern Union players killed during the war, any overall figures can only be approximations.

Douglas Clark on the Western Front

The most revealing wartime experiences among the Huddersfield players are recorded in the diary kept by Douglas Clark. In 2012 this diary was borrowed from the Imperial War Museum and transcribed by David Gronow, grandson of Douglas's Huddersfield and Great Britain teammate, Ben Gronow.

Douglas Clark arrived on the Western Front in 1917, just prior to the Battle of Messines which raged from 7 to 14 June. An NCO with the Army Service Corps Motor Transport division, Douglas was based at the 7th Siege Park, a munitions depot, on the Ypres Salient. He served with the 352 Siege Battery Ammunition Column (SBAC), primarily delivering munitions to artillerymen close to the front line. The first entry in his diary reads:

I shall never forget Messines … the bombardment simply awful.

Bombardments were standard preliminaries to an infantry charge. When the bombardment stopped at 2.50am on 7 June, the Germans anticipated the usual charge and raced from their underground dug-outs to the front line. It was a trap. The British had spent 18 months tunnelling under the German positions on the Messines Ridge. At the end of the tunnels were 19 chambers packed with explosives. At 3.10am the British began the detonation of these in sequence. Four hundred and fifty tons of high explosives killed 10,000 Germans. Then, protected by a creeping artillery barrage and gas attacks, the infantry advanced. After a week of attack and counter-attack the Messines Ridge was in Allied hands. This eradicated a major German salient, one of the few clear-cut British victories up to this time.

The 168th Brigade Royal Field Artillery which was raised in Huddersfield further enhanced their growing reputation in these attacks, but at a price. On 13 June Douglas Clark watched these 'Batteries from Huddersfield, each distressed, coming from the Messines battle.' He recognised and acknowledged about two hundred of them, and there was 'plenty of "Play up Huddersfield" to lift their spirits.

352 Siege Battery Ammunition Column; Douglas Clark is on the front row, second from the right

It was a busy and dangerous time for Douglas. Away from the immediate front line, the motor transport units were thought to be on a 'soft number' by some of the infantry, but as the use of spotter planes and observation balloons increased and the accuracy of longer range artillery fire improved, motor transport convoys were increasingly targeted.

Douglas experienced the perils of the job for the first time on 12 June when he set out with a convoy of five lorries to deliver ammunition to 156 Battery at Ploegsteert Wood, eight miles south of Ypres. On arrival they found that the Battery had moved. Delayed by German bombing of a nearby farm, which was ablaze, they had to abandon one lorry which sank up to its axle in mud.

Eventually they moved on, but were halted by an Officer who 'cursed' them for bringing the lorries up in broad daylight. Douglas quickly understood why. 'We can easily see Fritz's observation balloons and watch events with a very wary eye.' The Battery Officer reluctantly allowed them to unload at the ammunition dump before dusk, but they had just completed this when:

> … a German shell landed right on Dump, wounding Sgt of Battery in back. I would be 100 yards away on open road. Fritz shrapnel bursting all around … find myself on ground knocked off footboards by drivers of lorry running to cover ... Fritz is trying to get it. We lay flat in a ditch, shrapnel bursting all over our heads past lorries. Battery want us to remove vehicle, but my drivers refuse. A bit of shrapnel hits door covering my legs [with debris]. I run to lorry and try to take it to cover past our Battery, only to receive a curse from officer for drawing fire on them. I reverse it right back to Tree Avenue and Battery men give me a good cheer. Then officer thanks me. As soon as I get lorry under cover they stop shelling.

On 16 June, Douglas was on the road for twenty-one hours. Again heading south, his ammunition column salvaged shells from an abandoned Battery position, then transported Royal Garrison Artillery men to Le Bizet. En route, near 'Shrapnel Corner', he spotted someone signalling as each lorry passed. He recorded: 'I consider every person in civvies a spy round here and I am not alone on this point.' Shortly afterwards they were 'heavily shelled' and the small car that accompanied them was 'badly ditched.' They pulled it out, but its clutch was damaged, and it had to be towed back to a munitions dump.

On 7 July the 352 SBAC was moved to a Siege Park on the southern outskirts of Ypres. The 'nasty rumours concerning our new position' were borne out by regular delays on congested roads and frequent bombardments of gas bombs, sounding 'like some monster giant wheel crushing everything in its wake.' A narrow escape on 16 July precipitated daily gas drills, but these did not help Douglas on 24 July.

> We are about to unload. Fritz sends over shrapnel. Gets in Dump which spreads all over lorries and, of course, we get it. He kills one man and two lose their arms. I am very weepy. We help bandage poor fellow up. He sends over his beastly Chlorine gas. We put them in lorry. Driver missing. I take helmet off to call for driver, but have to put it on again. Driver turns up and takes wheel, nearly ditches us. I take off my helmet to drive, manage to get to hospital. Find two of wounded dead. I collapse and taken to gas hospital. Eyes, chest, throat very bad. Sick, sick."

Even the robust constitution of a professional rugby player took time to recover from the insidious gas, and Douglas was under treatment for the next ten days.

His diary records regular sporting activity at the siege parks of the ASC, where he wrestled and enjoyed games of chess, cricket and football – at least until 27 October when a bombardment destroyed their goalposts. On 16 October he delivered a talk about the 1914 British Northern Union tour of Australia.

Still under treatment for the gas, Douglas witnessed preparations for the most infamous battle of 1917, the Third Battle of Ypres, better known as the Battle of Passchendaele, scheduled to commence on 31 July. On 30 July he returned to hospital at Poperinge.

Douglas Clark

> … eyes not quite as well today. Guns quiet. RAMC men prepare for 50,000 wounded, marquees all along road. We receive our instruction re moving of guns after advance … bombardment to commence after midnight. After dusk, roads full of limbless and Red Cross. 12pm [midnight] Mr Preedy and myself take up our position to watch bombardment from top of lorries … at 3.50am witness the sight of our lives. 3 mines go off and guns open in full. Such a bombardment the like of which this war has ever seen. Then the line just looks white hot and Fritz is soon in trouble sending SOS Green and Red star shells up along the front. I have never seen fireworks half so beautiful. We all feel for poor old Fritz. He replies with shrapnel, but soon stops. The bombardment has not ceased for one moment, it is now 11am. We all wonder if it's possible for a human being to live in it ... but the left flank of enemy holds fast. We bombard this flank all day ... our men advance … but owing to such bad state of no-man's land, we cannot take guns up to support, and our men have to retire and start digging in 2 miles down. We bombard all night, but rain sets in. Conditions awful, out of question going over.

The weather and underfoot conditions continued to deteriorate. On 1 August, Douglas wrote: 'It never stops raining … ground awful', and on 2 August, 'Rains all day. Cook house blown down.' A 15-inch naval gun opened fire behind them, becoming an immediate target for German shells which whistled directly over their Siege Park. On 3 August, Douglas resumed duties, driving 200 rounds of pipe to 352 Battery and returning past the Cloth Hall in Ypres, commenting: 'It is enough to turn anyone grey, the destruction of this town.'

There would be only brief respites from the rain over the next four months. The Allies pounded the thirteen-mile battle front with 4.25 million shells until mid-August, but despite their successes they destroyed many of the dykes and ditches that drained the low-lying, clay-based terrain. It created the worst underfoot conditions for an attacking force in the history of the British Army. The water table was so high that there were few German trenches. Instead, the land was defended by dozens of pillbox machine gun posts with overlapping fields of fire.

Relatively stationary, protected by these outposts and by deep curtains of barbed wire, the Germans' quickly disrupted attempts by the Allies to coordinate artillery, tanks and infantry in the same attack.

On 16 August Douglas Clark received a widely circulated extract from a 'Zurich telegram' which informed all the troops: 'We must hold our positions between the seas and our lines or we shall lose the war entirely. The fate of Germany is now being decided in Flanders.'

That day he delivered 800 rounds of ammunition to three different batteries, but noted that the guns were 'not going forward.' In fact the Allied plans for the Battle of Langemarck (16 to 18 August) were wildly ambitious, and minor gains were dwarfed by the number of casualties. The Germans retaliated on 22 August and Douglas recorded: 'Early morning. Great bombardment raging which shakes our hut just like the endboards on a box cart.'

Shortly afterwards he was part of a munitions convoy that drove through Ypres to 352 Battery's position. He was unloading when …

> … a shrapnel shell … burst over my head. I gave myself up as a goner, about 15 pieces hit my steel helmet and my back. I thought of home, but luck was with me and my helmet. Shrapnel fairly splintered off it and nearly choked me with smoke. Cox was 10 yards from me and gave me up as lost. Pleased to report only damage, a cut on little finger, so I carry on.

The disasters of the Battle of Langemarck saw General Gough replaced by the more conservative Sir Herbert Plumer. He began the more cautious tactic of taking the German's lightly defended outer positions, and digging in. This method secured ground at the battles of Menin Road Bridge and Polygon Wood between 20 September and 3 October, after which the Allies possessed the ridge east of Ypres.

On a foggy 30 September, Douglas Clark set off from Ypres along the Menin Road to deliver ammunition to 352 Battery on the front line. Either side were dead bodies and improvised graves from the recent battle, and not just those of infantrymen as Douglas noted:

> Fritz is knocking hell out of it … man's greatest friend the horse, poor beasts, are lying dead or dying on this road this morning … would turn anyone.

Continuing his journey, Douglas arrived at his Battery just as the British guns began a bombardment.

> It's hellish awful, poor Bosch. I watch effects of barrage ... Fritz balloons up, look as near as ours, a beautiful sight indeed … Every make of gun in play, from 15 inch to rifle. Guns everywhere you look blending fire. This is a real war, a wonderful, splendid, inspiring, awful sight I shall not forget.

On 26 October, the Canadians progressed to within 500 yards of Passchendaele. That afternoon Douglas and the 352 SBAC made several deliveries, the last of them to the 352 Siege Battery almost a mile beyond Prazinburk Ridge, near St Jean. As Douglas recorded, their orders were taking them ever-closer to the front line.

> Death on every side. 12 tanks destroyed … count 20 horses and 8 men dead. Wounded coming in. Splinters from Fritz shell hit my legs. Flying everywhere. Our Battery is in line with field guns. 4.30, we see our lot going up, then all guns open up on poor Bosch guns, wheel to wheel. Pours with rain and up to knees in slush, no words could explain condition, still we all see what Salient looks like. We return to Park … have supper and turn in wet through.

Three days later they were again unloading at 352 Siege Battery's dump when …

> Fritz starts shelling, simply hellish. We have to unload ourselves as men have taken cover, horses and men flying for their lives. Grenadier Guards … are detailed to unload us. After one lorry they scoot and we never see them again. I have never seen anything so awful as this before, death at every side.

Then a shell struck part of the dump where the Guards' captain and some of his men were sheltering. Douglas tried to organise a rescue, but 'Three officers and lots of men refuse to help me, they run like March Hares.' Entering alone, he found them 'badly wounded from some burning cartridges' and helped them on to the relative safety of his lorry, before continuing his journey of deliveries.

> I breathe a silent prayer for four hours and think every minute my last. Words fail to express this scene, blood everywhere you look, dead men and wounded. Those fine stretcher bearers.

The pack mule drivers of the Royal Field Artillery unloaded on Prazinburk Ridge, as it was 'not fit to take horses further' yet Douglas and his colleagues delivered to 352 Siege Battery a mile further along the same road. There, the Battery men refused to leave their cover to help to unload the lorries.

> There's not a soul in sight excepting men trying to find a better hole ... You can see shell explode long before you hear the noise of shell travelling through air and explosion.

Shell fragments set fire to some of their shipment of cartridges. Douglas and his co-driver fled, fearing a major explosion, but returned when their wounded passengers could not make their escape. Extinguishing the blaze, they returned to the Siege Park. Douglas recorded briefly but movingly:

> The awfullest day in my life so far. My lucky star.

Field Marshall Douglas Haig was aware of such valour. In his Passchendaele despatch he referred to:

> ... Particularly good work ... by the Motor Transport drivers who have shown the greatest gallantry and devotion to duty ... under heavy shell fire and during long hours of exposure.

How long could Douglas's luck hold out, delivering ammunition through such extraordinarily dangerous, ferocious firepower? His next delivery to the same area was two days later. Six lorries left at about 5.30pm. Approaching Prazinburk Ridge the Military Police informed them that the shelling was worse there than over the ridge, so they proceeded over the ridge, keeping 200 yards between each lorry. As an extra precaution, they planned to wait until each lorry had not just unloaded but returned before the next one started out on the last 200 yards.

> It is now quite dark and wind favourable for Fritz gas. All guns his side of Bavaria House in action ... Mr Preedy and I rode on first vehicle. We had not gone very far until we found the gas very bad ... so we pulled up to warn drivers, Mr Preedy going back to following lorries. I took ours forward to unload ... the place was deserted, so first and second driver and myself started unloading. I pulled off my helmet 3 times, doing so I was almost overcome. At this point one of Fritz's green lights flared up, and then the place was turned into hell. I doubt if ever Fritz has sent over so many shells on such a small stretch as he did round us, even putting the shelling of the previous days in the shade. I received a nasty wound in the left arm and I thought it certain all would be killed. I ordered boys to go back and take cover near the other lorries. Here I found Mr Preedy and reported I was wounded. He wanted to take me to hospital, but I refused to leave lorries. Shells were falling in front, behind and on all sides ... we decided to get lorries out of this ...

With some difficulty, Douglas turned his lorry round. Then 'a shell burst, hitting me in the abdomen and chest and throwing me some distance.' The blast threw him over a hedge into a pool of water.

> I was bleeding very heavy from stomach and having lost my gas helmet, thought the end must be near. It's then a man starts to think of the dear ones at home and I prayed I might just be able to see them to say "goodbye", when another shell threw me back onto the road.

As the men emerged from cover they found Douglas lying on the road with almost all of his clothing torn off by the force of the explosions.

> I was picked up and taken to Ypres Dressing Station (the Prison) and my wounds dressed. The journey left me very weak from loss of blood, it was simply murder.

From there he was moved to Number 10 Casualty Clearing Station outside Poperinge. Doctors found that eighteen pieces of shrapnel had pierced his left arm, abdomen and chest, one piece penetrating perilously near his heart. Douglas's only chance was an immediate operation.

Douglas came round from the operation to remove shrapnel from his chest and abdomen at 4am on 1 November, about eight hours after receiving his injuries. He endured a 'very bad' 48 hours, but skilful surgery combined with the strength, endurance and determination developed as a coal man, rugby footballer and wrestler saw him through. On 9 November he was well enough to be transported to base hospital at Boulogne, where the ward was 'a large marquee with 32 beds and very comfy considering wild elements.' Three days later he was marked 'for Blighty.' He sailed from Boulogne to Dover on 14 November and by 17 November was in the Northern General Hospital, Lincoln.

The final fortnight of the Battle of Passchendaele featured an advance over dreadful ground by numerous Huddersfield troops in the 49th Division, which helped in the capture of the Passchendaele Ridges. The capture of Passchendaele village was accomplished on 6 November by some of the Allies' best infantry, the Canadian 1st Division, supported by some of their best artillery, the Huddersfield lads in the 168th Brigade RFA, who adapted their aim brilliantly to the muddy conditions in which their guns frequently sank up to their axles.

Germany had lost its strategic positions on a twelve-mile front and, for the Allies, the Ypres Salient was no longer an overlooked deathtrap. However, the whole operation had been much more difficult, time-consuming and costly than anticipated. The Allies had inflicted 260,000 German casualties, but suffered 310,000 in return. Germany would recapture much of this ground in their spring offensive of 1918.

On 27 November Douglas's parents visited their son in hospital from their home village of Ellenborough on the Cumberland coast. They were with him when he learned that his courage had earned him the Military Medal. Douglas was transferred to Huddersfield's Royds Hall War Hospital on 17 January 1918, and on to Honley District War Hospital ten days later where he completed his convalescence.

Invalided out of the war in a wheelchair, Douglas was told that he would jeopardise his life if he returned to his rugby and wrestling careers. He defied medical advice in spectacular fashion. Later in 1918 he rejoined his Motor Transport Unit on the Western Front. In the spring of 1919 the Fartown crowd cheered him to the echo as he took the field once more as part of the Huddersfield pack. Douglas's recovery from his wartime injuries to resume, with outstanding success, his careers in both rugby and wrestling, earned for him the reputation of 'strongest man on the planet.'

The End of the War

The Armistice was declared on 11 November 1918, but the country had lost three quarters of a million men killed in the fighting, as well as the many others who were temporarily or permanently invalided. The economy was geared to the needs of war not peace and many thousands of men in military service were anxious to return to civilian life as soon as possible. In these circumstances it would take some time for the Northern Union to resume a full programme of league and cup competitions. Could the Huddersfield club and the surviving stars of the Team of All Talents, who had lost four years – a significant percentage – of their careers to the war, resume where they had left off?

Chapter 7

Break-up of the Team of all Talents

Post-war

It will always remain a matter of conjecture as to what Wagstaff, Rosenfeld and their Huddersfield colleagues may have accomplished but for the intervention of the First World War.

The Yorkshire League resumed shortly after the Armistice, but only the clubs that had continued to play matches throughout the war participated. Others, such as Huddersfield, opted to play friendlies and await the demobilisation of the majority of their players from the forces.

At the outbreak of war the average age of the Huddersfield team was twenty-five. By 1919 most were around thirty. Could the ageing 'Team of all Talents' carry on from where they left off in 1915? How would the losses of several players affect them? In addition to the death of brilliant loose forward Fred Longstaff on the Somme, Herbert Banks had smashed an ankle working in a reserved occupation down the pit, Jim Davies had returned to Wales, and Aaron Lee would shortly emigrate to America. Douglas Clark's effectiveness following his multiple injuries at Passchendaele was uncertain.

Other clubs had, of course, suffered wartime losses too. Huddersfield's first post-war competition was the Yorkshire Cup, which was staged in the spring of 1919. Quickly into their stride, they beat Hunslet, Hull KR and Hull before conquering Dewsbury 14-8 in the final at Headingley to retain the trophy they last won in November 1914.

Later in 1919, as the sporting calendar approached normality, the Yorkshire Cup returned to its autumn slot. The draw did the Fartowners few favours but Halifax, Hull and Wakefield were overcome to set up a final against Leeds. Stanley Moorhouse ran in four tries, the record for a Yorkshire Cup final, as Huddersfield won 24-5 to become the first club to win the trophy twice in the same calendar year, a feat emulated by Bradford Northern in 1941 when war once again disrupted the sporting calendar.

With 29 wins from 34 league matches, the nucleus of Huddersfield's all-conquering pre-war side was still firing. Wagstaff's men comfortably won the Yorkshire League and headed the League Championship table. The Challenge Cup Final against Wigan was, according to Stanley Chadwick's *Claret and Gold: 1895-1945*, 'a great match, for the forwards of both sides were in form', Huddersfield retaining the trophy they had won in 1915.

Huddersfield v Wigan
Challenge Cup Final
at Headingley, Leeds, 10 April 1920

Huddersfield	21	Wigan	10
Tries: Pogson (2)		Tries: Hall	
Clark		Jerram	
Habron		Goals: Jolley (2)	
Todd			
Goals: Gronow (3)			

Huddersfield
Major Holland;
George Todd, Tommy Gleeson, Harold Wagstaff, Hubert Pogson;
Johnny Rogers, Bob Habron;
Arthur Swinden, George Naylor, Thomas Fenwick, Arthur Sherwood, Ben Gronow, Douglas Clark.

Wigan
Bill Jolley;

Vince Smith, Frank Prescott, Danny Hurcombe, Harry Hall;

George Hesketh, Syd Jerram;

Charlie Seeling, Ernie Shaw, Percy Coldrick, Tom Prescott, Dick Ramsdale, Jimmy Lowe.

Referee: F Mills (Oldham)   Attendance: 14,000

A repeat of the four trophies achieved in 1914-15 was on. Only the League Championship remained. The Championship had resumed under the pre-war system adopted in 1905-06, the Yorkshire and Lancashire clubs playing all the teams in their own 'county' home and away and in addition organising inter-county fixtures on an individual basis. With clubs playing different numbers of fixtures, positions were determined by the percentage of points each club had gained from those available.

Northern Rugby Football Union Championship 1919-20

Pos	Team	Pld	Won	Drwn	Lost	Points For	Agnst	Pts	%age Pts gained from Pts Available
1	Huddersfield	34	29	0	5	759	215	58	85.29
2	Hull	34	25	1	8	587	276	51	75.00
3	Leeds	32	23	0	9	445	208	46	71.87
4	Widnes	30	21	1	8	250	115	43	71.67
5	Barrow	32	22	1	9	477	202	45	70.31
6	Halifax	34	23	1	10	390	168	47	69.12
7	Rochdale Hornets	34	22	1	11	363	203	45	66.18
8	Oldham	34	21	1	12	333	226	43	63.23
9	Dewsbury	32	18	2	12	299	262	38	59.37
10	Warrington	30	15	2	13	236	198	32	53.33
11	St Helens Recs	28	13	3	12	329	196	29	51.79
12	Batley	32	15	2	15	223	319	32	50.00
13	Wigan	32	15	1	16	281	266	31	48.44
14	Leigh	28	12	2	14	175	228	26	46.43
15	Salford	32	14	1	17	202	269	29	45.31
16	St Helens	30	12	2	16	278	285	26	43.33
17	Swinton	30	12	1	17	201	274	25	41.67
18	Wakefield Trinity	32	11	4	17	229	494	26	40.62
19	Hull Kingston Rovers	32	10	2	20	250	325	22	34.37
20	Bramley	30	8	4	18	163	372	20	33.33
21	York	30	8	1	21	213	422	17	28.33
22	Hunslet	34	9	0	25	167	384	18	26.47
23	Broughton Rangers	32	7	2	23	184	460	16	25.00
24	Bradford Northern	32	7	1	24	177	479	15	23.44
25	Keighley	32	6	0	26	106	471	12	18.75

As some clubs may have had easier or more difficult fixture lists than others, a top-four play-off series, known as 'the supplementary competition', introduced in 1906-07, was used to determine the champions. Apart from the interventions of the World Wars, this system was retained, with a brief break in the 1960s, until 1973. Even allowing for vagaries in the fixture lists, the table indicates that free-scoring Huddersfield were the best team in the competition.

Before the supplementary (play-off) competition began, the Great Britain tour party set sail for Australasia. It included the spine of the Huddersfield team – forwards Douglas Clark and Ben Gronow, scrum half Johnny Rogers, full back Gwyn Thomas and captain and centre threequarter Harold Wagstaff. Stanley Moorhouse might also have made the trip had he not been suffering from a broken arm.

Huddersfield's 1920 Great Britain tourists,
Ben Gronow, Harold Wagstaff, Johnny Rogers, Gwyn Thomas and Douglas Clark

The five tourists enjoyed a couple of nights at the Rugby Hotel in London, which was run by Albert Bennett, the trainer of the Team of all Talents, who had moved to the capital in 1916 after over two decades with the Fartown club. They travelled across France to Marseilles where they joined the rest of the party, and were on the high seas when the semi-final kicked off before a tense Fartown crowd. The visitors, a dour Widnes team, had the best defence in the Northern Union, but Huddersfield were able to grind out a 7-5 victory to set up a Headingley final against Hull.

Captained by Albert Rosenfeld, Huddersfield led the final 2-0 with five minutes remaining. Then, dramatically, Hull's Billy Batten scored the game's only try to snatch a 3-2 victory. Huddersfield were within five minutes of winning all four cups for a second time, a feat no team ever achieved and which, since the shelving of the Yorkshire and Lancashire cups in 1992, is no longer possible.

It had, nevertheless, been an outstanding season. As well as the three trophies, winger Stanley Moorhouse was the league's highest try scorer with 39, and Ben Gronow had established new Northern League records of 147 goals and 330 points in the season. His 147 goals remained the Huddersfield club record until beaten by Danny Brough in 2013. The selection of five star players for the Lions' Australasian tour almost certainly cost Huddersfield all four cups for a second time.

The 1920 tour of Australasia was also disappointing. The Ashes were lost and Johnny Rogers had the misfortune to fracture his left leg at Auckland, keeping him out of football until January 1921. Ben Gronow enjoyed a happier time, kicking 65 goals and scoring two tries in sixteen appearances, setting up new scoring records for a tour.

Break-up of the Team of all Talents

Huddersfield were always competitive and added a respectable amount of silverware during the 1920s, but the 1919-20 season was a last hurrah for the Team of all Talents which gradually and inevitably broke up.

On 1 April 1922 Stanley Moorhouse shared a joint benefit with Arthur Swinden. Only Swinden played in the match, the attendance of which was disappointing, the receipts being £322. Placed on the transfer list at his own request, Moorhouse moved to Bradford Northern as player/coach in December 1923, but he never recaptured the form that made him such a success at Huddersfield, and made only five appearances for Northern in 1923-24. Subsequently, Moorhouse became a referee in the Yorkshire Senior Competition, later returning to Fartown as trainer/coach to the second team.

He was foreman-electrician at the Great Northern Street Works of the Passenger Transport Department, Huddersfield, where he had worked since 1906, except for a break of a few years in the twenties, and he played cricket with the Primrose Hill and Huddersfield clubs. Stanley Moorhouse died suddenly at his home in Almondbury, Huddersfield, on Monday 23 April 1951, aged 59.

One of numerous Harry Fieldhouse cartoons that appeared in the *Huddersfield Examiner* in the 1930s shows Stanley Moorhouse, drawn in 1934, when he was coaching the second team.

Johnny Rogers played in seven Test Matches, and for Other Nationalities against England in February 1921. He also added a League Championship runners-up medal to his collection when Huddersfield lost the Play-off Final 15-5 to Hull KR in 1923. Rogers signed for Wakefield Trinity on 9 January 1925 for a bargain of fee of £300. Staying in the north, he was licensee of the Plumber's Arms in Huddersfield until 1955, and continued to live there for three years after his retirement, until he died on 26 July 1958, aged 65.

Ben Gronow's career continued to flourish following his record points tallies for Huddersfield and Great Britain in 1920. In 1924 he was again selected to tour Australasia, at 35 one of the oldest-ever tourists. He was unable to add to his seven Test Match appearances, injuries restricting him to eight matches during which he kicked five goals and scored one try.

Gronow had a benefit match at Fartown on 8 March 1924, Huddersfield beating Dewsbury 9-3 before a crowd of 10,099 which paid receipts of £493. In June 1925 he left for Australia where he stayed initially with his old Fartown teammate Tommy Gleeson, and took up a position as player/coach to the Grenfell club.

B. Gronow, England's Champion Goal Kicker in Action.

He remained the only player from an English club to play for an Australian club until the late 1950s.

Returning to England in August 1927, he played mainly for Huddersfield reserves during 1927-28. His last game for Huddersfield was on 1 September 1928 at York, where he kicked 2 goals in a 10-2 win. Brief spells at Batley and Featherstone Rovers followed before he retired at the age of 41.

He later served for many years on the Huddersfield Football Committee and he was made a Honorary Life Member of the club a few months before he died, aged 80, on 24 November 1967,

Albert Rosenfeld played the last of his 287 games for Huddersfield on 2 April 1921 in a home cup-tie against Leeds, leaving a trail of club records in his wake. He had scored 5 tries on twelve occasions, 4 tries eight times, 3 tries twenty-seven times and topped the Rugby League try-scoring charts in four consecutive seasons from 1911/12 to 1914/15. His points tally of 1102 included a new club-record 366 tries which has only subsequently been beaten by his compatriot, Lionel Cooper, who ran in 420 tries between 1947 and 1955.

On 15 September 1921 Albert was transferred to Wakefield Trinity where he played for two seasons. Approaching 40 years of age, he moved to Bradford Northern, scoring his last-ever try in a 12-8 home win against Wigan Highfield on 26 January 1924. After retiring from the professional game he coached local amateur club Rastrick, continued to watch Huddersfield's home games, and kept an eye on the schoolboy rugby careers of his two grandsons.

His major interest outside of sport was repairing radios, but his day-jobs were not the sort usually associated with truly great sportsmen. He briefly ran a tobacconists and for many years drove a Huddersfield Corporation refuse cart. Later, well into his seventies, he worked as a dyer.

Albert received continuing recognition from the Australian Rugby League authorities as a survivor from their first-ever tour. On every tour of the UK they presented to him a special blazer, its badge emblazoned with the word 'Pioneer'. In 1964, Albert and Ethel celebrated their golden wedding anniversary by travelling around the world, culminating in a four month stay in Sydney. It was Albert's first return to his home city in 55 years, and he was welcomed and feted wherever he went.

The last survivor of the 1908-09 Kangaroos, Albert passed away on 4 September 1970 in the Huddersfield home that he and Ethel had occupied for half a century. He was 85. EE Christensen remarked in the *Sydney Daily Telegraph*:

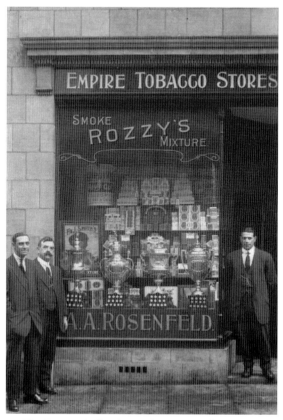

The Team of all Talents' four cups of 1914-15 displayed in Albert Rosenfeld's tobacconists window, next to the Empire Cinema on John William Street.

76

Rosenfeld achieved football immortality in Australia and England and was a remarkable man both in youth and old age … His record has never been approached and, nowadays, English club wingers feel proud of themselves if they can manage thirty tries in a season.

The *Huddersfield Examiner* simply stated: 'He was one of the most famous of all Rugby League players.'

Douglas Clark's extraordinary career as a professional sportsman continued well into middle age. He played his last match for Huddersfield at the age of 38, in the 1928-29 Championship-winning season, but had also continued his career as a Cumberland wrestler, winning the Grasmere Cup in 1922 and 1924.

In 1930 Sir Atholl Oakley began to formalise professional wrestling in Britain, organising the first World Championship tournament at the Lanes Club in Baker Street, London. Douglas beat Oakley in the final to become the first World Heavyweight Champion. He regained his title later in the decade and toured Australia in 1934 and 1936. His last major bout was against the devastating American Jack Sherry in 1938. Aged 47, Douglas lost to the younger man in two minutes, a result that saw Sherry acknowledged as the greatest heavyweight to that time. Douglas continued to wrestle until 1941, retiring at the age of 50.

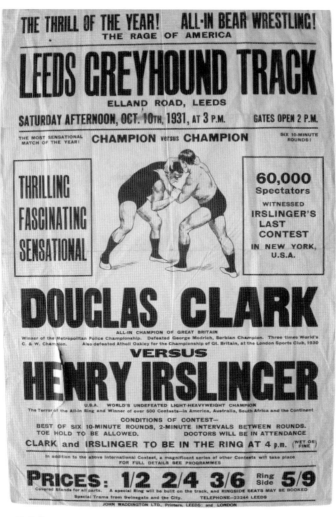

Top: Poster for one of Douglas's World Championship bouts, 1931
Left: Poster for Douglas's final World Championship bout against American Jack Sherry in 1938.
Right: A letter of advice from Douglas to the Huddersfield team, probably from one of his wrestling tours of Australia.

He continued to work as a coalman in Huddersfield, ran to keep fit, and frequently returned to favourite fishing rivers around his home town of Ellenborough in Cumberland. In 1951, aged 59, he contracted influenza. It developed into pneumonia and he died quite suddenly.

Harold Wagstaff's well-deserved benefit match came against Rochdale, his mother's home town, on 31 January 1920. A special train, and 'almost every motor vehicle in the town and surrounding district' were hired to bring Rochdale supporters to Fartown. Despite a wet and miserable day, 15,888 spectators paid gate receipts of £927 19s 2d, Huddersfield crowning the occasion by winning 22-8.

In 1921-22, Harold led the team that regained the Ashes on home soil. The deciding Test Match at Salford on 14 January 1922 proved to be his last. He may have played many more, but illness again restricted him. He had suffered stomach problems for years and he underwent an operation for a duodenal ulcer. After that he played in a corset to protect his abdomen, bowing out – curiously playing at full back – at Oldham on 23 March 1925, shortly before his 34th birthday.

Harold became licensee of the Boar's Head public house in Halifax, before returning to Huddersfield in 1932 to take over as landlord of the Swan With Two Necks in Westgate. The pub was renamed the Royal Swan in 1933.

In 1925-26 he had a brief, unsuccessful spell as coach at Halifax, and in 1935 acted in a similar capacity for the Broughton Rangers club. He was elected to the General Committee of the Huddersfield club in 1937, to the Football Committee in 1938 and subsequently made Vice-Chairman in 1938-39.

Great former Huddersfield players, Gwyn Thomas, Harold Wagstaff, Ben Gronow and Johnny Rogers, pictured in 1938.

Towards the end of 1938, Harold's health deteriorated. A severe dose of influenza caused heart problems and on 17 July 1939 he was admitted to a Huddersfield Nursing Home. Two days later he passed away, aged just 48.

Tributes poured in for a man who had played and conducted himself with extraordinary distinction, ever since his debut at such an unbelievable, young age that the Huddersfield club printed his birth certificate in a match day programme as proof. Frank Ellis Woodhead, who commented on the club's affairs in the *HDE* under the pen name 'Rouge' from World War I until his death in 1943, wrote Harold's obituary in the *HDE*:

> If in search of the secret of his success, the nearest one could get would be: 'Quick thinking combined with perfect technique.' No player ever demonstrated more thoroughly the importance of the split second in both attack and defence, and certainly none ever timed his efforts with greater success.

For Wagstaff, 'possession was nine tenths of the law.' Under him, Huddersfield became known, with a little exaggeration, as 'the team that never kicks.' His philosophy was, if you have possession of the ball, why kick it away to gain a few yards?

'Rouge' also quoted the testimonial presented to Harold by the club on his retirement.

> Huddersfield people will always remember with great pride the fact that throughout the whole of your lengthy career not one single instance can be recorded against you of an action out of keeping with the great name you have made for yourself and the Club.

'Rouge' added:

> Wagstaff … was rightly proud … that he had never been sent off the field for unsportsmanlike behaviour.

On Saturday 22 July 1939, hundreds lined the streets of Harold's funeral procession from the Royal Swan through the centre of Huddersfield, making the thoroughfare along Market Street almost impassable. On the coffin lay two wreaths – a cross from his widow and son, and a rugby ball comprised of golden lilies and claret carnations, bearing the inscription 'From the boys of the Fartown football team.' Eight of Harold's old team-mates carried the coffin into Holmfirth Parish Church where the Reverend TH Cashmore addressed the congregation:

> Holmfirth was rightly proud of a man who, in his own sphere, had carried her name far beyond their hills and valleys. He had great qualities of heart and mind and body that won for him the confidence and admiration of thousands.

Harry Fieldhouse's tribute to Harold Wagstaff, published on the day of his funeral

The blue plaque dedicated to Harold Wagstaff, opposite the Pump Hole in Holmfirth. Of 17 blue plaques in the Holme Valley it is the only one dedicated to an individual rather than to a building.

Halls of Fame

Huddersfield's 'Team of All Talents' won three Challenge Cup Finals, three Yorkshire Cup Finals, three League Championship Finals and six Yorkshire League titles. These 15 trophies represent an unrivalled period of success for the club, and were crowned by winning 'All Four Cups' in 1914-15. Their attractive, flowing, attacking rugby ensured that the Huddersfield supporters not only experienced the pride and joy of their team's successes, but were also royally entertained.

Huddersfield's greatest players of this era have been awarded the greatest honour the game can bestow. In October 1988, Harold Wagstaff and Albert Rosenfeld were among the original nine members of the Rugby Football League Hall of Fame. In 2005 they were joined by a further eight inductees who included Douglas Clark.

On 22 April 1999, at the McAlpine Stadium, the Huddersfield Rugby League Club Players' Association inducted 21 players to the club's Hall of Fame. Among these were Harold Wagstaff, Albert Rosenfeld, Douglas Clark and Ben Gronow. These players, and through them the Team of all Talents, are immortalised for as long as the game of rugby league is played.

Chapter 8

Mixed Fortunes Between the Wars

Inevitably, as the Team of all Talents broke up, the Huddersfield club entered a period of transition. Although there were notable successes, the 1920s were an anti-climax, the *Huddersfield Examiner* in a retrospective, 'Sixty Five Years of the Huddersfield Club' in November 1929, referring to a long period in the decade 'when disappointment followed disappointment.'

Club Finances and Management

Throughout the inter-war period and beyond, Huddersfield Rugby League Football Club continued to operate as a section of 'Huddersfield Cricket and Athletic Club' (HC and AC), the name continuing to reflect the club's origins in the summertime sports, although rugby had been the highest profile section of the club for several decades.

A General Committee of HC and AC co-ordinated and supervised all financial matters involving rugby, cricket, crown green bowling, the annual athletic festival, and any other activities at Fartown. Each section of the club, including a ground committee, was operated by its own sub-committee which reported to the General Committee. The surviving committee records and summaries provide insights into the financial affairs and management of the club between the wars.

In January 1927 the rugby section had 1917 members, paying annual subscriptions that ranged from 17 shillings (85p) to 37 shillings (£1.85p). Membership had increased to 2215 by January 1930. Not all members had the same status, as can be inferred from the range of membership fees. Sir Joseph Turner, KBE, JP, was President from 1922 to 1939. This continued the club's tradition of a figurehead who was the Chairman of the town's major chemical works, Read Holliday, even though this firm had been taken over by British Dyeworks Ltd as a wartime munitions factory in 1915. At each Annual General Meeting (AGM), usually held at the Temperance Hall on Princess Street, members were elected and appointed to the various committees and sub-committees that carried out the work of the club.

The Football Committee, typically comprising seven officers, was responsible for all aspects of the management of the first and second teams. This included picking the teams and, according to a minute from 8 July 1927, 'full powers to act in cases of emergency in regard to the signing on of players, in consultation with the Finance Sub-Committee.' Some famous players, such as Milford Sutcliffe and Harold Wagstaff, went on to serve on the Football Committee once their playing days were over. The Football Committee's hands-on control of the teams and players left the coach as little more than a physical fitness trainer. It resembles the running of most cricket teams, which are selected by committee before practice and on-field tactics are devolved to the captain, rather than the management structure of modern-day rugby league or soccer clubs, suggesting that it may have been copied from the club's earliest days as a cricket club. Such comprehensive control entailed a remarkable 92 meetings of the Football Committee during the year ending 30 April 1927.

Members of the Football Committee were elected by all the members present at each AGM, but in July 1927 the Articles of Association – the regulations governing HC and AC – were changed at an Extraordinary General Meeting. Among the changes, the General Committee could now …

... appoint the various Sub-Committees of the Club, particularly the Football Committee. This will prevent a recurrence of the difficulty that has arisen at the Annual General Meetings in the past when the Football Sub-Committee has been appointed by the members present and not by the General Committee.

Clearly the members of the General Committee wished to have more direct control over the Football Committee which was overwhelmingly the most important in terms of the club's annual income and expenditure. Even after this change, the minutes of the General Committee hint at continuing tension regarding the Football Committee's finances. What appear to be very minor matters were scrutinised, as in 1927 when the General Committee approved the minutes of the Football Committee except 'the employment of a woman to serve teas to officials at first team meetings' and the proposed use of 'collecting boxes at York Match at Fartown on behalf of Mr Frank Renton's Benefit.' Despite these disagreements, the committees provided opportunities for local participation in running the club and seem on the whole to have worked quite well.

The recollections of a committeeman from the 1970s, Trevor Kaye, shed some light on the club's autocratic ethos.

When you were [first] on the General Committee the only other committee you could go on straight away was the Catering Committee. So I ended up making sandwiches ... [the] Football Committee was the pinnacle of the Huddersfield Cricket and Athletic Club. So you went on the General Committee, and they said you must start on the Catering Committee to get the experience – and don't do anything, don't ask any questions, don't say anything at the meetings. This is how it was, so myself and a lad called Richard went on the Catering Committee. [Eventually] there became vacancies on the Football Committee, so I put my name forward. In those days there was Hubert Lockwood, Peter Gronow and Frank Dyson, who had played full back for Great Britain. Peter Gronow's father [Ben Gronow] had been an international. There were a lot of people on that Football Committee who had a lot of experience – and then little me and Richard.

They had a policy that the football committee was the be-all and end-all. You employed a coach ... who would coach the players on Tuesday and Thursday nights – Saturday as well maybe – but on Thursday night he would get a call to come to the boardroom for half past seven and he would be told what his team was going to be.

Little, apparently, changed in how the rugby league side of the club was run between the 1920s and the 1970s. It was still team management by committee, their reluctance to relinquish power diminishing the role of the coach.

It is extremely difficult to find details of the size of crowds at Fartown, as it is for all rugby league clubs, in the inter-war years. Although the Football League required crowd figures to be recorded as early as 1925, the same position was not adopted in rugby league until after the Second World War. The exceptions were for Challenge Cup matches and Australian tourists' games, for which the gate receipts were divided between the two teams. So, for example, full details are available for the Australian tourists' four matches at Fartown during the inter-war years – from which Huddersfield even achieved one famous victory.

Year	Result	Attendance	Gate Receipts (£ s d)
1921	Huddersfield 2 Australians 36	11,048	1,035 13 0
1929	Huddersfield 8 Australians 18	18,560	1,455 9 6
1933	Huddersfield 5 Australians 13	7,422	610 0 0
1937	Huddersfield 17 Australians 7	9,383	747 18 6

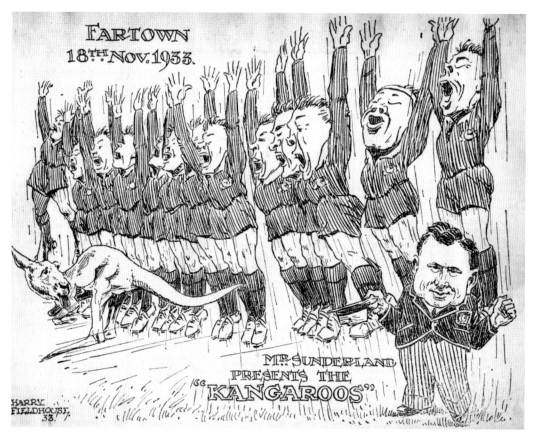

A Harry Fieldhouse cartoon celebrates the appearance of the 1933 Australians at Fartown.

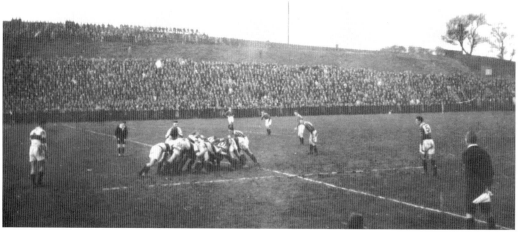

A sizeable Fartown crowd on the popular bank watches Huddersfield v St Helens in November 1930.

However, rugby league clubs did keep records of gate receipts and the annual accounts of HC and AC reveal trends in crowd numbers as well as key items of expenditure such as players' wages.

1918 to 1920

Financial details for the season 1918-19 are extremely sketchy but later reports indicate that 'this short football season was a financial success, in no small part because Huddersfield won the only competition they entered, the Yorkshire Cup.' The public embraced sport as one of the shared communal activities that symbolised and affirmed the gradual return to normality after the horrors and suffering of the war, the annual report for 1919-20 showing a profit on 'football activity' of just over £1684 and membership at a new record high of 1597. A new Fartown record crowd, 22,131, paid gate receipts of £1600 for the victory over Hull in the second round of the Yorkshire Cup. Nevertheless, in this first full post-war season, attendances away from home consistently exceeded those at home, which was 'not greatly to the credit of Huddersfield's reputation as a sporting centre', particularly as the team had also retained the Yorkshire League and the Challenge Cup.

The Huddersfield committee could not maintain the excellent quality of the team 'without adequate support.' In part the committee's concern about poor support expressed in the 1920 Annual Report was probably influenced by dramatic events at Huddersfield Town AFC. In November 1919, Town was experiencing financial difficulties and there was a sensational proposal to move the club to Leeds to replace Leeds City. Leeds City had been expelled from the Football League in October 1919 for making illegal allowances to 'guest' players during the war. Eventually, uproar in Huddersfield and impressive fundraising ensured that the football club stayed in the town. Meanwhile, Leeds City re-formed as Leeds United FC.

Huddersfield Town FC: Complete Record 1910-1990 contradicts the HC and AC's complaint about the lack of adequate support, stating:

> Huddersfield Town had, for years, been engaged upon the unprofitable task of serving up first-class soccer in an area which most markedly demonstrated its loyalty to the Northern Union game.

To emphasise the point it compares the Fartown receipts of £1600 for that November 1919 Yorkshire Cup tie against Hull to a gate of £90 from an attendance of 2500 at Leeds Road on the same day.

1921 to 1926

There were other exceptions to Fartown's 'disappointing' crowd numbers, most notably when 31,494, another new ground record, attended a second round Challenge Cup tie against Oldham on 12 March 1921, generating receipts of just over £2301.

By the standards of the great Huddersfield teams of the previous decade, results in the 1920-21 season were disappointing. As the Team of all Talents began to break up, for the first time in a decade no major trophies were won, the team slumping from first to 14th. Despite this, the football profit was still £1652. The annual report lamented the 'falling away' of players who had served the team so well in the past, and the need for urgent team building. Several players were past their prime and rebuilding began in earnest when the first of these, Albert Rosenfeld, John Willie Higson and Major Holland, left at the start of the following season.

The boom in the British economy that followed the end of the war broke abruptly in the winter of 1920-21. One consequence was that wages fell heavily in every industry. Textiles and coal mining, the traditional industrial mainstays of the Northern Union, were particularly badly affected. According to Tony Collins, almost every rugby league club had 'little more than a tenuous hold on financial health' throughout the remainder of the 1920s and 1930s. The first indications of strife at Huddersfield appeared in the 1921-22 annual report which attributed the football section's significant loss of £2127 to 'the great falling off in gate receipts due to bad trade and employment.' The attendance of 728 members at the annual meeting in the Town Hall was, despite the hard times, the highest in the history of the club, demonstrating the concern of the hard-core supporters.

Fifty of these members of HC and AC had met on 6 June 1921 in St John's School, Hillhouse, to discuss the formation of a Supporters' Club. A few days later a further meeting was held at the Friendly and Trades Hall on Northumberland Street with about 200 present. The formation of the Supporters' Club was endorsed and a committee was formed under the chairmanship of Mr H Hardy. The meeting agreed that: 'The objects of the Club are to secure and support suitable members to serve on the various Committees of the HC and AC, and also to use its influence in the general interests of the premier club.' The Supporters' Club was given official recognition and best wishes for success by HC and AC. It went on to organise trips to away matches and various fundraising activities, and had delegates on the club's committees.

From the 1920s, supporters' clubs played an important role in financing many of the professional rugby league clubs. The Huddersfield Supporters' Club raised nearly £5000 between 1921 and 1946. As Tony Collins points out, 'Ultimately, it was on this foundation of volunteer and community support that rugby league was built and which ensured its survival through the depression.'

The Northern Union held its annual meeting in Huddersfield on 14 June 1922. Considering its name 'too parochial' for a game now played in three countries, it adopted the name suggested three years earlier by the New South Wales Rugby League. After 27 years, the Northern Rugby Football Union became the Rugby Football League.

For four seasons from 1922-23 Huddersfield's financial records are extremely sparse. The rebuilding of the team was a partial success. In 1923 Huddersfield finished second in the league table and reached the Championship Final, which they lost 15-5 to Hull KR.

The continuing harsh economic climate was reflected in a loss of £960 in 1923-24. In 1925-26 another loss of £1729 was in part attributed to unfortunate draws in the Challenge Cup. Amidst these difficulties, in September 1924, William Hirst resigned owing to ill-health after many years of sterling service as secretary of HC and AC.

Some compensation for the lack of trophies at Fartown came in Huddersfield Town winning the FA Cup in 1922, and successive Division One (now the Premier League) titles in 1923-24, 1924-25 and 1925-26. This unprecedented level of success produced a very significant increase in Town's level of support compared to the precarious uncertainties of 1919. It is difficult to gauge the extent to which this was associated with a loss of support and lack of success at Fartown. However, Tony Collins suggests that, although the success of soccer teams was often at the expense of local rugby league teams, Huddersfield appears to have been an exception, where the two codes co-existed successfully. This is consistent with the recollections of many older supporters who watched the local rugby and soccer clubs on alternate Saturdays during the 1930s and 40s. Nevertheless, the HC and AC committee was very aware of the potential threats from the soccer team. In June 1927 the minutes of the General Committee reported that:

> The Chairman of the Football Committee (Mr J W Priestley) reported that Huddersfield Town had arranged for Home Matches on Easter Saturday, Easter Monday and Easter Tuesday next season. This matter was fully discussed and it was decided that a complaint be lodged with the Rugby League and that they be asked to take the matter up with the Football Association.

Such complaints to the association football authorities were not uncommon or confined to rugby league. The Lancashire Cricket League complained several times about the football season encroaching further into the cricket season and, as recently as 1960, suggested that the FA Cup Final, no less, should be switched to a morning kick-off as playing it in the afternoon was affecting their gates!

From 20th August 1926 to 19th August 1932 the Huddersfield Cricket and Athletic Club's Minute Books, including annual reports and accounts, are intact. The rugby football club's income and expenditure over this period are summarised in the following table.

Huddersfield Cricket and Athletic Club
Rugby Football Club Income and Expenditure for Year Ending 30 April

	1927	1928	1929	1930	1931	1932
INCOME						
First Team Gate Receipts	5832	7247	7941	6922	5774	5307
(Less Entertainment Tax)	(929)	(994)	(1134)	(904)	(883)	(861)
(Less Money Paid to Other Clubs)	(1186)	(1119)	(829)	(557)	(506)	(546)
Receipts from Cup Ties and Special Games	1573	1503	1533	1166	2512	2901
First Team Gate Money (Net)	5290	6637	7511	6627	6897	6801
Second Team Gate Money (Net)	145	237	123	142	186	151
TOTAL GATE MONEY (NET)	**5435**	**6874**	**7634**	**6769**	**7083**	**6952**
Transfer Fees Received	625	30	270	315	200	300
Profit on Programmes Sales	179	212	261	200	192	171
Sundry Receipts	0	0	0	12	11	11
TOTAL INCOME	**6239**	**7116**	**8165**	**7296**	**7486**	**7434**
EXPENDITURE						
First Team Wages	2791	3387	3396	2970	3269	3303
Second Team Wages	535	777	349	466	438	357
Match and Ground Expenses, Outfits, Printing, Travelling etc	1574	1552	1558	1936	2004	1611
Insurance Premiums and Medical	522	337	283	463	286	405
Transfer Fees, Bonuses and Expenses for New Players	1017	2515	1102	2104	859	484
Trainers' and Attendants' Wages	287	260	260	269	269	286
Huddersfield and District Junior League	105	46	46	95	108	53
TOTAL EXPENDITURE	**6831**	**8874**	**6994**	**8303**	**7233**	**6499**
TOTAL INCOME	6239	7116	8165	7296	7486	7434
TOTAL EXPENDITURE	6831	8874	6994	8303	7233	6499
PROFIT OR (LOSS)	**(592)**	**(1758)**	**1171**	**(1007)**	**253**	**935**

(all amounts rounded to the nearest £)

First team gate money, indicating trends in levels of support, was just over £5800 in 1927. This increased quite substantially over the next two years, before falling slightly in 1930, despite a second successive Rugby League Championship title. Two more years of decline followed until the gate money in 1932, £5307, is the lowest of any of the six years.

The next line of the income account shows Huddersfield, like other sporting clubs, paying 'entertainment tax'. Introduced in 1916 as a temporary wartime measure, this much-loathed tax would continue to be a burden on rugby league clubs until 1957, although it was abolished for rugby union and cricket in 1953. The accounts show the club paying between 13% and

16% of their gate receipts in this form of tax. Even second team gate money was taxed in this way. In depressed economic conditions this tax was onerous for all forms of entertainment that charged an entrance fee. Even amidst the patriotic fervour of World War I, organisations quickly adopted avoidance methods. Within days of the tax becoming law, the Huddersfield bowls committee, whose clubs were required to pay ½d tax on entrance fees of 2d and 1d tax on fees of 3d to 6d, announced that 'because of the amusement tax no charge to be made at bowls cup matches until the semi-final stage.' Such a measure would not prevent them taking a voluntary tax-free collection from spectators in the earlier rounds.

Throughout the inter-war years, gate receipts for cup games and special games were usually shared between the clubs involved. For example, a letter dated 1 January 1932 from Halifax Football Club acknowledges receipt of £406 from Huddersfield and mentions a cheque for £340 sent to Huddersfield. These sums represent the shared gate receipts from the annual festive season games played on Christmas Day ('fine day with trams and buses running', according to a handwritten note on the list of Huddersfield gate money) and Boxing Day 1931.

The trend for attendances away from home to exceed those at home, bemoaned by the committee in 1919, may have continued as, in every season from 1926 to 1932, Huddersfield received more from away gates for cup ties and special games than it paid out to other clubs. However, this might be explained by the classification of matches played at neutral venues, such as cup semi-finals and finals, as away matches.

Ernie Mills, spotted in Australia by Ben Gronow who recommended him to the Fartown club.

The 1933 Challenge Cup semi-finals, Huddersfield v Leeds at Wakefield, and Warrington v St Helens at Swinton, show how such receipts were allocated. The gross gate receipts were £2300 at Wakefield and £2055 at Swinton. Expenses such as tax and police costs were deducted along with a ten per cent share to the host clubs. The remaining money, £3136, was then forwarded to the Rugby League which deducted one third, (£1045) for the league and divided the remainder equally between the four competing clubs, each receiving £523. All that appeared in the accounts of HC and AC was the £523 received, boosting income from 'away' cup matches.

The profits made on selling programmes at Fartown ranged between £171 and £261 per year and, as would be expected, vary very much in line with gate money receipts.

The largest item of expenditure was, unsurprisingly, first team wages, although virtually all the players were part-time with full-time jobs outside the game. For the year ended April 1928 the standard rates of pay for players at Huddersfield were: £4 10s for a win; £3 10s for a draw; and £2 10s for a defeat. Star players at some clubs might be paid significantly more than the standard rates. Some players' pay was commonly boosted by employing them to work on the grounds, but these payments were charged to the overall HC and AC account, not to the football account. Thus in 1928-29 eight Huddersfield players received payment for working on the grounds at Fartown. This enabled the great Australian winger Ernie Mills, for example, to add £83 to his earnings of £276 for his exploits on the rugby field.

Between 1927 and 1932 players' wages ranged between 45% and 52% of net first team gate receipts. It has been suggested by Tony Collins that by this time many clubs were struggling to generate enough gate money to cover the costs of players' wages so it appears that, despite the harsh economic climate, Huddersfield was achieving a balance between wages and income.

Huddersfield v Wigan at Fartown, April 1931

Transfer fees received from selling players were relatively modest and were always exceeded by the amount spent on acquiring new players. A major cause of this was the signing-on fee paid to a new player, an inducement to join the club, that could range from £2-£10 for a local player to £200-£300 for a young player of outstanding talent or a prestigious signing from a Welsh rugby union club. Shortly after the start of the 1931-32 season, Huddersfield paid a signing-on bonus of £200 to the Welsh international stand-off Gwyn Richards. Some established Australian imports to English clubs received signing-on fees of £1000 or more. At a time when a factory worker might be fortunate to earn £150 in a year, such lucrative signing-on fees, which were paid in addition to any transfer fee between the clubs, were a significant expense and made any overall profit on transfers unlikely.

Gwyn Richards

Of course not all signings were successful; in 1929 the Australians Albert Carr and Sydney Harris simply packed their bags and returned to Australia halfway through their three-year contracts with the club.

The wages paid to trainers and attendants were low and varied very little from year to year. In 1926-27, Huddersfield's highest-paid trainer, Littlewood, received £42, about 12% of the £339 earned by the highest-paid player, Len Bowkett. With the Football Committee picking the team, and therefore influencing its tactics, the trainer focused very much on physical fitness, his low wage and status possibly reflecting the view of Douglas Clark in 1925 that 'when fit and playing every week, men

Harold Fieldhouse cartoon from 1930, paying tribute to trainer JT Withers

THE BIG 6.

FARTOWN'S FORMIDABLE FORWARDS

A RIGHT HANDFUL

TRAINER WITHERS. WHO IS ALWAYS WITH US.

following an everyday occupation require very little training.' For the typical rugby league player, the day job itself would be physically demanding.

Match and ground expenses vary little from 1927 to 1929, rising to a peak of just over £2000 in 1931 before falling again in 1932. Modest payments were also made to the local Junior League, to encourage the development of players who might make the grade at Fartown.

The annual reports overwhelmingly prioritise finance and the first team's performance. With the Team of all Talents and their four cups etched into living memory, subsequent teams inevitably suffered in comparison. In 1926-27, winning the Yorkshire Cup clearly did not compensate for finishing 23rd out of 29 clubs in the league:

> The Football Section are to be congratulated once again on winning the Yorkshire Cup, but on the whole the season from a playing point of view has been disappointing.

The team was significantly strengthened over the next twelve months. The game's ban on signing overseas players was lifted in June 1927 and Huddersfield jumped in first, capturing wing-threequarter Ernest Mills from Australian club, Grenfell, whose player/coach, Ben Gronow, arranged the signing. Mills made his debut in August 1927 and quickly confirmed his reputation as 'faster than any player in England.' In total Mills made 336 appearances and scored 290 tries for Huddersfield. This was one of several significant transfers that help to explain the financial and playing conclusions in the 1928 report:

> The Football Section, although shewing [sic] a loss ... shews [sic] increased Gate Receipts. The Football Sub-Committee feel that with the new players at their disposal the prospects for the forthcoming season are much brighter.

Indeed they were. The 1929 report was euphoric:

> The Football Section (as anticipated in last year's report) has had a most successful season and are to be congratulated on having won the Yorkshire League, the Northern Rugby League and the Rugby League Championship Competition. They were also

successful in winning the Halifax Infirmary Cup. The Football Committee feel they can look forward with confidence to the forthcoming season and are sparing no effort to retain the position they now hold.

The tradition of annual matches to support local hospital services can be traced to 10 September 1924 when Huddersfield Town played Heart of Midlothian to raise funds for the Huddersfield Royal Infirmary and the Victoria Nurses' Association. In 1925, the Huddersfield and Halifax rugby league clubs played for the Huddersfield Infirmary Cup. The principle was extended to support Halifax Infirmary, and by 1945 these annual matches by the association and rugby football clubs had raised £7649 for the infirmaries and the Nurses' Fund.

The only regret of the 1928-29 season was missing out on the first Challenge Cup Final to be staged at Wembley, where Wigan beat Dewsbury. The final table saw Huddersfield at the top with a percentage of 73.68. In the semi-final of the Championship play-offs, fourth placed Salford were despatched 13-5 with tries from Young, Morton and Mills, and two goals by Brook. In the other semi-final Leeds beat Hull KR 7-4. The final at Thrum Hall was a classic, the *Leeds Mercury* reporting:

> It was all very enlightening, a revelation to those who think the Rugby League game on the wane, and an example of what can be done when the play is according to the spirit of the laws. Full of thrills with the result always in the balance ... here was a game with the milk of quality ... Huddersfield survived one of the hottest, fastest games of football I have seen for years.

'Rouge', reporting in the *HDE*, concurred:

> A fellow scribe who saw the Cup final at Wembley, said that the Thrum Hall display would have impressed the Londoners much more than did the game between Wigan and Dewsbury.

Such eulogies may seem a little strange for a game which Huddersfield won 2-0 through a penalty goal from Brook. But the pace, skill, intensity and tension were compelling, and Huddersfield were deserving winners of their fourth Championship title. The team returned on Saturday evening to a large, rejoicing crowd in St George's Square for a dinner at the George Hotel.

Huddersfield v Leeds
League Championship Final
at Thrum Hall, Halifax
11 May 1929

Huddersfield   **2**   **Leeds**   **0**

Goal: Brook

Huddersfield

J Brook;

E Mills, L Bowkett, G Parker, F Smart;

S Spencer, E Williams;

CW Morton, C Halliday, J Rudd, L Gee, P Carter, H Young

Leeds

JW Brough;

G Andrews, MA Rosser, AF O'Rourke, AC Lloyd;

J Moores, W Swift;

JF Thompson, W Demaine, D Pascoe, W Davis, AG Thomas, F Gallagher

Referee: F Fairhurst (Wigan)   Attendance: 25,604   Receipts: £2028

The Huddersfield team that played in the
League Championship Final
at Thrum Hall on 11 May 1929, beating
Leeds 2-0
Back: J Brook, C Halliday,
P Carter, L Bowkett, S Gee, H Young,
J Rudd, CW Morton
Front: JT Withers (Trainer), S Spencer,
E Williams, E Mills, G Parker, F Smart

Forward Harold Young chases a loose ball.

Forward Clifford Morton, who helped to uphold
Huddersfield's reputation in rugby league and in music.

Huddersfield's optimism at the quality of their signings had proved justified, but the transfer policy could only continue whilst finances allowed. In October 1929 shock waves from the Wall Street Crash reverberated around the developed world. The Great Depression of the 1930s, the greatest financial crisis of the 20th century, loomed, and the club's Annual Report of 1930 suggested that the financial brakes might have to be applied.

> … The Football Section shows a loss … which is accounted for by heavy transfer fees and bad weather, but they are to be congratulated on the winning of the Yorkshire League and the Rugby League Championship for two years in succession, also the winning of the Huddersfield Royal Infirmary Charity Cup.

In 1929-30 Huddersfield finished second in the league, behind St Helens, with a percentage of 68.42. Salford were again beaten in the semi-final at Fartown, 15-10, before a crowd of over 15,000. In the other semi-final, fourth-placed Leeds beat St Helens 10-6 to set up a repeat of the 1928-29 final, this time at Belle Vue, Wakefield. On the back foot from the moment Banks was sent-off for 'laying out' Adams of Leeds, Huddersfield survived to draw 2-2.

Leeds had missed their chance and Huddersfield took control of the replay at Thrum Hall, played two days later. Tries from Thompson and Parker, supplemented by a conversion and a penalty goal by Stocks, gave the Fartowners a decisive 10-0 lead at half time. Huddersfield then adopted a 'what we have we hold' strategy and there was no further scoring. 'Rouge', writing in the *HDE*, was fulsome in his praise of Fartown's pocket dynamo Stanley Spencer, adding:

> To say that Leeds were completely outplayed is a mild form of expression. They were never in the hunt. During the whole of the first half only one scrummage was formed in Huddersfield's '25' ... Bowkett played his best game of the season. His defence was rock-like and in the first half he combined effectively with his mates. Here it may be

said that the thrills were all provided in the first half. Then Huddersfield were doing their best to get something on the board. In the second they concentrated on stopping the other fellow.

So, for the second year in succession, and for the fifth time in total, Huddersfield were champions.

Huddersfield v Leeds
League Championship Final Replay
at Thrum Hall, Halifax
12 May 1930

Huddersfield   **10**   **Leeds**   **0**

Tries: Thompson
         Parker
Goals: Stocks (2)

Huddersfield
JW Stocks;

E Mills, L Bowkett, G Parker, F Royston;

E Thompson, S Spencer;

J Rudd, C Halliday, L Gee, T Banks, H Tiffany, H Young

Leeds
JW Goldie;

S Smith, TC Askin, MA Rosser, AF O'Rourke;

E Williams, L Adams;

W Demaine, D Pascoe, JF Thompson, AG Thomas, DR Jenkins, A Evans

Referee: AE Harding (Broughton)   Attendance: 18,563   Receipts: £1319

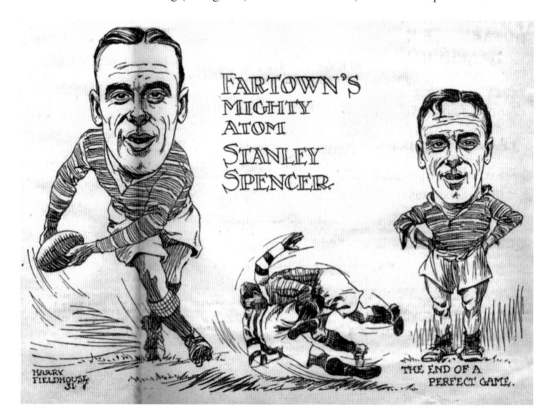

FARTOWN'S MIGHTY ATOM STANLEY SPENCER.

THE END OF A PERFECT GAME.

HARRY FIELDHOUSE 3L

Huddersfield's share of the gate money from the play-off matches justified a loan of £1050 from the RFL, taken out by HC and AC on 26 August 1930 to improve the Fartown football ground. The annual rate of interest was 4%. Willie Fillan, jeweller, and Percy Hague, master baker, acted as the official guarantors, and within the club this risk was spread more broadly, four other members signing a memorandum to reimburse Willie and Percy for any loss they might incur. In fact, the club had repaid the loan by April 1935.

Although there were fewer major incoming players, Huddersfield's strong team continued to thrive, the financial profit over each of the next two seasons owing much to some exciting runs in the cup competitions and appearances in major finals. In 1931 they won the Halifax Infirmary Charity Cup and were runners-up in the Yorkshire Cup, injuries in the latter part of the season torpedoing their challenge for one of the top four positions.

The 1932 report acknowledged that:

> The Football section shews a profit ... after including receipts from the Rugby League Championship … and is to be congratulated on the team having finished at the head of the Northern Rugby League, and also winning for the eighth time the Yorkshire Challenge Cup. They were not, however, successful in the Final of the Northern Rugby League and [we] congratulate the winners St Helens on this achievement. The increased accommodation in the Members Stand was found very useful on the occasion of the Semi-Final of the Rugby League Challenge Cup, Halifax versus Leeds, on Saturday, the 19th of March, 1932, when a RECORD attendance of 32,158 paid £2431 for admission.

Harry Fieldhouse cartoon published on the day of the 1932 League Championship Final, showing Huddersfield and St Helens eyeing the trophy. St Helens won 9-5.

1933 to the Outbreak of War

With the Rugby League Challenge Cup Final now firmly established as a Wembley occasion, Huddersfield supporters were beginning to feel their team, one of the strongest of the era, was overdue a trip there. However, as rugby league historian Stanley Chadwick remarked, Huddersfield's league form at the beginning of the 1932-33 season 'did not suggest they would reach Wembley.' That was until new signings Ray Markham, Fred Brindle and Leslie Adams inspired 'a wonderful change.'

Ray Markham and Leslie Adams made an immediate impact at Fartown.

Ray Markham evades a tackle.

Left: Harry Fieldhouse promotes Huddersfield's first round Challenge Cup tie against Dewsbury.
Right: Harry depicts Len Bowkett as the prolific Australian batsman Don Bradman, in celebration of his 'cricket score' of 12 points – six successful conversions from six attempts – in Huddersfield's 30-8 victory over Leeds in the semi-final.

Huddersfield's 1932-33 Challenge Cup campaign began with a 19-7 victory over Dewsbury, but the second round threw up the sort of tie on which many a cup campaign has run aground – Barrow, away, in the worst blizzard for thirty years. All the other ties were postponed and Huddersfield eventually escaped with a nil-nil draw, before scrambling through the replay 2-0. A 12-5 win over Swinton in the 3rd round set up a semi-final against Leeds at Wakefield which Huddersfield won with surprising ease, 30 points to eight. Warrington awaited in the final.

Wembley Fever: Mrs Bowkett buys husband Len, the Huddersfield captain, a souvenir before the team set off for the capital.

There was great excitement in the town and the Supporters' Club organised two trains to take 1066 passengers from Huddersfield, one to Euston Station and the other to St Pancras, leaving at 6am and arriving back in Huddersfield at 4.45am and 5.38am respectively. The more serious-minded could go on an organised tour of the Houses of Parliament, whilst the rest were free to enjoy the delights of London before and after the game.

Sowing Seeds for Wembley:
some of the methods that had helped the Fartowners to the 1933 Challenge Cup Final.

97

Their trip was made worthwhile by a tight contest between two evenly-matched teams. Warrington shaded the first half and led 10-9 at the break, Huddersfield's points coming from a try by Brindle converted by Len Bowkett and two penalty goals by Bowkett. Just as the game appeared to be slipping away, Huddersfield raised their game in the last twenty minutes. First, Ernie Mills ran in the best try of the match, then ten minutes later Gwyn Richards adding another. Both were converted by Bowkett who also kicked another penalty goal to make the final score Huddersfield 21 Warrington 17.

Huddersfield v Warrington
Challenge Cup Final
at Wembley Stadium
6 May 1933

Huddersfield	21	Warrington	17
Tries:	Brindle	Tries:	Davies (2)
	Mills		Dingsdale
	Richards	Goals:	Holding (4)
Goals:	Bowkett (6)		

Huddersfield
T Scourfield;
E Mills, S Brogden, L Bowkett, R Markham;
G Richards, L Adams;
H Sherwood, C Halliday, T Banks, H Tiffany, F Talbot, F Brindle

Warrington
WJ Holding;
T Blinkhorn, WJ Shankland, W Dingsdale, T Thompson;
J Oster, DM Davies;
J Miller, N Bentham, S Hardman, A Evans, R Smith, C Seeling

Referee: F Fairhurst (Wigan)   Attendance: 41,874   Receipts: £6465

Cup Final images:
Left: London Underground poster advertising transport to the 1933 Challenge Cup Final.
Right: Tom Scourfield moves in to tackle Warrington captain Bill Shankland.

Gwyn Richards scores Huddersfield's controversial final try in the 1933 Challenge Cup Final. Warrington's Bill Holding appeals to the referee. Looking on, left to right, are Warrington's Blinkhorn and Shankland and Huddersfield's Stanley Brogden

Left: Len Bowkett collects the Challenge Cup from HRH the Prince of Wales in 1933.
Right: Len Bowkett carried by Herbert Sherwood and Cyril Halliday on the lap of honour around Wembley. Other Fartown players are, left to right Les Adams, Tom Banks, Tom Scourfield, Ernie Mills and Gwyn Richards. On the extreme left is long-serving club secretary Charlie Reynard; extreme right is club chairman Richard Lockwood.

Harry Fieldhouse's caricatures of captain Len Bowkett and trainer-coach Chris Brockbank

Above: A happy band of Huddersfield supporters at Euston Station after the match. Their mascot brought luck to the team.

Right: London, Midland and Scottish Railway Company flyer for the 1933 Challenge Cup Final

The 1932-33 Challenge Cup-winning team

Back Row: CL Reynard (Sec), FB Hoyle (Comm), H Brook (Comm), HG Roebuck (Vice-Chairman), Sir Joseph Turner (President), R Lockwood (Chairman), M Sutcliffe (Comm), F Wright (Comm)

Middle Row: C Brockbank (Trainer), H Tiffany, C Halliday, F Brindle, E Norcliffe, H Sherwood, F Talbot, W Overton (Asst Trainer)

Seated: G Richards, T Scourfield, E Mills, L Bowkett (Capt), R Markham, S Brogden, G Parker

Front: L Adams, S Spencer

A rapturous reception met the team on their return to Huddersfield, the *Fartown Supporters: 1921-1946* booklet recalling:

> After winning the cup in 1920 at Leeds, no more than a couple of dozen people were in the "Square" to welcome home the team, but following our success at Wembley in 1933 an estimated crowd of 15,000 people were awaiting the return of Bowkett and his men.

Despite their cup triumph, the HC and AC accounts for 1932-33 showed a loss of £1693. This was attributed to the large sums paid out in wages owing to the successful cup ties and the 'meagre' £350 received from the Wembley gate-money of £6465. The expenses at Wembley Stadium must have been very significant to account for this surprisingly low payment, which is even less than the £523 received from the RFL from the Cup semi-final gate receipts of £2,300. A letter from the RFL to the club dated 16 May 1933 simply states: 'enclosed find cheque for £379/13/8, being amount due to your club in connection with the Cup final plus fares.' The rail fares for players and officials added £29 13s 8d to the club's £350 share of the gate, but unlike the semi-final, there is no detailed breakdown of income and expenditure.

Huddersfield's 1933 AGM was told that the 'reserve fund was now exhausted.' This must have been a notional reserve fund as no such item is shown in the available accounts or balance sheets of HC and AC. Playing success – in particular winning the Challenge Cup for a record fourth time – did not equate to financial success, particularly during the Great Depression.

No financial information is available for 1934 which, on the field, was very disappointing, 12th place being the lowest for seven seasons.

Four stalwarts of the 1930s, loose forward Fred Brindle, full-back Tom Scourfield threequarter Stanley Brogden and prop Reginald Roberts

Despite the recent statement about the reserve-fund, 1935 saw the committee continue team-building, spending £2054 on 'transfer fees, bonuses and expenses for new players.' These included amongst others: Stanley Pepperell a half-back from Cumberland; Stanley James Mountain a rugby union player from Newport; and Dai Morgan Davies a scrum half from Warrington, Huddersfield's Welsh contingent growing to eight. Transfer fees contributed significantly to the loss of £402 on the football account.

The investments almost brought further silverware to Fartown in 1935, Huddersfield suffering their first defeat in a Challenge Cup Final, 11-8 to Castleford before a crowd of 39,000.

Fartown's Welshmen 1935-36:
Tom Scourfield, Stanley Mountain, Dai Evans, Gwyn Richards, Glyn Prosser, Idris Towell, Billy Johnson, and Dennis Madden.

There is no further financial information until March 1938, when, after defeat by Leeds in the second round of the Challenge Cup, the Football Committee shocked supporters by announcing that they would consider any good offer for any player. They had, effectively, put the entire squad up for sale, a strategy of last-resort associated with clubs facing liquidation or administration. The club's finances were far from healthy, showing an overdraft of £2000, but Stanley Chadwick believed that the Football Committee's decision was partly based on their belief that some players had neglected their training. The committee had over-reacted and shortly afterwards the club issued an official statement to the effect that it was solvent and no wholesale transfer of players was being considered. It was one of many low points in the 1937-38 season. Huddersfield returned to the 23rd position they had occupied eleven seasons earlier, and the Football Account showed a loss of £1519.

The unrest continued into the close season. A petition dated 10 June 1938, signed by over 100 members of HC and AC, requested changes to the rules of the club, including a requirement that 'existing members of the Football Sub-Committee shall retire at the Annual Meeting in 1938 ... and the election shall take place at the Annual Meeting.' This was an attempt to revert to the pre-1927 system of voting, before the changes which empowered the General Committee to appoint the Football Committee. The petition also proposed much greater autonomy for the Football Committee:

Henry Tiffany grabs the Castleford number 9 as Huddersfield defend their try-line in the 1935 Challenge Cup Final. The other Huddersfield players are, from the left, Willie Watson, Dai Davies, Fred Talbot, Tom Scourfield and Herbert Sherwood.

> The General Committee shall not have power to vary or rescind any Resolution of the Football Sub-Committee and the General Committee shall adopt any contracts entered into or authorised by the Football Sub-Committee.

There was clearly a strong feeling that the General Committee had been interfering unduly and adversely with the Football Committee. Only two members of the Football Committee survived the vote at the 1938 AGM and the new members soon made their mark, banning the players from attending any social events on Thursday or Friday nights before games. This certainly did no harm. A marked improvement in performances saw Huddersfield win the Yorkshire Cup for the ninth time and climb 19 places to finish fourth in the league. No financial information is available to reveal whether on-field success was reflected in the balance sheet.

Profit or Loss?

For the twenty seasons from 1918-19 to 1937-38, Huddersfield's football accounts show a profit in five, a loss in nine, with no detailed accounts available for the other six. The fourteen seasons for which figures are available show a net loss of £6092.

The financial situation across the whole of British sport and leisure would have been much more positive without the unwelcome millstone of the government's entertainment tax. By 1939 Huddersfield's total entertainment tax contributions from rugby alone were about £20,000.

Like all accounting figures, the accuracy of the overall loss incurred depends on the accounting conventions used. Some expenditure, such as wages paid to players employed on ground maintenance, was borne by HC and AC, reducing the expenditure and the loss on the Football Account. Some income, such as part of the membership fees, is credited to HC and AC Account and not the Football Account, exaggerating the loss.

Nevertheless, the rugby club's playing successes during the inter-war years did not produce an overall profit, and there is strong evidence that success came at a price.

Chapter 9

World War II

Huddersfield, Yorkshire Cup winners in 1938-39, began 1939-40 in a manner that suggested a successful season. That summer the club had renewed their lease at Fartown for a further 21 years, the terms reflecting the continued influence of Lord's Day Observance by stipulating that 'cricket shall not be played on Sundays.' It was taken as read that rugby football on Sundays was unthinkable, but the war would soften attitudes towards Sunday leisure time activities. Post-war, playing sport on Sundays would become an increasing part of community life, professional rugby league taking the plunge in 1967.

Internationally, echoes of 1914 resounded as the 1939-40 Rugby League season opened on 26 August. On 2 September, Huddersfield beat Featherstone 56-10 at Fartown to make it two wins from three matches, but the following day the country was once more at war with Germany.

Anticipating air raid attacks over heavily populated areas, the Home Office banned all large gatherings of people, ordering places of entertainment, including sports grounds, to be closed. This unpopular measure was soon relaxed, with the proviso that well-publicised evacuation procedures were in place should the air raid siren be sounded.

Even so, the requirements of the armed forces and other demands of the war were inevitably and immediately disruptive to all sports. The regular rugby league season was abandoned and the RFL quickly established two War Emergency leagues, comprised of 12 teams in Lancashire and 15 teams in Yorkshire, thus reducing travel times and fuel consumption.

Player availability was an issue from the start as conscription, introduced tentatively by degree in World War I, was immediately enforced. This did at least spare professional sports the scrutiny and moralising about whether or not they should continue to be played. Unlike World War I, they could not be accused of unpatriotically depriving the forces of young men, and the RFL felt able to standardise an unconditional wartime payment of ten shillings per match, including expenses, to professional players. The players at Huddersfield, Halifax and Bradford threatened strike action and on 11 October the RFL doubled match pay for players and referees to £1, plus 5s broken time for matches at Hull and Barrow.

The Great War had also established that the continuation of sport and other leisure activities was valuable, providing brief escapes from the practical and psychological pressures of wartime, and opportunities for fundraising.

Fartown re-opened for a friendly match against Hunslet on 16 September 1939. The War Emergency leagues commenced later in the month and Huddersfield were in contention at the top of the Yorkshire Section all season. Harsh winter weather prevented any play for two months following the traditional Christmas matches against Halifax, and the season was eventually extended into June so that the Yorkshire Cup competition could be completed. Playing 28 League matches and a handful of Yorkshire Cup ties, Huddersfield finished second behind Bradford Northern in the League and were beaten 23-9 by Dewsbury in the second round of the Yorkshire Cup.

Huddersfield dropped a place to third in 1940-41, but by August 1941 ten of the 27 clubs that played in the first wartime season had suspended operations, including all the 'Lancashire' contingent except Oldham, St Helens and Wigan. For 1941-42, the RFL amalgamated the remaining 17 clubs into one War Emergency League. By 1942-43 there were only 14 competing clubs. These 14 completed every wartime season, which was a triumph for every one of them, particularly Huddersfield which, although stubbornly mid-table for the rest of the war, played 139 wartime league matches, five more than any other club.

As in World War I, all clubs used the guest-player system. This allowed the participation of players working or stationed away from home, or whose own clubs were no longer playing, and helped the remaining clubs to field competitive teams. Fielding and organising a team each week was, nevertheless, a huge challenge. During the second wartime season, 1940-41, 46 different players represented Huddersfield, of whom 24 were guests, borrowed primarily from Lancashire clubs which were in abeyance. At Keighley in September 1941, still a man short at kick-off, the Fartowners were reduced to drafting in trainer Fred Ashworth to play at loose forward.

Matches were squeezed in among tight wartime work schedules and reduced rail timetables. In the spring of 1941 time ran out for some of the Castleford players at Fartown. Their second round Yorkshire Cup tie ended 3-3, but several visiting players were unable to stay for extra time, which Alex Fiddes kicked-off with no opponents on the field. Belshaw ran on to the kick-off, touched down and converted the try, the Yorkshire RFL Committee confirming Huddersfield as the winners.

Fred Ashworth became the Huddersfield's trainer in August 1939, just prior to the outbreak of war, and unexpectedly found himself playing loose forward at Keighley in 1941.

There were other unusual wartime sights at Fartown. As in World War I, the rules were relaxed about the participation of players from rugby's league and union codes in the same matches, providing they were servicemen. Just six weeks into the war, Fartown hosted a challenge match, played under rugby union rules, an Anti-Aircraft Battery XV playing a Huddersfield XV which included a number of high profile rugby league players.

Huddersfield players, including captain Alex Fiddes and the Pepperell brothers Russ and Stanley, featured in several rugby union charity matches played by Northern Command. In December 1945 Northern Command played Western Command at Fartown, with Hubert Lockwood, a former Huddersfield player and future club Chairman, at full back. At the time, Hubert was a prolific full back for Halifax, where he set club career records of 817 goals and 1652 points.

Perhaps the most unusual wartime occasion at Fartown came on 11 August 1943, when 2400 spectators watched an exhibition baseball match between two teams of American servicemen.

IN THE HOOD

"Dai" Evans Presumed Lost

A Former Fartown Footballer

David Morgan Evans, the former Fartown forward, is presumed to have gone down with the Hood. His wife, Mrs. Evans, of Neath Crest, William Street, Crosland Moor, has received an official telegram stating that her husband is missing and presumed killed.

"Dai" Evans

DEATH OF HERBERT SHERWOOD

BURIED IN RIO DE JANEIRO

FINE PLAYING CAREER AT FARTOWN

HERBERT SHERWOOD, who was the Huddersfield Club's front-row forward for thirteen years up to the outbreak of the war, has died on active service.

This news has been received by his wife, who is staying with her mother at Aire Street, Castleford. Sherwood, who was an Acting Able Seaman, died in Rio de Janeiro, Brazil, on October 14, and was buried there the following day.

Sherwood, who was still on the books of the Huddersfield Club, joined the Royal Navy in the early part of the war and had not played in war-time football.

He was a member of probably the best-known Rugby family in the West Riding, for at one time five brothers and five of their sons were playing football. He was a nephew of the late "Clon" Sherwood, former captain of the Huddersfield Club for many seasons, who died only a few months ago, and the elder son of Sam Sherwood, who was killed in the last war.

CUP-TIE AT HEADINGLEY RECALLED

Sherwood, who was thirty-three years of age, played for Yorkshire and was once reserve for England. For a period he was the regular goal-kicker for the Fartown side, and during his career he kicked some brilliant goals for the Club. One occasion will be remembered by both supporters of the Huddersfield and Leeds Clubs. It was a cup-tie at Headingley when Sherwood's goal-kicking put Huddersfield into the next round.

He had a knack of kicking goals

NEWS OF MEN IN THE FORCES

Death of Kenneth Gronow

Huddersfield sportsmen will regret to hear of the death of Sergeant Kenneth Gronow, which took place in the Middle East on November 28. It was not known that he had been ill, and it was this morning that Mr. and Mrs. Ben Gronow, Bracken Hall Road, received news that their son had died of polio-myelitis (which is inflammation of the grey matter of the spinal cord).

Sergeant Gronow, who was twenty-seven years of age, had followed his father as a member of the Fartown side. His football career began with Bradford, for whom his father was for some time coach and trainer, but most of his playing career had been with Huddersfield. He was a forward, and when the war broke out he was establishing his place in the team, usually turning out as loose forward and sometimes in the second row. Though hardly so spectacular a player as his father, he had the instinct for positional play that is the mark of the class footballer. That and keen following up helped him many, many times to come up at the last moment to make the extra man and score a try, so that he was able to figure among the scorers rather more prominently than is usual for a forward.

The summer game claimed his quiet enthusiasm also. He played with Bradley Mills, for whom he made several useful innings, and since he had joined the Army he made many good scores with Army sides in the Middle East.

Sergeant Gronow joined the Army at the beginning of the war, serving with R.A.S.C. He took part in the evacuation of Dunkirk, and went through the siege of Tobruk. He is the eldest of four brothers, all serving. Gwynn is now in hospital making good progress after suffering the fracture of both legs; Peter is also in the Middle East, and Sydney is in the Navy.

Before joining the Army, Sergeant Gronow was employed as a printer by Messrs. Netherwood and Dalton, Ltd.

The *HDE* reports the deaths on active service of Huddersfield players Dai Evans, Herbert Sherwood and Kenneth Gronow

With most of the Huddersfield players on active service there were inevitable casualties. They included Dai Evans, who had enlisted for the Royal Navy. On 24 May 1941 he was serving on HMS Hood when it was sunk during the Battle of Denmark Strait, probably by a shell fired by the German battleship Bismarck.

In October 1943 the club received more dreadful news. Another popular forward, 33 year-old Herbert Sherwood, also serving in the Royal Navy, had drowned off the coast of Brazil. He was buried in Rio de Janeiro. A Huddersfield player since 1928, Herbert was due a benefit match, which went ahead in support of his widow and family on 29 January 1944. Despite wartime austerity, a crowd of 2000 paid receipts of £150, which was raised to £488 by additional collections.

About the time that Herbert Sherwood perished, Kenneth Gronow contracted polio in the Middle East. He died just over a month later. The son of the Team of all Talents' Ben Gronow, Kenneth was just breaking into the Huddersfield first team in 1939. Prior to his ill-fated final posting, he served with distinction through two of the war's most demanding and notorious episodes, the evacuation of Dunkirk and the Siege of Tobruk.

Happier times: Harry Fieldhouse's tribute to Herbert Sherwood in 1932

Perhaps prompted by these losses, Huddersfield became proactive in team-building, signing four players in the 1943-44 season. The best of these was Jeff Bawden from Whitehaven. A quick, classy wing three-quarter, a proven try-scorer and a prolific goal-kicker, he was the leading points-scorer in the Rugby League in 1945-46 and 1946-47, helping to establish Huddersfield as contenders in post-war rugby.

Hints of future successes came mainly in the wartime cup competitions. Huddersfield reached the 1942-43 Yorkshire Cup Final, losing 7-2 over two legs to Dewsbury. Appropriately, in 1945, the 50th

Jeff Bawden

anniversary of the birth of the game, Huddersfield reached the Challenge Cup Final. Victories over Leeds, Barrow and League runners-up Halifax set up a daunting final over two legs against League Champions Bradford Northern. Huddersfield, ninth in the League, earned a narrow 7-4 advantage from the first leg at blizzard-lashed Fartown. Favourites Bradford were expected to overturn this at Odsal, but Jeff Bawden had other ideas, running in two tries as Huddersfield won 6-5, and 13-9 on aggregate. Bawden contributed 43 of the 83 points scored by Huddersfield during their cup campaign.

Captain Alex Fiddes lifts the Challenge Cup at Odsal, 5 May 1945

Huddersfield's 1945 Challenge Cup-winning team

The omens were good as the League returned to its full complement of 27 clubs for the first post-war season, 1945-46. The pack was led by outstanding Cumberland second row forward Bob Nicholson, who earned an England cap against Wales in November 1945. The following summer he was the only Huddersfield player to tour Australasia as part of the 'Indomitables', playing one Test Match against New Zealand.

After an inconsistent autumn, two factors caused a marked improvement by Huddersfield in the second half of the 1945-46 season. The first was a major signing, John 'Jock' Anderson, a

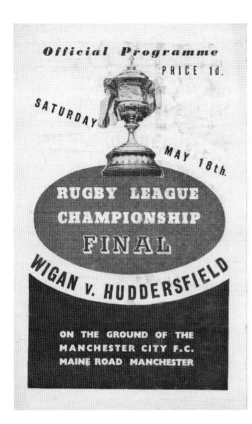

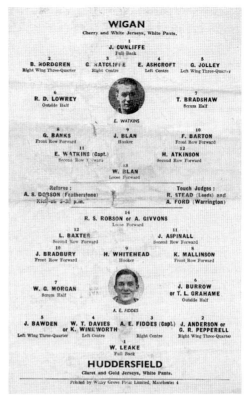

FITTING FINALE TO RUGBY LEAGUE'S VICTORY AND JUBILEE SEASON

BY "OBSERVER" OF "THE DAILY DISPATCH"

NO more fitting finale to the Rugby League's Victory and Jubilee season could have been wished for than the meeting of the two clubs on view to-day.

For a consistently high standard of the best type of Rugby, Huddersfield and Wigan possess records probably unequalled by any other two clubs.

Not even two world wars and the passing of a generation or two have undermined the traditions of these organisations. So the stage is set for what should be a thrilling game this afternoon.

This "play off" method of deciding the League Championship is open to criticism from many angles, but that it has become a real "money-spinner" to the clubs and the League is evidenced by the fact that two semi-finals last Saturday pulled in aggregate crowds of 67,573 and £6,418.

Assuming the weather conditions are good to-day, expectations are that the 69,504 attendance on this ground on May 13, 1939, when Salford defeated Castleford by 8 points to 6, will be surpassed. Almost certainly the receipts of £4,301 will be exceeded.

May Be World Record

INDEED, the world's record attendance for a Rugby League match, established in Australia on the Sydney Cricket ground in June, 1932, of 70,204 (£5,739 15s. 3¼d.; I wonder how they got that halfpenny), may be beaten. In any case a big crowd is assured, and the game should be worthy of the occasion.

Wigan headed the League table with 60 points out of a possible 72, and Huddersfield finished second with 55 points. Wigan can be acclaimed the most consistent side of the season, for this is the third final they have contested.

In the last stage of the Lancashire Cup v Warrington last October they succumbed by a narrow margin to one of McCue's "master" moves, and their dramatic last minute defeat at Wembley in the Challenge Cup final a fortnight ago is fresh in the memory.

Up to now the only tangible reward they have received for their brilliant consistency is the championship cup of the Lancashire League, in which they gained 44 points out of a possible 48. Wigan, beyond any question, have paid dearly for the sacrifice involved in sending the touring team to Australia.

Wigan have contributed to that team four players who obviously cannot be replaced. On the other hand, Wakefield Trinity, their conquerors at Wembley, have only one tourist, and that also applies to Huddersfield. That is no fault of these clubs. They would just as readily have released any of their players chosen for the "greater glory" as Wigan have done.

This "country before club" spirit of Rugby League clubs is something to be proud of, and is an answer to those who think the sporting element has been submerged by financial and selfish motives.

Not Met This Season

THE strongest argument in favour of this "Play Off" system is probably that under existing conditions all teams cannot meet each other in ordinary League fixtures. For example, in the season which concludes to-day Lancashire clubs have played only six Yorkshire opponents and Wigan and Huddersfield have not previously met this season.

Huddersfield have had a much easier late-season programme than Wigan because of their early dismissal from the Challenge Cup by the ultimate winners, and they have revealed their power by winning nine of their last 10 matches.

The improvement can be traced largely to the return of several of their players from the Forces. The problem of the committee now is "whom to leave out." Leake is a promising young full-back from the Featherstone district. Anderson is the Scottish winger signed in January after he had helped his country to defeat the Kiwis, and Russell Pepperell is one of three Cumberland brothers to have worn the Huddersfield colours and I believe is a nephew of that great forward and world-famed wrestler Douglas Clark.

Alec Fiddes, the captain and right centre, has rendered brilliant service to the club for more than a dozen years. He came from the Scottish border town of Hawick via Fartown this season by Anderson and loose-forward Robson, a farmer. Fiddes is not only a great schemer but a splendid leader as well as a scorer of tries and goals.

SIMILAR remarks apply to W. T. Davies, left centre or full-back, who joined Huddersfield after a big reputation in Wales, and has enhanced it here. Ken Winkworth, I believe, is a product of Manchester junior Rugby and a youngster well thought of.

Broke Club Record

A good many will be interested in left-wing three-quarter, Jeff Bawden, whose scoring feats around Eastertide hit the newspaper headlines. In one match he scored 10 goals and five tries (35pts.), a Huddersfield club record for one match. He hails from Whitehaven, Cumberland.

Tommy Grahame, out half, is an Australian recently demobbed from the Royal Navy, and he and Glyn Morgan have struck a happy partnership in the vital key department. Burrow is a versatile Cumbrian, who has played full-back for his county this season.

Interesting personality of the forwards is Joe Bradbury, the Wigan-born front-row man, who was in the Salford side which beat Castleford here in the 1939 final. Robson is by many considered unlucky to have missed the tour, and Alec Givvons joined Huddersfield after service with Oldham.

*   *   *

WIGAN are much the younger set. They expect to field the team defeated at Wembley, which comprises locally born, one Welshman, Eddie Watkins, the captain, one Yorkshireman, George Banks, one Cumbrian, Lowrey, and a New Zealander, Nordgren.

Watkins was a Cardiff and Welsh international before coming North and gained a lot of honours during his war service with the R.A.F. Banks is the oldest man in the team—37—but he can last out the game with many younger Nordgren has only been in England under ten months. He is credited with exceptional pace, and Wigan will wish him better luck in goal-kicking than at Wembley.

Wigan's three-quarters are all young, speedy, and enthusiastic, and in scrum-half Tommy Bradshaw have a vastly improved player who may exert a big influence on the game. The two Blans are brothers, and "J." has the responsible job of "hooker" in the absence of the tourist, Egan. So with Cutliffe, who has been called upon to deputise for the League's No. 1 full-back, Martin Ryan, Wigan have made the best of their difficulties, and can be relied upon for a bold bid to-day. Tailpiece: Salford lost the Challenge Cup final at Wembley in 1939 before winning the League Championship. Will history be repeated?

SOME RECORDS BY THE CLUBS

Huddersfield

WON Rugby League Championship five times (runners-up four times). In 1914-15 won all four cups and narrowly failed to repeat in 1920 when, with five players on tour, they lost League championship by half by 3 points to 2. Won Rugby League Challenge Cup five times, Yorkshire Cup nine times, and Yorkshire League eight times. Scored 119 points against Swinton Park in 1914. Their winger, Rosenfeld, scored 80 tries in season 1913-14. In 1914-15 Huddersfield played 47 matches and scored 1,269 points (207 goals, 285 tries).

Wigan

WON Rugby League Championship four times (runners-up one time). Won Rugby League Challenge Cup twice (runners-up three times), Lancashire Cup seven times (runners-up 10 times), Lancashire League (11 times runners-up six times). Highest score 116 points against Flimby and Fothergill in 1925. Full-back and captain kicked 200 goals in 1933-34 season and over 100 goals every season between 1921-22 and 1938-39.

THE SCORING

A Try counts 3 points   All Goals count 2 points

The programme for the 1946 Championship Final, one folded sheet,
reflected the rationing that continued for several years after World War II

Scottish Rugby Union international who had recently scored two tries against the All Blacks at Murrayfield. This burly winger made his Huddersfield debut in January 1946 and soon became a crowd favourite. In seven seasons at Fartown he made 114 appearances, scored 74 tries and kicked 21 goals, before returning to his native Hawick. The second factor was the return of players from the forces.

Winning nine of their last ten matches, Huddersfield rose to second position in the league and qualified for the Championship Final against League leaders Wigan, played at Maine Road, Manchester. Unfortunately, the Central Park side proved too strong. An inspirational half-time talk from their legendary coach Jim Sullivan helped Wigan to take control in the second half, and they won 13-4.

As they had after World War I, crowds flocked to sporting arenas after World War II. Attendances in England for soccer, rugby league and cricket, peaked in the late 1940s. Fartown's highest-ever attendance was 35,136 for the 1947 Challenge Cup semi-final between Leeds and Wakefield Trinity. This increased affluence was evident in rising transfer fees. A new rugby league record transfer fee, £1,650, was set when Dewsbury bought full back W. T. (Billy) Davies from Huddersfield in 1947. This record was to be broken five times in the next two seasons.

But no club could surpass the quality of signings that Huddersfield was about to make. Through a combination of excellent recommendations from their contacts, and good fortune, the Fartown club was about to hit the jackpot.

Huddersfield secretaries before and after WWII, CL Reynard and Arthur Archbell.
Both signed excellent players for the club.

Chapter 10

Post-War Successes

After World War II, the public embraced the community activities that represented and affirmed the return of peacetime normality. National enthusiasm for rugby league, association football and cricket grew, peaking in 1949, as post-war rationing was gradually relaxed and people began to enjoy a little more disposable income. Consistent with the national pattern, the highest-ever attendance for a Huddersfield match at Fartown, 32,912, came on 4 March 1950 for the visit of Wigan.

Huddersfield capitalised on this extraordinary, popular period for spectator sport by making a succession of top quality signings, easing the team's inevitable post-war period of transition.

Retirement of Alex Fiddes

The testimonial match of long-serving Scot Alex Fiddes – a 41-11 victory over Hull Kingston Rovers on 26 May 1947 – marked the passing of the baton to the next generation. Signed from Hawick Rugby Union FC in 1933, Fiddes had been an astute centre, captained Huddersfield for 13 seasons, and in 1945 became the only Scot to lift the Challenge Cup. He scored 200 tries, kicked 166 goals, and only Douglas Clark and Ken Senior have played more than his 467 matches for the club.

By 1947 the captaincy was already in the safe hands of Cumbrian Russ Pepperell for the first of his two spells in the role. Pepperell, who played for Huddersfield alongside his brothers Stanley and Albert, could fill any of the back positions, and represented England and a British Empire XIII in addition to his 365 matches for Huddersfield.

A signed photograph and a collectable Ogden's Cigarette Card of Alex Fiddes.

Russ Pepperell, who succeeded Alex Fiddes as captain, dives over for a try at Fartown

Three Fartown Aussies

Fiddes' career overlapped by two months those of outstanding signings from the Eastern Suburbs club in Sydney, powerful wingman Lionel Cooper and innovative full-back, Johnny Hunter.

Cooper was Australia's player-of-the-year in 1946. He was recommended to Huddersfield by Eddie Waring, the future BBC rugby league commentator who had covered the 1946 'Indomitables' tour of Australia for the *Sunday Pictorial*. Leeds had first refusal on Cooper, but he did not want to travel to England alone. His insistence that the relatively unknown Johnny

The Fartown scoreboard; Maurice Oldroyd 'wangled' a superb view by persuading the officials to let him put up the tins, for which he was paid a shilling per game.

Hunter came with him deterred Leeds and opened the door for Huddersfield. The impact of these two players on the club and on the English game could not have been predicted when they disembarked into the freezing English winter of 1947.

Lionel Cooper was an extraordinarily powerful wingman. His capacity to burst through opponents as well as sidestep them, combined with his powerful hand-off, upset the best of defences. The sight of Cooper on the charge thrilled the Fartown crowd.

Johnny Hunter was a stylish, enterprising full-back, who introduced new dimensions to this traditionally defensive role. Supporter and future founder of the British Amateur Rugby League Association (BARLA), Maurice Oldroyd, commented:

> At that time the full backs used to have kicking duels. I can remember Huddersfield full back Bill Leake having a kicking duel with Jimmy Ledgard, who was an international full-back from Dewsbury ... it was almost like Wimbledon ... heads right, left, right, left ...

Johnny Hunter's instinct was to use possession to turn defence into attack, not kick it away for quick, safety-first territorial gain. It helped that he possessed brilliant ball skills. Often standing a little deeper than an orthodox full back, he would catch the high ball on the run and startle the opposition with the ground he made before the chase arrived. If a kick threatened to gain ground by just finding touch, he could reach over the touchline and catch one-handed. He was equally alert for opportunities to make the extra man in the line, unbalancing defences to create and release a spare man, or going for the line himself. In December 1950 AN Gaulton wrote in *Rugby League Review*:

Johnny Hunter and Lionel Cooper

Hunter … spends more time in his opponents' '25' than any other full-back playing. This feature of his play causes great concern to the many purists in the Fartown crowd, but would it be wise to curb so ebullient a nature?

Maurice Oldroyd, in his foreword to *Three Fartown Aussies: Hunter, Cooper, Devery*, describes an example of such ebullience.

… Hunter caught the ball in the in-goal area by the corner flag, and … ran across until he met the goalpost. With his non-ball carrying hand he swivelled around the post at 90 degrees, wrong-footed everybody and then ran the length of the field, beating man after man and scored a sensational try.

Neil Shuttleworth, a supporter for over 60 years, remembered that Hunter …

… had a style that was entirely his own. He could catch the ball like no one I've ever seen – and it was a big, wet, heavy leather ball in those days on muddy fields. He would turn defence into attack and he was gone like a will o' the wisp. You never knew what would happen. He could throw the ball into the crowd, he could find a winger from 40 yards.

He was fearless. On one occasion he caught the ball, hit the line of defence, bounced off two defenders, went down, played the ball, got up, headed for the try line and dived over for a wonderful try. The only problem was, it was his own try line. When he hit the tackle he spun round completely and got up facing the wrong way.

In the first 25 years after World War II, HC and AC published many testimonial booklets and a series of detailed yearbooks. It was part of a wider pattern as, belatedly, the recounting of rugby league's current affairs and its rich social and sporting history moved from the largely oral to include much more literature. The HC and AC's testimonial booklets usually included a poem about the beneficiary, written by Brian Donaldson. Below are abridged versions of the poems he wrote about Lionel Cooper and Johnny Hunter.

The Mighty Lionel
by
Brian Donaldson

Who is this man called Cooper,
This man all wingers fear,
This man who's always dangerous
Whenever he gets near?

This sturdy-built Australian,
Since visiting our shores,
Has proved a man of power,
A man for making scores.

"We know just how to deal with him,"
They all say that at first,
But he's quite difficult to stop
When once he's on the burst.

Opposing wingmen make their vows
That he'll not score again,
But, somehow, it's beyond their powers,
Their efforts seem in vain.

Half of the team can wait for him,
He is afraid of none.
It's nothing new to see him cross
With three men hanging on.

If they decide to tackle him
By going on his knees
Just when they think they've got him taped
He'll hand them off with ease.

But these are not the only ways
In which he scores his tries.
His side-step baffles many teams
And takes them by surprise.

Who is this man called Cooper?
Spectators well might ask,
The man who has to keep him marked
Receives no easy task.

Exhilarating Johnny

by

Brian Donaldson

When Johnny Hunter plays full-back
He likes to join in the attack,
He enjoys every match he plays
And has exhilarating ways.

To him there is no greater fun
Than when he makes a zig-zag run;
He races down the field "all out,"
That he enjoys it there's no doubt.

Then very often, if he can,
He comes and makes the extra man
To turn a move into a score;
And this has brought him tries galore.

Sometimes if Johnny's in a fix,
He'll use one of his long range kicks
And follow up to take his man
Or gain possession if he can.

Beside his own abilities
He has his little "oddities,"
And one to which he's quite devout
Is that of coming "last man out."

Let's hope he'll have a few years yet,
Crowned with success he won't forget.
Then, when he's finished his career,
He'll not forget his visit here.

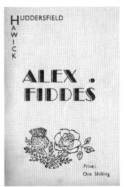

The first testimonial booklets published by the Huddersfield club were for Ben Gronow in 1924 and for Douglas Clark a year later. Above left, from Gronow's booklet, is an image of his caps and medals. Above centre is the cover of Clark's booklet.

The next such booklet was for Alex Fiddes' testimonial in 1947 (above right). Two other early post-war booklets were for the testimonials of international forward Bob Nicholson in 1951 (below left) and Jeff Bawden in 1953 (below centre). The first Fartown Year Book was published in a similar size and format in 1952 (below right). Nineteen consecutive year books were published until 1970.

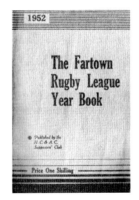

Left: Lionel Cooper looking to burst through a Hunslet tackle at Fartown in 1949
Right: Johnny Hunter cuts a typical swathe through the opposition.

Three more pieces in the Huddersfield jigsaw: Pat Devery, Dave Valentine and Billy Banks

In October 1947, a third Australian, Pat Devery from Sydney's Balmain club, arrived at Huddersfield on a three-year contract worth £1300 in total, plus match pay. In addition to his income as a part-time rugby league professional, like his compatriots Cooper and Hunter he was guaranteed a job, a relatively easy condition for the club to fulfil in the post-war labour shortage. Cooper was a rep for Fina Petroleum, Hunter was a plumber and later a carpet salesman and Devery gained experience of English schools in his profession as a teacher.

Pat Devery was a terrific all-round player. He had a great kicking game and quick feet in possession, creating openings by timing his passes superbly. In defence he had terrific positional sense and a smother tackle from which there was no escape for man or ball. 'Elia II', wrote in *Rugby League Review*:

> The principal difference between modern Rugby League and the old-style play is that speed and science are rapidly ousting muscle and brawn ... If you observe Devery closely you will see the ideal co-ordination of brain and muscle; movements being worked out with almost mathematical precision rather than charging up and down the field like a rampaging bull.

Devery's leadership qualities were soon apparent and he was appointed captain for the 1948-49 season. Starting at stand-off, he moved to left-centre where he formed a superb partnership with Cooper. Maurice Oldroyd remembered ...

> ... the excitement came when the ball came out of the scrum to Billy Banks. He fed Russell Pepperell, then on to Pat Devery, and when Devery pulled his hands back a big roar went down the terrace ... because the ball was going to go to Lionel Cooper.

Huddersfield continued to build, signing from Hawick 21-year-old loose forward Dave Valentine, a Scottish rugby union international who had recently played against England at Twickenham. Valentine quickly adapted to the thirteen-man game and made his home in Huddersfield.

The jigsaw was not quite complete, but Huddersfield had assembled a force to be reckoned with and finished third in the 1947-48 season, eventually losing 17-5 to Warrington in the play-off semi-finals. They were also runners-up in the Yorkshire League.

A team taking shape; Huddersfield at Halifax for the Annual Charity Match in August 1948.
Back: John Daly, Bob Nicholson, Bob Robson, Mel Meek, Lionel Cooper, John Maiden
Front: Johnny Hunter, Jeff Bowden, Russ Pepperell, Stan Walsh, Pat Devery,
Paddy Reid, Dave Valentine

Match Day at Fartown

Lively Welsh scrum half Billy Banks was signed in the summer of 1948. Other teams were also improving, but Huddersfield's potential was apparent in a 24-5 victory over Challenge Cup holders Wigan in the second match of the 1948-49 season. The visitors could not handle the opportunist skills of Johnny Hunter, described in a glowing report in *Rugby League Review* as 'more than a footballer … an entertainment.' The Fartown crowd of 24,589 was another cause for optimism. Every match day had become a huge event in Huddersfield, as fledging supporter Nancy Beaumont recalled:

> … there used to be huge queues of trolleybuses in St George's Square just ferrying people to the match and back. When we went to the match it was fourpence from Golcar down to Huddersfield, tuppence on the trolley, sixpence to go in, and tuppence for a programme.

Harold Mitchell Jowett regularly travelled to Fartown from his Greetland home.

> I'd walk down to West Vale, get the trolley to Blacker Road and walk down. Blacker Road would be full of people. It was just like Greetland village when the mills closed at tea time. The roads would be full of people walking. There weren't a lot of cars about. Then I'd walk into Huddersfield to get the trolley back because you couldn't get on at Blacker Road – they would be full.

Neil Shuttleworth often left ten minutes before the end to catch the trolleybus back to St George's Square.

Oh, the smoking upstairs on the double-decker buses … the smell of 40 men, in wet raincoats, in flat caps, in mufflers, smoking Woodbines … that's a memory, the football special.

Smoking was not limited to the top deck of the buses, as Gerald Furness recalled from his first visit to Fartown on Christmas Day 1946:

My biggest impression was this cloud of tobacco, of smoke, all over the stand.

The match day routines of thousands of regular supporters included, if possible, standing in the same spot on the terraces, close to familiar faces who had their spot nearby. Harold Mitchell Jowett stood on the terrace side:

We always stood in more or less the same place. You could see the fog when it rolled up the valley. There were blokes [who stood nearby] and you'd see them regular. There were a joiner from Outlane called Wilf Pilling. He used to give the referees some stick all the bloody game. There were a little ref called Laurie Thorpe from Wakefield. He only refereed between the 25s because he couldn't keep up with 'em. He copped for some stick from Wilf.

I've been in the old stand but it was a death trap – all wood – it could have set a-fire like Bradford.

Drawn by J. Forster

"Tut, tut, surely that isn't the Referee's real name!"

"He admits he started his run in a game at Fartown and got lost in the fog. But he says even if he has touched down at Odsal in the wrong game, such a run is still worth a try."

Cartoons from *Rugby League Review*, December 1946 (left) and January 1950 (right)

David Thorpe remembered the thrill of entering the terrace side.

We used to enter the ground from the turnstiles at the top … the feeling of being so high up was amazing … You had such a fantastic view … the terrace was so steep, there was such a depth between each of the steps … it was certainly the highest, steepest terrace of any rugby league ground.

Roger Armitage, who first watched Huddersfield in 1948 at the age of six, recalled that he was

The vast crowd on the terrace side watches Huddersfield v Wigan in 1948

put against the railings at the front of the Paddock with the other youngsters, before growing and graduating to join his grandfather and father on the spot where his grandfather had stood for many years.

> My Grandad would always have a trilby on – he was more a trilby person than a flat hat. Everyone would be wearing big overcoats so they would be more formally dressed. Most of them would work in the mills anyway and it helped to keep the production going for them to wear the woollen and worsted cloths.

Such garments would often include waistcoats and jackets, the scene altogether more drab than the colourful sea of replica shirts at modern day rugby league matches.

Another feature of home matches was the Lockwood Brass Band, as Neil Shuttleworth remembered.

> They used to march round the pitch then settle on either the stand side or the terrace side and play. They had these collectors going round the pitch with this grey army blanket and it became great sport to forget the blanket and try to hit the collectors with your coins.

In September 1949, the engagement of the prestigious Band of the Coldstream Guards for the visit of Leeds earned the Huddersfield, Yorkshire and RFL committees a scathing rebuke from the editor of *Rugby League Review*, Stanley Chadwick. At half time, instead of the five minutes 'allowed by Law 50(i)' …

> … the interval was extended to eighteen minutes while they performed a funeral march cross the playing area … the Huddersfield club had asked and received permission … to extend the half-time interval to fifteen minutes because the Coldstream Guards Band had refused to play for a shorter period … Drastic punishment should be meted out to the men responsible.

The second half eventually began after the crowd had heard not only the band, but the result of the St Leger and the half time score from Leeds Road, where the crowd of 20,822 to watch Huddersfield Town v Arsenal was over 4000 fewer than the crowd at Fartown. With local amateur association football, rugby league and cricket also being played, these three sports engaged around 50,000 players and spectators in Huddersfield and District that afternoon, over half of them in rugby league.

119

1948-49: A Season to Remember

On 18 September 1948, three weeks after their impressive win over Wigan, another huge crowd – 26,053 – watched Huddersfield take on the Australians. From the start there was animosity from the tourists towards Huddersfield's Australian trio, who had arrived shortly before the Australian Rugby League Board of Control imposed a ban on any further Australian players signing for overseas clubs. The match degenerated into a series of bruising, bad-tempered confrontations, but the few flowing moves came from Huddersfield who emerged with a deserved and famous victory, 22-3. Australian wingman John 'Whacka' Graves signed off by knocking Johnny Hunter unconscious, and the baying crowd needed no further incitement. On the final whistle large numbers climbed the railings and headed across the pitch in Graves' direction. Anticipating trouble, Huddersfield secretary Arthur Archbell instructed the Duke of Wellington's West Riding regimental band to play the National Anthem, at which the hordes stood to attention whilst Graves escaped to the changing rooms.

This victory probably cost a battered Huddersfield team any chance of success in the Yorkshire Cup. Two days later they were knocked out 19-12 by Bradford Northern at Odsal.

Huddersfield returned to Odsal for the Challenge Cup semi-final the following April, strengthened by international loose forward, Ike Owens, signed in January from Castleford for a new club-record fee of £2750. Before another huge crowd of 64,250, Huddersfield were surprisingly beaten 11-10 by Halifax. Long-time supporter Dave Thomas recalled watching from the packed Odsal banking.

> Frightening. There was no terracing as such. It was just a steep bank and you sort of had to dig your way in and make a flat bit to stand comfortably ... but ... it doesn't matter how big the crowd was, there wasn't pushing or shoving or people acting stupidly, because it was dangerous. If the ones at the top fell you'd all end up in a pile at the bottom!

A run of nine straight victories followed as the Fartowners secured the Yorkshire League title and third place in the Championship behind Warrington and Wigan. An all-ticket crowd of 42,700 at Central Park watched Huddersfield beat Wigan 14-5 to set up the 1949 Championship Final against Warrington at Manchester City FC's Maine Road ground.

On 14 May 1949 tens of thousands of Huddersfield supporters crossed the Pennines to Manchester either by train, or on coach trips organised by pubs, amateur rugby league clubs, and by the Huddersfield Supporters' Club. At Golcar Station, Nancy Beaumont had to leave the platform and run alongside the track even further than usual to find a compartment with a seat on the corridor-free train.

Lionel Cooper sprints away from the Australian defence at Fartown in 1948.

... nobody much had a car. The petrol was still rationed ... the train was so long with supporters it wouldn't fit into Golcar Station and the porters used to have to lift us up into the train.

Over 75,000 people were packed into Maine Road. Unfortunately, to the acute embarrassment of the RFL, match referee Frank Smith was not one of them. His appointment document had been lost in the post. After a short delay, touch judge Matt Coates took his place and another referee, Paul Cowell, was dragged from the crowd to run the line.

There was consternation among some Huddersfield supporters when one of the women among them fainted. Dave Thomas recalled:

> It was my mother. It doesn't seem to happen now, but somebody fainted at nearly every game in those days. If somebody passed out, all the guys used to wave a white handkerchief ... St John Ambulance would know there was somebody not so good and they'd trot across to attend to them. They put my mother on the side of the ground until she came round.

A first half of Huddersfield pressure was rewarded when Dave Valentine pounced on a defensive fumble to send John Daly in under the posts, Devery converting. Warrington responded dangerously and only great covering tackles by Hunter and Valentine, the latter to stop great Australian wingman Brian Bevan in his tracks, kept Huddersfield in front. Then, just before half time, a slick combination between Banks and Devery created a gap from which Devery put Cooper in at the corner to give Huddersfield an 8-0 lead.

Huddersfield increased their lead when Devery accelerated onto an Anderson dribble and made a smart pick-up to touchdown under the posts, his conversion extending the lead to 13-0. Again, Warrington responded. Sustained pressure yielded a penalty. Then, in the last ten minutes, two quick converted tries reduced Huddersfield's lead to just one point. Warrington looked the fresher team, but marshalled by man-of-the-match Devery, a tiring Huddersfield hung on grimly. The full-time whistle was greeted by rapturous and relieved cheering. The Fartowners had secured the club's sixth Championship and the first since 1930.

Huddersfield v Warrington
League Championship Final
at Maine Road, Manchester
14 May 1949

Huddersfield	**13**		**Warrington**	**12**
Tries:	John Daly		Tries:	Billy Jackson
	Lionel Cooper			Roy Francis
	Pat Devery		Goals:	Harry Bath (2)
Goals:	Pat Devery (2)			Harold Palin

Huddersfield
Johnny Hunter;
Jock Anderson, Arthur Ferguson, Pat Devery, Lionel Cooper;
Russell Pepperell, Billy Banks;
John Maiden, Mel Meek, John Daly, Ike Owens, Bob Nicholson, Dave Valentine

Warrington
Leslie Jones;
Brian Bevan, Albert Pimblett, Billy Jackson, Roy Francis;
Jack Fleming, Gerry Helme;
Bill Derbyshire, Harold 'Ike' Fishwick, William Riley, Harry Bath, Jim Featherstone, Harold Palin

Referee: Matt Coates (Pudsey)   Attendance: 75,194   Receipts: £11,073

For those unable to attend such occasions, the Saturday night sports' newspapers were an eagerly anticipated treat. Roger Armitage, who watched rugby league at Fartown and Huddersfield Town at Leeds Road on alternate Saturdays, recalled his Saturday evening ritual.

> From being 8 or 9 ... I'd catch the 6 o'clock bus from Holthead to Slaithwaite with a few pennies in my pocket and go to the newsagents ... usually the papers came just in time to catch the bus back at 5 and 20 to seven. So we would by that time have a minute-by-minute report of the matches, both Fartown and Town.
>
> I'd fetch a paper for ourselves, Grandad and probably Uncle Fred ... we lived in a row of 3 cottages. We would all be waiting to find out the details, although we would probably know the result already having listened to the sports programme on the BBC, the Light programme as it was then.

Captain and man-of-the-match
Pat Devery lifts the
League Championship Trophy
at Maine Road in 1949

I don't know how they managed to publish it so quickly, I believe by ringing in reports and setting it up in the old typesetting as they went along.

Just occasionally we might treat ourselves. The green one was a Leeds paper I think and the pink one was a Bradford one ... occasionally we'd have a treat and have a green or a pink one but for our family the Examiner was the one we relied on.

Published by the Fartown Supporters' Club

HUDDERSFIELD RUGBY LEAGUE TEAM   Season 1948-49
Winners of the Northern Rugby League and Yorkshire League Championship

S. Williams   H. Lockwood   B. Gronow   W. Cunningham   H. V. Wood   J. Wood. Beever   A. Dews   W. Stoker
R. Nicholson   J. Maiden   J. C. Daly   R. S. Robson   D. D. Valentine   J. L. Davies   I. A. Owens   G. V. Hughes
A. Archbell   G. Wilson   J. Anderson   J. Bawden   P. C. Devery   L. W. Cooper   J. C. Hunter   M. Meek   A. E. Fiddes
S. V. Pepperell   W. Banks   The Yorkshire League Cup   The Northern Rugby League Cup   G. R. Pepperell   A. Ferguson

Postcard published by the Supporters' Club to celebrate
Huddersfield's League Championship and Yorkshire Cup successes of 1948-49

Cartoon from *Rugby League Review*, January 1950.

"This is the B.B.C. Light Programme. We regret that owing to a technical hitch we have given the Rugby League results. The person responsible has, of course, been dealt with."

Contenders

In April 1949, as Huddersfield coach Alex Fiddes negotiated the end-of-season fixture congestion by rotating his players, eighteen-year-old local boy Frank 'Spanky' Dyson made his debut. Dyson would spend several seasons as understudy to Johnny Hunter, but learned plenty from the Australian's generous advice, and emerged to become one of the most distinguished players to don the claret and gold.

1949-50 was another successful season. Huddersfield were the Yorkshire League winners for the tenth time, runners-up in the Yorkshire Cup and again in contention for the League Championship. Despite losing 27-8 at Fartown in March, Wigan beat Huddersfield into second place in the Championship table, and the two sides met again in the Championship Final at Maine Road.

Huddersfield were overwhelming favourites. The Lions party to Australia had already disembarked and, inexplicably, not one Huddersfield player had been selected. Wigan, in contrast, had eight players on the tour and were compelled to field most of their 'A' team in the final. Yet Wigan's tight, determined, disciplined defence frustrated Huddersfield time and again to produce one of the biggest Championship Final upsets. Sidney Crowther, who reported affairs at Fartown in the *HDE* for almost 40 years under the pen name 'Autolycus', summed up the humiliation thus:

Roses are red, Violets are blue,
Wigan got 20, Fartown got 2.

In September 1950, Huddersfield added speed on the opposite wing to Lionel Cooper by signing Peter Henderson, a double international who had been capped seven times by the New Zealand rugby union All-Blacks and had represented his country in the sprint and sprint-relay events at the 1950 Empire Games. Dave Thomas described him as …

> … a spectacular runner … the finest player I think I've seen … Cooper always stopped on his wing but I've seen Henderson track across field and tackle on the opposite wing. His work was tremendous.

123

Henderson was used as a utility man for significant periods of his first season, 1950-51, filling in when Johnny Hunter returned to Australia to get married, and when Pat Devery was injured and had a groin operation. Whilst Huddersfield's playing strength was the envy of many clubs, a Yorkshire Cup triumph, 16-3 over Castleford at Headingley, was the least the Fartown faithful expected from their talented but maddeningly inconsistent team.

There was a marginal improvement in 1951-52 when they finished top of the Yorkshire League and fourth in the Championship, losing narrowly 18-15 in the play-off semi-final away to Bradford Northern. Highlight of the season was Lionel Cooper's club-record ten tries in a 48-3 victory over Keighley in November, at least seven of them after beating three or more men. Cooper's total for the season was 71 tries, the most prolific of his eight seasons at Huddersfield in which he was never lower than fourth in the League's try-scorers.

Peter Henderson

Huddersfield v St Helens in 1950

Huddersfield celebrate their 1950 Yorkshire Cup win over Castleford.

Another loyal servant, forward Ted Slevin joined the club from Wigan in November 1951. At first he divided opinions among Huddersfield supporters. His tubby 'endomorph' body prevented him from running quickly and at first some saw him as merely plodding from one breakdown to the next. Eventually, all would realise his true value to the side. An astute ball-playing forward and a brilliant reader of the game, Slevin's best work – short accurate off-loads that released other players – often went unnoticed. Gerald Furness remembered:

> Ted never appeared to be doing anything but when he gave Bowman the ball there was always an opening for Bowman. He made Ken Bowman.

In the days of unlimited tackles, Slevin could organise play so that his team retained possession for considerable periods. A great club player of his era, he represented Great Britain twice and only three players have played more than his 441 matches for Huddersfield.

1953 and All That

Huddersfield retained a settled, injury-free side for much of the 1952-53 season, and it showed in more consistent results. The Yorkshire Cup was secured with an 18-8 victory over Batley in November fog at Headingley. The Fartowners embarked on the Challenge Cup trail by defeating Castleford in the first round, but the draw made progress difficult for them. Championship challengers Barrow were beaten 21-7 at Fartown in the second round, but that only earned an away tie to reigning champions Bradford Northern. An Odsal crowd of 69,198 saw Slevin and Valentine dominate the Bradford pack in a 17-7 win, setting up a return visit for the semi-final against Wigan. Despite heavy rain which left standing water on the Odsal pitch, 58,772 turned out to watch an attritional, mud-laden affair. Valentine made the crucial opening score after 49 minutes, touching down under the posts from Henderson's cross-kick, and Huddersfield went on to win 7-0.

The Fartowners were back at Wembley for the first time since 1935, but opponents St Helens were top of the Championship, three places above Huddersfield, unbeaten away from Knowsley Road all season, and strong favourites.

The nation was on a television-buying spree in anticipation of the Coronation of Queen Elizabeth II six weeks hence on 2 June. Although some recent finals had been televised, the first in 1946, the RFL banned live television coverage, fearing that it would affect the attendance. Supporters who could not travel were restricted to radio coverage on the BBC Home Service.

Captain Russell Pepperell leads out the Huddersfield team at Wembley, 1953

St Helens' surprisingly aggressive approach antagonised many in the 89,588 crowd who booed the Saints during and at the end of the game. Huddersfield withstood the challenge and in the 29th minute Slevin broke through the Saints' forwards. He fed Peter Ramsden who sensed that the two covering defenders had one eye on a two-man overlap on the right. Cutting inside, he burst through Alan Prescott's tackle and dived over, Devery converting. George Langfield responded with a penalty, and from the re-start Saints went the length of the field for wingman Steve Llewellyn to score.

No escape from the clutches of Pat Devery, Jack Large and Lionel Cooper

Pat Devery converts Peter Ramsden's opening try.

Five-all at the break became 8-5 to Saints when, against the run of play, Langfield scored near the posts. Huddersfield breathed a little more easily when he missed an easy conversion, but their prospects looked bleak when Hunter was flattened by Llewellyn and stretchered off, and a leg injury reduced Devery to a passenger on the wing. Maurice Oldroyd recalled the glum Huddersfield faces on the terraces.

> There were no subs then and if you were a man down for any period you'd had it.

Suddenly, scrum half Billy Banks negated Saints' numerical advantage. Darting from the base of the scrum, he shot over the line. Cooper took over kicking duties from Devery and converted to give Huddersfield an improbable 10-8 lead.

With eight minutes left, St Helens manoeuvred a drop goal opportunity which Langfield took to level the match at 10-10. At that point, as Maurice Oldroyd remembered, 'Hunter charged back on to the field and a thunderous roar went up.' The match remained on a knife edge until, with four minutes to play, Valentine and Bowden made a break through the centre, interpassing until Bowden flicked the ball right to release Ramsden. The nineteen-year-old romped inside the last, isolated defender and over for the winning try, Cooper's conversion making the final score 15-10. Peter Ramsden was named man-of-the-match and remains the youngest-ever winner of the Lance Todd Trophy.

Peter Ramsden dives over for Huddersfield's third try

Huddersfield v St Helens
Challenge Cup Final
at Wembley Stadium
25 April 1953

Huddersfield	**15**		**St Helens**	**10**
Tries:	Peter Ramsden (2)		Tries:	Steve Llewellyn
	Billy Banks			George Langfield
Goals:	Pat Devery		Goal:	George Langfield
	Lionel Cooper (2)		Drp Gl:	George Langfield

Huddersfield

Johnny Hunter;

Peter Henderson, Russ Pepperell (captain), Pat Devery, Lionel Cooper;

Peter Ramsden, Billy Banks;

Ted Slevin, George Curran, Jim Bowden, Jack Brown, Jack Large, Dave Valentine

St Helens

Glynn Moses;

Steve Llewellyn, Douglas Greenall, Don Gullick, Stan McCormick;

Jimmy Honey, George Langfield;

Alan Prescott, Reg Blakemore, George Parr, George Parsons, Bill Bretheron, Ray Cale

Referee: George Phillips (Widnes)   Attendance: 89,588   Receipts: £30,865

No finer feeling: Russ Pepperell collects the Challenge Cup from the Duke of Norfolk.

Huddersfield's season was far from over, but the players were out on their feet. The Challenge Cup Final was the tenth of 13 matches in 36 days. Three days after the final they beat Castleford 38-5. Two days later they beat Hull KR 46-2, pipping Barrow to fourth place and qualifying for a play-offs re-match against league leaders St Helens at Knowsley Road.

The match kicked off just 42 hours after the full time whistle had blown against Hull KR. The *HDE* commented:

> Huddersfield were lifeless, there were times when it seemed that as much they could do was to drag one leg after another … there was no freshness in them, they played as a side who were suffering from brain fog and from being leg weary … they were slow in thinking as well as slow in moving.

St Helens, who had not played since the cup final, took full advantage and crushed Huddersfield 46-0.

The 1953 Cup Final marked the beginning of the end for Huddersfield's great post-war squad, although the decline was gradual. Sixth place in the 1953-54 Championship was respectable, but on Easter Monday 1954 Pat Devery announced his retirement. His groin injury, operated on in 1951, had continued to impede him and he was ready to return to Australia. In 223 appearances for Huddersfield he kicked 401 goals and scored 98 tries, a total of 1,096 points. His tally of 322 points in 1952-53 was a Huddersfield club record which stood for many years. His leadership would be greatly missed.

Lionel Cooper, still a potent force on his day, played his last match for Huddersfield twelve months later. His Huddersfield records of ten tries in a match and 420 in his career may never be equalled. Along with his compatriot Brian Bevan, Cooper was the great wingman of the immediate post-war period. He went on to coach Dewsbury for a season before returning home to Australia.

Jeff Bawden, who was consigned to the 'A' team towards the end of his career, also retired in 1955. In a letter to the Football Committee, he wrote:

> Huddersfield has been my first and only club, and I feel very proud indeed in having the honour and pleasure of wearing the famous claret and gold colours during the past twelve years.

Russ Pepperell also played his last match in 1954-55. He briefly coached Keighley before emigrating to Australia.

Such quality and experience could not be replaced overnight, not even by top-quality signings such as Tommy Smales, a scrum half from Featherstone Rovers, and Mick Sullivan, who initially took Devery's place at centre.

The First Rugby League World Cup

Huddersfield's stars were fully involved in a concerted effort to raise the profile of international rugby league after World War II. In 1949 a British Empire squad comprising seven players from Huddersfield, four from Workington, three from Leeds and one from Warrington played two matches in France.

Four months later an Other Nationalities team was added to England, France and Wales to create a four-team European Championship which was played on a round-robin basis for the next five seasons. The teams were well-matched. England and France were champions twice each, and Other Nationalities once, but the title was usually decided on points difference. Only once, in the final season when England won all three of their matches, was any team unbeaten.

The Australian trio of Hunter, Cooper and Devery were regulars in the Other Nationalities team, alongside Scot Dave Valentine, Irishman John Daly and Kiwi Peter Henderson. Scottish full-back George Wilson also featured. Billy Banks was a mainstay of the Welsh side and wingman Dick Cracknell broke into the England team in 1951.

The series produced one infamous match, the 1951 'Battle of the Boulevard'. Marseille policeman Eduoard Ponsinet set the tone by knocking out and hospitalising Australian forward Arthur Clues before the ball had come to earth from the kick-off. Cooper and Henderson were

The Other Nationalities team that lost 30-22 to England at Wigan in November 1953 included Dave Valentine (second right, back row), Pat Devery (furthest right, front row), and captain Lionel Cooper (front row, ball at his feet)

Dick Cracknell runs in a try on Huddersfield's right wing.

among several Other Nationalities players who had to be removed for treatment to injuries as the French repeatedly and robustly crossed the line of fair play, Ponsinet eventually being sent off. Captained by Cooper, who insisted that his team should not retaliate but 'keep on playing football', the Other Nationalities prevailed 17-14, all their points coming from Cooper (3 tries) and Devery (4 goals).

In addition to the European Championship matches, Huddersfield contributed players to all four teams in two matches – Great Britain v Australasia, and an Empire XIII v Wales – staged as part of the Festival of Britain celebrations in May 1951.

The obvious next step, following the example of the FIFA World Cup, which had begun in 1930 and which England entered for the first time in 1950, was a Rugby League World Cup. Staged in France in the autumn of 1954, the inaugural tournament was a four-team round-robin on the lines of the European Championships, but featuring Australia, France, Great Britain and New Zealand. Huddersfield was represented in the Great Britain side by Dave Valentine, who was captain, and by wingman Mick Sullivan, who was just starting out on a distinguished international career. Scrum half Billy Banks,

" Don't bother writing it. Here's my card. I stock 'em for these occasions."

Cartoon from *Rugby League Review*, November 1949

hooker Harry Bradshaw and versatile back Ron Rylance were also in the squad. It was no surprise that all the matches were keenly contested, nor that two teams finished level on points at the top, France and Great Britain both beating the southern hemisphere nations and drawing 13-13 when they met.

A hastily arranged play-off gave the tournament the showpiece final it deserved. A crowd of 30,368 flocked to Paris's Parc des Princes to see Great Britain come from behind to beat the French 16-12. Dave Valentine was the pride of Huddersfield as he became the first captain to lift the Rugby League World Cup trophy.

End of an Era

Dave Valentine, Mick Sullivan and Johnny Hunter all played for Huddersfield until 1957. After the last of his 332 matches for the club against Warrington on 13 April, an emotional Hunter stripped off his jersey and threw it into the Fartown crowd. He returned to Australia leaving many friends in the spheres of rugby league and league cricket, which he played with distinction as an attacking batsman for Bradley Mills in the Huddersfield League, Salts and Lightcliffe in the Bradford League, and Rochdale in the Central Lancashire League.

Johnny Hunter narrowly missed Huddersfield's first trophy for four years, a 15-8 victory over York in the Yorkshire Cup Final at Headingley in October 1957. It was a success on which the club was unable to build. Four days later, against the wishes of the Huddersfield committee, Mick Sullivan left Fartown. In the early hours of 23 October Wigan secured his signature with a cheque for £9,500, a record transfer fee at the time. Mick was subsequently sold to St Helens in 1961 for £11,000, another new record. Such fees reflect his standing as one of the all-time great wingmen. In total, he won 46 caps for Great Britain, a record he shares with future Huddersfield player-coach Garry Schofield, and he scored an unmatched 41 tries. He played in two further World Cups in 1957 and 1960, Great Britain winning the latter to make him the only player to represent Great Britain in two World Cup-winning teams.

A month to the day after Sullivan's departure for Wigan, Dave Valentine broke his ankle at Hull. It was the third time he had broken the same ankle within fourteen months. He subsequently announced his retirement from the game. Although he briefly came out of retirement in 1960, Huddersfield had lost all of the stars who had graced the post-war era.

New player coach, Ernie Ashcroft, signed from Wigan in 1958, faced the challenge of moulding a team from the remnants of the old plus several new signings. His charges included

Mick Sullivan, the greatest left wing of his time, scored 93 tries in 117 appearances for Huddersfield, a similar ratio to his Great Britain record of 41 tries in 46 appearances. In 2013 he was inducted to the Rugby League Hall of Fame.

local players Brian Curry, Ray Haywood and Alan Redfearn, Ken Noble, a second row forward from Featherstone Rovers, outstanding hooker Don Close, signed from Allerton Bywater, second row forward Ken Bowman from Heworth, and former rugby union players Aidan Breen from Broughton Park and Mike Wicks from Torquay. Huddersfield finished 19th in 1958-59, the club's lowest position since 1937-38, but Ashcroft's classical style of play proved to be an inspiration and he was able to halt the decline.

Ken Bowman, a mobile, powerful second row forward
who played for Huddersfield from 1956 to 1965

In 1959-60 the Fartowners were challenging for top-four honours in February. They eventually finished 12th, which was scant justice for the quality of their play. Mike Wicks had an outstanding season, scoring 20 tries in 20 matches, and Frank Dyson reached a century of goals for the fourth time, earning selection at full back for Great Britain against Australia, and captaining Yorkshire in all three County games. A protégé of the generous teachings of Johnny Hunter, Dyson had bided his time and emerged as one of the best full backs in the game. Against Wakefield Trinity in April 1961, he stroked the ball between the Fartown posts to pass Ben Gronow's long-standing aggregate of 673 goals for the club. When he left for Oldham in the summer of 1963, Dyson had set Huddersfield club career records which still stand of 958 goals and 2072 points.

Ernie Ashcroft left for Warrington in October 1961, but he had passed on a great deal of guile, craft and experience. He was succeeded by Dave Valentine, who had made a surprising comeback in 1960, playing one 'A' team game then featuring at loose forward in the 1960 Yorkshire Cup Final against Wakefield at Headingley, Huddersfield losing 16-10. Valentine answered his critics by his ability to stay the pace, as he did in the subsequent nineteen games he would play in that season.

Valentine was a shrewd coach, and his squad was kept in peak condition by trainer and physiotherapist, Mel Meek. Kevin Brook, a ball-boy at the time, witnessed an unusual occurrence behind the Fartown scenes and was sworn to

Frank 'Spanky' Dyson

secrecy by Dave Valentine. Kevin kept his promise for half a century, speaking about it for the first time in 2013.

> I got down early before a game and there was a chap there on the table under the hands of Mel Meek, treating his injury. I thought, 'Who's that? He's a big chap.' Dave Valentine said to me: 'You mustn't say anything about this gentleman being here,' … and I never have until now. The chap on the treatment table was the British Lions and Scottish [rugby union] captain Michael Campbell-Lamerton. If he'd been caught in a rugby league club at that time that would have been the end of his rugby union career.
>
> He was the commanding officer of the Duke of Wellington's West Riding Regiment and a lot of the rugby league lads who'd done national service with him, like Brian Curry at Huddersfield and Roy Sabine at Keighley and others who knew him, advised him that the person he really needed to see about his injury was Mel Meek at Huddersfield.

Tommy Smales

Guided by Valentine, and marshalled around the park by captain Tommy Smales, Huddersfield exceeded all expectations in 1961-62. In contention for a top four spot all season, they also progressed in the Challenge Cup with victories over York (8-7), St Helens (13-2) and Castleford (10-4), the latter in a replay after a 4-4 draw. In the semi-final against Hull KR at Odsal, three goals from man-of-the-match Frank Dyson secured a 6-0 win. Huddersfield were back at Wembley, but the achievement did not detract from their League form. Five wins from their last seven matches, including a decisive 18-10 triumph over fifth-placed Workington, secured fourth position and a play-off semi-final away to League Leaders Wigan.

Huddersfield had lost 41-3 at Central Park less than a month earlier and, playing their ninth match in three weeks, were written off by the media, one of whom described them as 'a side whose moderate capabilities fall well short of their ambitions.' They were also underestimated by experts within the game, including the national selectors who met in March and chose just one Huddersfield player, Ken Noble, for the Lions' summer tour of Australia and New Zealand.

Undeterred, the Fartowners produced their most resilient display of the season to restrict Wigan to one try whilst running in three of their own, Close, Smales and Haywood scoring to edge a nerve-wracking contest 13-11.

Only Wakefield Trinity, opponents in the Challenge Cup and League Championship finals, stood between Huddersfield and a glorious double. Challenge Cup Final day, 12 May 1962, has lived long in the memory of many supporters. The Supporters' Club worked overtime to book transport and tickets to Wembley. Two special trains, appropriately named 'Claret' and 'Gold', ran from Huddersfield, whose supporters outnumbered the Wakefield contingent in the 81,263 crowd.

Unfortunately, the opposition included the game's most prolific points-scorer in top form. Neil Fox ran in a first half try and kicked three drop goals to keep Huddersfield at arms-length. A brilliant individual try by Smales reduced the deficit to 5-3, and Peter Ramsden resumed his love affair with the occasion, crashing over in the second half to make it 10-6, but Fox struck

Wembley 1962

Top: Leo Booth is introduced to Earl Alexander of Tunis.

Centre: Ken Noble and Tommy Smales hunt down a loose ball.

Bottom: Try-scorer Peter Ramsden passes to the left wing as Leo Booth looks on.

again to secure a 12-6 victory for Wakefield. It remains the only Challenge Cup Final in which not one penalty goal or conversion was kicked.

Seven days later, back at Odsal, Wakefield were fully expected to add the League Championship to the Yorkshire League, Yorkshire Cup and Challenge Cup, thereby following Hunslet, Huddersfield and Swinton as one of the clubs to win all four trophies in the same season. Huddersfield made two changes from their Wembley line-up, Austin Kilroy replacing Mick Clark in the forwards, and Gwyn Davies coming in at half back to allow Harry Deighton to move back and replace Ray Haywood at centre. This time it was Huddersfield who got their noses in front with a try by Mike Wicks that Dyson converted. The outcome was in doubt until the last minute when Tommy Smales nipped over for a match-sealing try.

Neil Shuttleworth was among the Huddersfield supporters.

> Somebody had to deny Wakefield joining the elite band of four-cups winners and we did … it was the first and only time I ever invaded the pitch … it was just outstanding. Having lost at Wembley to three drop goals that we couldn't do much about, to beat them well and truly at Odsal was absolutely wonderful.

The joyful Huddersfield supporters were cleared from the pitch and Frank Dyson's conversion completed a well-earned 14-5 victory. To come from fourth place to win the Championship trophy was a rare and remarkable achievement.

Huddersfield v Wakefield Trinity
League Championship Play-off Final
at Odsal Stadium
19 May 1962

Huddersfield	14	Wakefield Trinity 5
Tries:	Mike Wicks	Try: Neil Fox
	Tommy Smales	Goal: Neil Fox
Goals:	Frank Dyson (4)	

Huddersfield

Frank Dyson;

Aiden Breen, Harry Deighton, Leo Booth, Mike Wicks;

Gwyn Davies, Tommy Smales (captain);

Ted Slevin, Don Close, Ken Noble, Austin Kilroy, Ken Bowman, Peter Ramsden

Wakefield Trinity

Gerry Round;

Fred Smith, Alan Skene, Neil Fox, Ken Hirst;

Harold Poynton, Keith Holliday;

Jack Wilkinson, Milan Kosanovic, Don Vines, Brian Briggs, Albert Firth, Derek Turner (captain)

Referee: NT Railton (Wigan)   Attendance: 37,451   Receipts: £7979

Neil Shuttleworth continued:

> We knew where the team was going and we followed them up to this pub at Outlane … we had a drink of champagne, beer and God knows what else out of the Championship Cup.

Huddersfield owed much of their success in the 1961-62 season to the leadership, prompting and tactical nous of their scrum half and captain Tommy Smales and the intuitive passing game of prop forward Ted Slevin.

Slevin had continued to live and work in Wigan, and from 1951 to 1963 made the five-hour round trip to home matches and to training on Tuesday and Thursday evenings. Neil

A civic reception for the victorious team

Shuttleworth recalled his superhuman commitment.

> Ted worked down the pit in Wigan. After his shift he would come up from the pit, have a wash, get the train from Wigan to Manchester, the train from Manchester to Huddersfield, a bus from the station to the ground, train, go back the same way, and back down the pit the next morning.

Ken Senior, the outstanding player amongst the next generation at Fartown, made his Huddersfield debut in October 1962 and worked a 40-hour week in engineering.

> Week-to-week you weren't that much better off being a professional, because if you couldn't work Saturday morning at time and a half you were losing pay, so it almost cancelled it out.

Standard pay for Huddersfield's first team players at this time was £10 for a win and £2 for losing or drawing but, as Ken explained, there were some windfalls.

> I got a £250 signing on fee, £200 after playing 20 first team matches, and another £150 after another 20 first team matches. After I had played 19 of my second lot of 20 matches, I was reserve for the next match at Wakefield. We got to Wakefield and Tommy Smales didn't turn up, so they had to play me. I always wondered whether Tommy Smales knew that it was my 20th match, but I don't know.

Another windfall for players who gave ten years' service to the club was a testimonial. Ted Slevin could hardly have chosen a better moment for his, four days after the 1962 Championship triumph. A crowd of 5000 supported his testimonial match, a 34-all draw between a Huddersfield XIII and Ted Slevin's XIII at Fartown which realised £303 for the beneficiary. After the match, Slevin completed a lap of honour with the Championship trophy, mobbed by hundreds of supporters. Two years later, there were similar scenes at his last-ever game. Neil Shuttleworth recalled the emotional scenes.

Everybody loved Ted. They made him captain for the game, and as the players came up the tunnel, the rest of them stopped so that Ted came out on his own, and everybody gave him this rapturous applause.

In 1999 Ted Slevin was inducted into the Huddersfield RLFC Hall of Fame.

Huddersfield had started the 1960s on a high. At the time, no one could anticipate that it would be decades before the club and its supporters would again experience such success and euphoria

Above: Ted Slevin in support as Ken Bowman makes a tackle

Right: Ted Slevin

Chapter 11

The Amateur Game

Adapting to the Birth of the Northern Union

Amateur rugby continued to be an important part of the sporting scene in Huddersfield after the formation of the Northern Union in 1895. Most but not all local amateur clubs followed the town's parent club in switching to the Northern Union code. Rugby union continued to struggle on, its clubs having to travel further afield to find opponents as Huddersfield became a Northern Union stronghold, but no local rugby union clubs from 1895 have survived. The oldest rugby union club in the district is the Huddersfield Old Boys, founded in 1909.

Immediately after the 1895 split, there were 23 clubs competing locally, with most of the villages represented. The Holliday Challenge Cup, in its eleventh season, continued as the most important amateur rugby competition in the district. In the 1895 final, held at Primrose Hill in October, Meltham lifted the Cup for the first time with a 3-0 victory over Lockwood. Charles Brook, a local mill owner and President of the Meltham club admitted that the final was the first rugby match he had seen, but he 'hoped it would not be the last.' Social status was apparently more important than enthusiasm for the game when appointing the figureheads of local clubs. On returning home, the team was led by the village's fire brigade and brass band to the centre of Meltham 'where festivities were sustained with much enthusiasm.'

Holliday Cup winner's medal presented to 21-year-old William Sykes of Meltham in 1895

Whilst the Holliday Cup helped to sustain interest, particularly in the more successful clubs, the pattern of clubs disbanding, forming and re-forming, evident since the earliest days of club rugby in the district, gained fresh impetus in the inevitable turmoil that followed the breakaway of the Northern Union. The administrative and financial resources of amateur clubs could be quickly overwhelmed by the game's new and volatile financial demands. In addition to competition for decent pitches which pushed up the rent, the erratic market for players, many of whom expected, at the very least, recompense for broken time and expenses, exposed and shattered the more fragile clubs.

Nevertheless, the Huddersfield and District Union retained a core of its strongest clubs, and in 1904 formed two divisions, eleven teams in each. In addition, Underbank Rangers, was admitted to the Yorkshire Senior Competition, effectively only one division below the Huddersfield club which was relegated to Division 2 of the Northern Union League in 1903-04. Attracting regular crowds of about 1000, Underbank had emerged as the strongest 'amateur' club, their high standing further emphasising the exceptional quality of Harold Wagstaff, who made his first team debut for them at the age of 14 in 1905.

Huddersfield and District Amateur Rugby League

On 27 April 1908 the Huddersfield and District Union became the Huddersfield and District League. Formed at a meeting in the Pavilion at Fartown, it is still in existence today. During the following two months, a constitution was drafted, officials were appointed – Mr W Fillan as President, Mr HG Roebuck as Secretary and Mr E Kaye as Treasurer – and 32 teams expressed an intention to participate. Of these, 21 actually entered. Twelve of these teams formed the Junior Division (over-18), while the remaining nine teams played in the Intermediate Section (under-18).

The annual Holliday Challenge Cup continued, and two new trophies were introduced. The Sam Wood Cup, named after its donor, a Vice President of Huddersfield Cricket and Athletic Club (HC and AC), was awarded to the winners of the Intermediate League. The winners of the Junior Division competed for the Charles Sykes Rose Bowl, presented by Mr Charles Sykes, local textile mill-owner, philanthropist and the President of the HC and AC. This trophy was later renamed the Sir Charles Sykes Rose Bowl after its donor was knighted towards the end of World War I, mainly in recognition of his leading role in organising the wartime woollen industry across West Yorkshire, which was a centre of khaki production.

Underbank Rangers, winners of the Charles Sykes Rose Bowl and Holliday Cup in 1908-09

MARSH N.R.U. FOOTBALL CLUB, 1911-12.
Winners of the Huddersfield and District Holliday Challenge Cup.
Winners of the Huddersfield and District N.R.U. Intermediate League (under 18).

Underbank, now back in the local league, were the first winners of the Rose Bowl. They also won the Holliday Challenge Cup, defeating Paddock 6-2 in the final at Fartown in April 1909. The Sam Wood Cup was won by Hillhouse, the first Champions of the Intermediate section.

Confirming the growing popularity of the game, the town's first workshop competition, staged at Fartown in 1908, attracted 44 entries. Reluctantly making up the numbers for the Acre Mills team was a young amateur association footballer from Halifax, Major Holland. A novice at Northern Union, he was a revelation, quickly catching the eye of the Huddersfield officials who signed him almost immediately. A talented full back and natural goal-kicker, Major Holland went on to play a key role in the development of the Team of all Talents. In 218 matches between 1909 and 1921 he scored 542 points for Huddersfield.

The Huddersfield and District League, urging its members to develop young players, retained its under-18s (Intermediate) Section for the 1909-10 season, but restricted the Junior Division to under-21s. There was also a senior competition. This arrangement continued until the autumn of 1914 when the Intermediate Section was suspended, wartime demands leaving many of its clubs bereft of both players and finance. The senior league also lost clubs, but some managed to struggle on, among them Holmbridge, Outlane and Kirkheaton. The final of the Junior Division was played at Fartown in April 1915, but was very one-sided, Rastrick crushing Holmbridge 53-3. The League continued to organise a Junior Section amidst increasing difficulties, but the introduction of conscription in 1916 left a number of clubs with no option but to drop out of the League. Some of these clubs, like the players who were killed, incapacitated or aged by the war years, were lost to the game for good.

Prosperity Post-World War I

Post-war, the Huddersfield and District League slowly recovered as young men were demobilised and people flocked to share the communal activities that they had sacrificed and fought for, and which affirmed the return to peacetime normality. The Huddersfield and District League grew from just six clubs in 1919, and had 25 clubs participating in some or all of its four sections – open-age, under-20, under-18 and under-16 – by the early 1920s. Of the clubs that joined or re-joined the League in the 1920s, a high percentage were from outlying villages. Flockton, Lindley, Marsden and Slaithwaite all competed successfully and interest was high. In March 1926, Lindley's visit to Rastrick attracted gate receipts of £26, a sum that was the envy of a number of professional clubs. Sadly, the League's open-age section declined towards the end of the 1920s, and by 1930 had been replaced entirely by an under-21 league. Clubs still running open-age teams had to find their fixtures elsewhere.

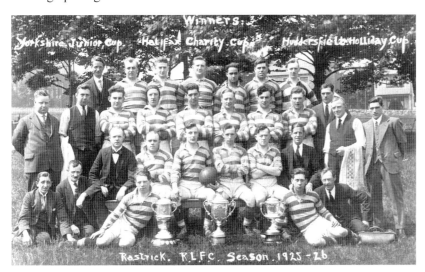

Rastrick, one of the district's strongest clubs from the 1910s to the 1950s

Lindley joined the Leeds and District League and carried the flag for the Huddersfield club game in this period, not least in the Rugby League Challenge Cup. In 1929 Lindley beat several amateur clubs to qualify for the first round and were drawn at home against St Helens. The professional club offered Lindley £100 to sacrifice home advantage and the tie was switched to Knowsley Road. Lindley lost 32-2 but put up great resistance to keep the score down and obviously benefited financially. In 1931 Lindley again reached the first round and were drawn at home to cash-strapped Rochdale Hornets, who could not afford to offer a cash inducement to switch the game. Over 2,000 spectators surrounded Lindley's Acre Street pitch, and with no score at half time a shock was distinctly possible. Unfortunately, an injury to Lindley's scrum half Clarke reduced the home team to twelve men for the whole of the second half. Rochdale gradually wore their amateur opponents down and finally scraped home 13-2. Reaching the first round again in 1932, Lindley gave a 'courageous' performance at Barrow where they lost 65-6, 'outclassed but not disgraced.'

Photo. W. E. TURTON   **1930 — LINDLEY RUGBY LEAGUE F.C. — 1931.**   BIRKBY
Winners of the Huddersfield Holiday Cup, Sir Charles Sykes Rose Bowl, Yorkshire Junior Cup, Leeds League Cup, Leeds Challenge Cup

The Lindley squad that lost to Rochdale in 1931, but won the Holliday Cup,
Sir Charles Sykes Rose Bowl, Yorkshire Junior Cup, Leeds League Cup and Leeds Challenge Cup

The Great Depression

The 1930s was a very difficult time for amateur sports clubs, which often exist hand-to-mouth financially. The desperate economic conditions of the Great Depression triggered by the Wall Street Crash of 1929 blew away the most vulnerable, and impacted severely on the rest. The Rugby Football League (RFL) had an informal policy of paying for rugby shirts for amateur clubs, and while this helped, the cost of renting grounds was a major millstone, as explained in the Huddersfield and District League's annual report of 1931-32:

> Field rents are as usual a great drawback. There has not been a great difficulty getting them, but the excessive rent asked ... is very big for clubs to shoulder. £10 for the season is as little as any owner seems to think of asking.

A 1933 report by the RFL into the state of amateur rugby league noted that there were no amateur clubs in Bradford, no adult clubs in the Dewsbury/Batley area, seven clubs in Leeds and just three – Lindley, Rastrick and Underbank – in Huddersfield and district. The amateur game, declining in the late 1920s, was decimated.

For men fortunate enough to be in employment there were some opportunities to play rugby league in the end-of-season workshop competitions, although most teams only existed for the duration of their competition.

From the mid-1930s, the Huddersfield District League began to recover alongside the economy, regaining some of its playing strength from earlier years. In 1936-37 the newly formed under-17 section gained five clubs and in 1937 the open-age section was revived, with seven clubs playing regularly. Lindley were the 1937 champions, beating Saddleworth 15-0 in the final, while Rastrick beat Underbank 15-7 to win the Intermediate Section. A feature of this mini-revival was a growing number of overseas players. One of the first was Norman Gibbons who first played at Underbank in 1933 and retained lifelong friendships there. It was a sad day for the club when, in 1995, Underbank Chairman Gerald Parr received a letter to inform club members that Norman had died at his Australian home.

Despite all the difficulties faced by the Huddersfield and District League in the 1930s, Huddersfield's senior club was still able to recruit and rely on local players. Between 1930 and 1939 the District League supplied no fewer than 46 players to the Huddersfield club, 30 of whom played first team football. In 1939 there were twelve local players on the Huddersfield books, including six who played regularly for the first team.

Nine clubs attended the District League's AGM of 1939, far from the numerical strength of the early 1920s, but the most for ten years and enough to organise a meaningful competition. Then came a fourth major disruption – following the 1895 breakaway, World War I and the Great Depression – that blighted progress and continuity. Britain was once more at war with Germany.

World War II

The outbreak of World War II brought immediate problems. Conscription was introduced from the start, and nearly all the young men were either lost to the forces or working flat out in reserved occupations. Factories and mills adopted extremely long shift patterns and working weeks, leaving little free time or energy to play sport.

Mr H Littlewood, the secretary of the Huddersfield and District League, in his report to the RFL recorded problems experienced during the first year of the war, recognising that some of them were insurmountable.

> Dear Sir,
>
> I submit herewith my Annual Report to your committee on the past season's working, attaching Balance Sheet, also the League Table and meeting attendances.
>
> I don't propose to dwell on the difficulty under which we have carried on, that is too well known, and I think under the circumstances this District has done wonderfully well to continue, and I thank the clubs we have had and the Management Committee for their loyalty and sacrifices in fulfilling their matches and attending our meetings.
>
> At our last Annual General Meeting it appeared we were to have our strongest Intermediate League for a good many seasons with the following clubs:
>
> Rastrick, Meltham, Moldgreen, Netherton, Slaithwaite, Underbank, Deighton, David Brown & Sons and Waterloo, but on the outbreak of the War, Slaithwaite, Underbank and Waterloo could not run due to conscription, etc, and we started the season with six clubs.
>
> It was decided to play each other four times in the League, play the Yorkshire Intermediate Cup and our District cups.

Up to December all engagements were fulfilled without trouble, then D Brown & Sons had to withdraw due to the extensive overtime worked by the firm, depriving them of their players.

Their matches had to be expunged from the table leaving five clubs to finish the season, which they did, and in addition, played through the cup-ties for the Rose Bowl.

I also arranged matches with different Regimental Units, who were very delighted to obtain matches with us.

I took a League Team to play the local Territorial Unit at Otley, and we had a very happy time and were entertained by the OC, officers and men.

All our clubs played the 287 AA Battery up to December until their removal from the district.

The terrible weather in the New Year made matters worse, and it appeared that the clubs would cease to exist.

Here again, with a further effort, I was able to get them going, and they fulfilled all their League fixtures … nine players have been dismissed from the field, this I consider very low to say that the clubs have played each other at least four times.

We made good repairs to the field at Netherton which has been in the League's hands for many years, and it is hoped to continue to hold this field for future use.

The Netherton club has taken on a new lease of life and is likely to be a good club once again.

Rastrick are yet the best club we have … Moldgreen continue to produce boys from nowhere and keep a good playing side season after season.

Deighton have done wonderfully well for a new club in their first season, and there would appear to be plenty of scope in this district for players and more than one club could be run if workers could be found.

Meltham have gone to seed and only one worker is left, it would be difficult to reorganise at this once-strong centre … Underbank, Slaithwaite and D Brown & Sons cannot be reorganised until after this War has been won.

No good purpose can be served by prophesying what will be done in this District in the future, and if there is any point upon which you require any information I can supply, I will do so upon hearing from you.

The decline in playing numbers had not sufficiently reversed by 1945 for the open-age section to resume. Some men were still to be demobilised from the forces, some had been permanently incapacitated, some had lost a large proportion of their rugby careers to the war and were now too old or disinclined to play, and, of course, some would never return. Available players were restricted to playing for the Huddersfield 'A' team or to amateur clubs from outside the district. Some of these players were then also lost to the local clubs for good. The floundering Huddersfield and District League did not begin to recover its pre-war strength until the 1947-48 season, when some amateur clubs were able to re-form.

During this paucity of local 13-a-side rugby, seven-a-side tournaments – more practical given the reduced numbers required – became very popular. Such competitions were played at Fartown in April and May, proved very attractive to spectators, and raised funds for the League. Teams from other districts were encouraged to enter and in the 1946 sevens competition, Batley Carr beat Buslingthorpe Vale in the final to win the Sam Wood Cup, awarded by Jeff Bawden, Huddersfield's prolific try scoring wingman.

Another Post-War Boom

Sustained by the sevens tournaments, local amateur rugby league snowballed after 1947. In 1950-51 the Huddersfield and District League had 31 teams, with open-age, under-21, under-18 and under-16 sections all operating successfully. Netherton was one of the most prominent clubs in the first half of the 1950s, equalling Rastrick's four consecutive Holliday Cup wins and dominating the open-age section.

Netherton, the strongest club in the district, ran two teams in 1949-50, their open-age team enjoying the first of a record-equalling four consecutive Holliday Cup triumphs

The League celebrated its Golden Jubilee in 1958 with a hugely successful county seven-a-side competition at Fartown, over 2000 supporters watching Reckitts from Hull win the final. Guests at the League's Celebration Dinner, held on 29 April at Heywood's Café, were entertained by principal speakers C Horsfall, Chairman of the RFL, Bill Fallowfield, RFL Secretary, and Eddie Waring, then the Northern Sports Editor for the BBC.

In the early years of the 1960s Moldgreen became the leading club in the district. They won the Holliday Cup in 1961-62 and reached the final qualifying round of the Challenge Cup in 1962-63. Drawn to play York Imperial, the tie was postponed several times because of the weeks of freezing conditions that afflicted the country. It was eventually played at Widnes, but it was the York side that triumphed, 9-0, to progress to the first round.

In 1963, surprising many in the amateur game, the Huddersfield and District League amalgamated with the Halifax District League to form the Huddersfield and Halifax Joint League. This initiative was considered a big success as it provided clubs with a greater variety of competition than was possible in a single town.

In the late 1960s Tom Keaveney, the Huddersfield and District League secretary, actively encouraged local youth clubs to field teams. As a result the under-19 and under-17 sections of the Joint League went from strength to strength. St Joseph's was the dominant open-age club at this time. They enjoyed successful runs in the Yorkshire Cup, reaching the final in 1973 when they were beaten 31-7 by West Hull.

Crosland Moor, Huddersfield and District League Champions 1958-59.
Their coach, back left, was former Huddersfield player Peter Gronow,
son of the Team of all Talents' Ben Gronow.

The number of amateur clubs was, however, once again declining rapidly across the game. Tom Keaveney believed that, with greater assistance from the RFL, more junior teams would participate in the district league competitions. Instead, the RFL had stopped grants to fund kit for amateur clubs. There was a groundswell of opinion that lack of support from the RFL was a major cause of the crisis in the amateur game.

Birkby Civic Youth Club Under-17s, 1963.
The tallest player in the centre is future Huddersfield prop forward Ian Van Bellen,
who made his first team debut at Fartown a few months later.

The Birth of BARLA

To address this widespread disillusionment, Tom Keaveney and two of his Huddersfield and District League colleagues, Jack Clayton and Maurice Oldroyd, instigated a meeting on 4 March 1973 at Greenside Working Men's Club in Huddersfield. The meeting was momentous for the amateur leagues, who voted almost unanimously to form the British Amateur Rugby League Association (BARLA), effectively removing administration of the amateur game from the RFL. In hindsight, Maurice Oldroyd regretted not imbuing this meeting with even greater historical significance by holding it at the George Hotel.

Tom Keaveney, who was awarded the MBE for his services to amateur rugby league

The timing was unfortunate for Maurice, who had progressed through the ranks of referees, and at the time of the BARLA breakaway had been appointed to take charge of a prestigious junior international between the RFL's youth team and the Australian Schoolboys. Maurice recalled:

> When the RFL realised that I was involved with the breakaway, they replaced me with Billy Thompson 48 hours before the game. I'd stuck my neck out and got my head chopped off!

Maurice, who was Chairman and Press Officer of the Huddersfield Referee's Society, had no hard feelings towards Billy Thompson, describing him and his colleagues Mick Beaumont and Clarrie Sutcliffe as …

> … real characters and great referees. Billy was world-class. The Australians even flew him out to referee the very first State of Origin game between New South Wales and Queensland.

As one door closed another one opened, and Maurice was appointed as Treasurer of BARLA, with Tom Keaveney as Secretary. Maurice recalled:

> Tom was wheelchair-bound, but a formidable negotiator, Jack Clayton worked for the council so he had contacts and knew his way round the bureaucracy, and altogether we were a good team.

From an initial bank balance of £25, BARLA gradually expanded. Later in the decade an office was established in Huddersfield and Maurice was appointed the Association's full-time National Administrator.

BARLA takes on the Establishment

To achieve its task of reviving amateur rugby league, it was essential that BARLA was recognised and accepted by the RFL. In 1973, the RFL voted 29-1 to reject BARLA, but from the meeting it was clear that BARLA had two powerful allies in Huddersfield's Hubert Lockwood, the RFL Chairman, and Tom Mitchell, the driving force behind Workington's post-war successes. Campaigning by these two and by the BARLA officials reversed the vote in 1974, the RFL voting unanimously to accept and work with BARLA.

Having tackled the RFL, BARLA's next target was the government after Maurice read that a national dance group had received a grant from the Sports Council. He realised that BARLA's key to unlocking public funds was the community of volunteers working right across the amateur game.

> Volunteering has kept amateur clubs going across all sports for many decades. As a purely amateur body, separate from the RFL, we were well-placed to apply for grants.

The breakthrough was a grant for £2000 from the Sports Council to take the amateur international team to France. Other grants snowballed from there. About three or four years later we took our Great Britain team to Australia, New Zealand, Papua New Guinea, Samoa, Tonga and Fiji.

BARLA also set about ending rugby union's life-bans on anyone who had played amateur rugby league. Maurice recalled that the intransigent RFU was eventually undone by the tenacity of the BARLA officials.

We met their big gun, Brigadier Dennis Shuttleworth, in the Hilton at Leeds – we were taking on the establishment. We presented our case, they thought a bit, then the Brigadier said "Maurice, we've heard everything you've said and we can either make a decision or not, and we're pretty damned good at the latter." I couldn't help but smile.

Nothing changed in 1973 but we won the battle in the end, in 1988, after fifteen years of letter-writing. We got the Sports Council involved and the rugby union were politely told that if they didn't allow free movement of amateur players, there was no public money! Q.E.D.

The Pennine and National Leagues

Meanwhile, BARLA had considerably expanded its activities and amateur rugby league was beginning to thrive again. The amateur tour of Australasia in the late 1970s was the tip of a growing iceberg. In five years from 1973 the number of amateur clubs doubled to over 300, there were over 20 district leagues and a national knockout competition. Clubs were being founded in the Midlands, Wales and the south of England. By 1990 BARLA had over 500 member clubs.

Locally, the revitalised open-age section of the Huddersfield and Halifax League merged with leagues in Bradford, Oldham and Rochdale to form the Pennine League. This new regional league stimulated interest by providing fixtures for clubs of all abilities and strengths.

Following the formation of the Pennine League, Underbank dominated the local open-age scene, producing a number of players for the Huddersfield club and winning the Holliday Cup three seasons in a row in the late 1970s. In the early 1980s the Huddersfield League introduced a Supplementary Cup, a competition that was run on a handicapped basis and provided opportunities for some of the less successful clubs to reach a final.

Moldgreen, centenary winners of the Holliday Cup at Fartown in 1985

In 1986 BARLA formed a National League for amateur clubs, a pyramid structure through which clubs could progress. It has been hugely successful, providing the best amateur clubs in the country with a level of competition that improves playing standards. The prerequisite that clubs meet minimum standards to join this League has driven up the quality of playing facilities. With support from the RFL and with the co-operation of BARLA, the National League became the National Conference League in 1993.

Moldgreen, the strongest club in the Huddersfield and District League at that time, was one of the founder members of the National Conference League. They were promoted to Division One in 1993-94 and reached the third round of the Challenge Cup in 1997, losing to Featherstone Rovers 48-14, a margin that did scant justice to Moldgreen's battling display. Sadly Moldgreen were forced to withdraw from the National Conference League at the end of the 1997-98 season.

A second Huddersfield club joined the National Conference League in 2002. Formed at Huddersfield YMCA and called Huddersfield Sharks, the club moved to Syngenta Sports Club on Leeds Road but struggled to attract enough quality players to compete successfully and was forced to withdraw from the League in 2006.

Initially, after the professional game adopted a February to October season in 1996, the amateur game continued its traditional winter season. This began to change with the introduction in 2003 of the Rugby League Conference for amateur clubs that wished to play in the summer. Underbank Rangers took the plunge and, in addition to its winter commitments, entered a team into the Rugby League Conference's Premier Division. When the National Conference League switched to the summer in 2011, Underbank moved its summer team into Division 3, confident that they could compete after reaching the Rugby League Conference Grand Final in 2009, which they lost 38-22 to Bramley Buffaloes. They soon appeared in two further finals, lifting the trophy with a 40-18 win over Kippax Knights in 2011, and losing 17-10 to Hemel Hempstead Stags in 2012.

Maurice Oldroyd, fourth from the left, at the unveiling of the plaque to celebrate Underbank Rangers' 125th anniversary in 2009. Maurice captained Underbank in the 1960s. Also present are, left to right, Darrel Turner (Mayor's Consort), Julie Stewart-Turner (Mayor of Kirklees), Neil Fox MBE (former Underbank coach and rugby league's all-time record points-scorer), Paul Dixon (Underbank, Huddersfield and Great Britain), Dave Berry (Chairman, Underbank Rangers), Bob Mortimer (Chairman, Huddersfield and District Amateur Rugby League) and Gerald Parr (President, Underbank Rangers).

Huddersfield and District's Amateur Rugby Union Teams 1848-95, and Northern Union/Rugby League teams 1895-present.

Of these 100 teams, the eight teams in bold were playing in 2015, all eight competing in the 2015 Holliday Cup competition.

Almondbury
Armitage Bridge
Birkby
Birkhouse Rangers
Bradley
Bradley Civic Youth Club
Brighouse Rangers
Brighouse St James
Britannia Works (Hopkinson's)
Brook Motors
Brookfoot
Central Iron Works (Thomas Broadbent's)
Central Lads' Club
Cowcliffe St Mark's
Crosland Moor
Crosland Moor Juniors
David Brown & Sons (Park Works)
Deighton
Deighton Civic Youth Club
Emley Moor
5th Duke of Wellington's W Riding Regiment
Flockton
Golcar
Great Northern Street
Hepworth
Highfield Rangers
Hillhouse and Birkby
Hillhouse Congregational
Hillhouse Free Wesleyans
Hillhouse Star
Holmbridge
Holmfirth
Holset Engineering
Honley
Honley Clarence
Huddersfield Clarence
Huddersfield Crescent
Huddersfield C & AC 'A'/Colts
Huddersfield (C & AC) Supporters
Huddersfield Hornets
Huddersfield St Josephs
Huddersfield Sharks
Huddersfield Technical College
Huddersfield Wanderers
Kirkburton
Kirkburton Black Watch
Kirkburton Rovers
Kirkheaton
Leeds Road
Leeds Road Clarence

Leymoor
Lightcliffe Road Juniors
Lindley
Lindley Swifts
Linthwaite
Lockwood
Lockwood Church Choir
Lockwood Crescent
Lockwood Rangers
Longwood
Marsden
Marsh
Meltham
Meltham All Blacks
Meltham Mills
Milnsbridge
Moldgreen
Netherthong
Netherton
Nethroyd Hill
Newsome Clarence
Newsome Panthers
Northgate Juniors
Northumberland Street Rangers
Nortonthorpe
Outlane
Paddock
Primrose Hill
Rastrick
Rastrick United
Scapegoat Hill
Scissett
Shelley
Shepley
Shorehead
Skelmanthorpe
Slaithwaite
Slaithwaite Clarence
Slaithwaite Hornets
Slaithwaite Juniors
Slaithwaite Saracens
St Augustine's
St Joseph's
St Patrick's
St Paul's
St Thomas's
Underbank Rangers
Waterloo
Waverley
Wooldale United

Holliday Cup Records				
Most Wins		**Most Consecutive Wins**		
St Joseph's	14	Rastrick	1937-38 to 1940-41	(4)
Underbank Rangers	13	Netherton	1949-50 to 1952-53	(4)

Underbank Rangers v Newsome Panthers in the 2012 Holliday Cup semi-final

Players Who Progressed from Local Amateur Clubs to become Internationals				
Player	**Local Club**	**Country**	**Debut Opponents**	**Year**
Harry Huth	Huddersfield C & AC	England RU	Scotland	1879
Ernest Woodhead	Huddersfield C & AC	England RU	Ireland	1880
Jack Dyson	Skelmanthorpe	England RU	Scotland	1890
Milford Sutcliffe	Nethroyd Hill	England		
Percy Holroyd	Paddock	England	Australia	1908
Harold Wagstaff	Underbank Rangers	England	Australia	1908
Stanley Moorhouse	Hillhouse Congregational	England	Australia	1914
Dick Cracknell	Central Iron Works	Great Britain	New Zealand	1951
Frank Dyson	Central Iron Works	Great Britain	Australia	1959
Ken Senior	Moldgreen	Great Britain	New Zealand	1965
Bob Irving	St Joseph's	Great Britain	France	1967
Henderson Gill	Huddersfield Supporters	England	Wales	1981
Paul Dixon	Underbank Rangers	Great Britain	France	1987
Anthony Farrell	Huddersfield Colts	England Wales	Australia Cook Islands	1995 2000
Keith Senior	Milnsbridge	Great Britain	Fiji	1996
Darren Fleary	Moldgreen	Great Britain	New Zealand	1998
Paul Reilly	Moldgreen	England	France	2004
Eorl Crabtree	Underbank Rangers	England	Russia	2004
Marcus St Hilaire	Moldgreen	Ireland	Wales	2009
Leroy Cudjoe	Newsome Panthers	England	Australia	2010

The Huddersfield League clubs that continue to play in the winter have had some successes in the the Pennine League and the BARLA Yorkshire Cup, notably Lindley which won the Yorkshire Cup in 2001 with a thrilling 16-11 victory over Hunslet Warriors. Moldgreen and Slaithwaite have followed Underbank's example and begun to play summer rugby as part of the recently formed Yorkshire Men's League. Meanwhile, the local cup competitions are still played annually. The Holliday Cup Final, usually played at Easter, continues its traditional importance in the town's sporting calendar.

The British Amateur Rugby League Association

A Royal Souvenir

Sponsored by British Nuclear Fuels

Official Opening by:
HER MAJESTY THE QUEEN
of
BARLA'S HEADQUARTERS
West Yorkshire House, Huddersfield
on
30th November 1990

BARLA's souvenir brochure commemorating the opening of their new
headquarters at West Yorkshire House, New North Road, Huddersfield,
by Her Majesty the Queen on 30 November 1990

BARLA's administrative base remains in Huddersfield, in headquarters opened by Her Majesty the Queen in 1990. In 2013 long-serving Huddersfield and District League official, Sue Taylor, was appointed as BARLA's first-ever woman Chair, a further sign of the growing role of women in the game and in society. Sue followed husband John's playing career at a string of local clubs – Underbank, St Joseph's, Paddock and Moldgreen – and in 1989 the couple set up Newsome Magpies, which is still going strong as Newsome Panthers. She described her progression through the administrative ranks.

> I went round the touchline selling raffle tickets, got the food ready for the players and took the minutes of meetings. At Underbank I was secretary for a time and I did similar jobs at St Joseph's and Paddock. I then became treasurer and secretary of the Huddersfield Amateur League and later the Pennine League.

The impact on rugby league of BARLA is incalculable, but this brainchild of its Huddersfield pioneers, Tom Keaveney, Jack Clayton and Maurice Oldroyd, ranks alongside Super League and summer rugby in the great rugby league innovations of modern times.

The Huddersfield and District League too continues. It has, since 1908, provided the opportunity for thousands of young men to play amateur rugby league, and has supplied many players for the town's senior club, some of whom have gone on to play for their country. Eorl Crabtree and Leroy Cudjoe are two current internationals who signed for Huddersfield Giants after playing junior rugby for Huddersfield-based amateur clubs.

Amateur rugby league in Huddersfield has a proven resilience, surviving and recovering from several buffetings since the explosion of clubs in the 1880s. The continual need to inspire the next generation of youngsters has not changed since then, but the challenges in doing so have. Where once providing the basic kit was the main issue, now the challenge is to compete for youngsters' time and attention with the multiple distractions of the digital age. Role models at the Huddersfield Giants, leadership from BARLA and the RFL, the Giants' community organisation, and the structural pathways for clubs, players and coaches, all have their part to play. But the common thread, unchanged since the 1880s, is the need for volunteers to run the amateur clubs. The number of local clubs has been stable at eight for several years, testimony to their consistency of effort in organising teams and in coping with that relatively new phenomenon for amateur sport, eye-watering levels of bureaucracy. The administrative burden has increased partly because more clubs have developed clubhouses that include a social club, and partly because of edicts, mainly from central Government about health and safety, child protection and standards that must be met to access grants.

There will always be scope for more clubs, but Huddersfield has a well-run, hard-working core flying the flag, assisting the development of the district's young players and perpetuating the game.

Chapter 12

A Sport for All:
Women's and Schools' Rugby League

Huddersfield Schools' Rugby League

The Huddersfield and District League's emphasis on youth from its inception in 1908 was consolidated by the development of Northern Union rugby in local schools prior to World War I. By 1913, a competition for local schools, the Hoyle Cup, had been introduced. In the 1913 final, a curtain-raiser to a Huddersfield first team match at Fartown, South Crosland beat Hillhouse Council School 21-3. As champions of Huddersfield, South Crosland qualified for the Yorkshire Schools Cup, and defeated two Leeds schools, Kirkstall Road and Jack Lane, to reach the final.

The South Crosland boys had the thrill of playing in front of a huge crowd as the curtain-raiser to the League Championship Final between Huddersfield and Wigan at Wakefield Trinity's Belle Vue ground. Hull Lincoln Street provided the opposition. In 'a ding dong struggle' South Crosland took an early lead with a converted try, but two unconverted tries gave the Hull side a 6-5 lead at half time. There was no further score until the final minute when a South Crosland try sealed an 8-6 victory to become the first school from Huddersfield to be crowned Yorkshire Champions. South Crosland continued their domination of the local schools competition in 1914, winning the Hoyle Cup for the second year in succession.

An official at the 1913 Hoyle Cup Final suggested that enthusiasm for Northern Union in local schools was outstripping the available facilities, most specifically that a shortage of playing fields was impeding the development of the game.

There are no records of local schools' competitions during World War I, but on 8 April 1918 the *Huddersfield Daily Examiner* (*HDE*) reported a schoolboys' match between Huddersfield and Wigan. It was refereed by Harold Wagstaff, who was somewhat affronted when one of the boys not only challenged a decision, but contemptuously sneered 'What do you know about the game?'

In 1919 a number of teachers from rugby-playing schools met at Fartown and formed a committee which was tasked with the organisation of inter-schools fixtures, the Hoyle Cup and the Town Boys team. Ten schools took part in the 1919 Hoyle Cup and more were attracted over the next two years so that, in 1921, the competition was split into two sections to accommodate them. Meanwhile, the representative team, the Town Boys, played fixtures against other schools associations.

In the mid-1920s Hillhouse Central was the dominant school in Huddersfield and emulated South Crosland's pre-war success by winning the Yorkshire Cup in 1926. The Huddersfield senior club, appreciating the value of the sport to the boys and to the long-term prosperity of the club, was very supportive throughout the decade. They allowed Fartown to be used for matches and for occasional training sessions. In addition, collections and curtain-raisers were held at Huddersfield's matches, and the activities of the Schools Rugby League were covered in the club's match-day programme notes.

In the 1930s, a sharp decline in the number of local schools and amateur clubs playing rugby league was largely explained by the Great Depression. The families of many boys who wanted to play could not afford to buy rugby boots. To address this, the Association allocated the money raised from one of the curtain-raisers at Fartown to buy boots for schools. As the economic situation improved, an under-11 league was formed and the number of schools playing in the senior schools' and under-11 sections began to increase. It seemed that the next major disruption to continuity and progress was never far away, and at the outbreak of World War II in 1939 formal schools' competitions were suspended. Delayed post-war by rationing and austerity, the competitions did not resume for eight years, pretty much the entire school life of children born during the Great Depression.

In 1947 the schools' competitions were kick-started by grants to the Schools' Association of £40 from Yorkshire Schools and £30 from the Huddersfield club. Kit remained an issue as clothing coupons were required for the purchase of shirts, but the number of inter-school fixtures increased, the Town Boys team was re-formed, and in 1949 an under-13 league was introduced. Reflecting the sporting boom of the late 1940s and early 1950s, a number of senior schools began to field two teams, and a shortage of pitches once again became an issue. To assist, the Huddersfield club allowed Fartown to be used one evening per week and the Education Committee made available two pitches on Leeds Road Playing Fields.

From a high point of participation in the early 1950s, changes to the education system wrought a decline in schools' rugby. As Secondary Modern Schools and 'Comprehensive' schools were created, a number of strong rugby league schools closed or amalgamated with other schools. The strength of the schools' game in the early 1950s led, towards the end of the decade, to the founding of youth leagues and junior clubs, backed by the Huddersfield District League. Some of these new clubs had a negative impact on the senior schools' competition as boys were encouraged to play for their club rather than their school.

During the 1960s it became increasingly difficult to persuade schools to take part in inter-schools fixtures. Some of the new High Schools, such as Colne Valley and Honley, were more interested in playing rugby union, which was unfortunate when the majority of local opportunities to play rugby on leaving school were in rugby league. At the same time, the Huddersfield club was also reducing its support for schools' rugby league. The Town Boys team, which won the Sproxton (Yorkshire County) Cup in 1959 and 1963, was able to function but the number of schools providing players for the team continued to decline.

In 1966, local boy Russell Mulvihill of St Augustine's played against France Schools in the first international of a new body, the English Schools Rugby League (ESRL), which had taken over the organisation of the game in schools. The ESRL was, however, unable to arrest the slide. By the early 1970s, schools' rugby league in Huddersfield, and elsewhere, was in serious decline. Fewer teachers had the time or the energy to organise school teams. The British Amateur Rugby League Association (BARLA), founded in 1973, attempted to bridge the gap by establishing an under-16 league which also had a massive impact on schools' fixtures.

By the mid-1980s inter-school fixtures had all but disappeared. The ESRL and the Huddersfield Schools' RL both folded, and the Town Boys team only limped along for a few more seasons because of the involvement of officials from the Huddersfield District League. If any final nails in the coffin of schools rugby league were needed, they were hammered home by three policies from central Government.

Firstly, during the 1980s, the Government chose to sell many school playing fields to private developers. This was followed by the introduction of the National Curriculum and OFSTED inspections in the early 1990s, both of which deluged teachers with new mountains of bureaucracy. The communications revolution had equipped the Department for Education with a capacity to produce and disseminate material like never before. Many of the new initiatives were worthy in isolation, but there was no joined-up thinking about their sudden cumulative effect on the workload of teachers. Many teachers felt that they were committing more time to justifying the existence of Whitehall bureaucrats and less time working for the benefit of the children in their care. Frequent comments from Government Ministers that undermined teachers' authority and implied a lack of trust in their commitment and professionalism intensified the pressure to achieve a good report from the next OFSTED inspection. Whilst some of the new paperwork was a legal requirement, much of it was purely to provide evidence for the next inspection, and had little or no impact on the children. To add insult to injury, whilst inspectors might check that the paperwork was in place, there was so much of it that most of it went unread.

These impositions took precedence over the unpaid voluntary time that teachers had previously committed to extra-curricular activities, distorting their priorities and withering their goodwill. Across the country, and particularly in primary schools, teachers reduced or terminated the extra-curricular activities they ran, many of them with a heavy heart after seeking direction from their headteacher or union official. The impact on sport in schools was devastating. For schools' rugby league in Huddersfield, any lingering hopes that it might once again flourish as it had in the 1920s and 1950s, with many schools participating in season-long competitions across different age groups, were over.

In 2015, schools in Huddersfield still play some rugby league, but the lessons, extra-curricular practices and matches are mainly arranged by Huddersfield Community Trust, the community arm of Huddersfield Giants RLFC and Huddersfield Town FC. Informal tournaments are popular, and a few local schools enter the RFL's annual 'Champion Schools' competition, won in 2013 by Honley High School's Year 8 team. Meanwhile the huge pressure on teachers to attend meetings and complete onerous administrative tasks, in addition to preparing lessons and marking work, continues to torpedo any possibility that regular inter-school fixtures will return.

Women's Rugby League

The first mention of women in relation to local rugby football comes from a report of Huddersfield's match against Leeds Grammar School Football Club in April 1870.

> A large group of spectators were in and about the grounds including several groups of ladies; and the oft-repeated bursts of cheering and waving of handkerchiefs sufficiently evinced their interest in the game.

Women were an integral part of the football crowds of this period, as Tony Collins, in *Rugby's Great Split*, pointed out.

> ... women's attendance at matches may have been encouraged by the fact that most grounds allowed women into matches free ...

Free entry of women to matches, common practice as early as the 1860s at club cricket matches in industrial Yorkshire and Lancashire, was one of numerous transferrable customs that cross-pollinated the cultures and traditions of cricket, association football and rugby football.

Tony Collins' assertion that: 'many women were active spectators and keen supporters of their chosen teams', is substantiated by the intimidating conduct of the female supporters of Hipperholme and Lightcliffe RFC. The *Todmorden Advertiser* reports that, on Christmas Day 1886, the referee was menaced into awarding Hipperholme a controversial try by their notorious followers, 'a group of formidable and vociferous women' known as 'the Amazons.' These women became ever louder as the lack of seasonal cheer degenerated into a mass brawl between the Hipperholme and Todmorden players and the match was abandoned.

By 1900 most clubs were charging women for admission, but at Huddersfield such charges were only applied at big matches. On 13 November 1909 the club responded in its programme notes to criticism of this apparent unfairness:

> I have always advocated free admission for ladies. Their presence subdues, and keeps in check, language which the ''lords of creation'' might otherwise use too liberally. Besides, they brighten the appearance of any gathering, for you must admit there is nothing very picturesque in the clothes of the ordinary man, even if you have 10,000 together. I hope our lady supporters may increase and continue to add colour and charm to our crowds.

Huddersfield's female supporters were apparently of a more gentile nature than those at Hipperholme. The club appealed to them directly on 5 March 1910, a week before a cup-tie against Ebbw Vale:

> To our Lady Supporters. The Committee, I am pleased to state, have reduced the price of admission for ladies to the Ebbw Vale cup-tie as follows – Terrace Side 6d, Pavilion side 6d, Covered Stand 1/- extra, and no extra charge is made for the uncovered stand. Ladies have free admission to league games as before.

The committees of sports' clubs were, for decades, all-male preserves. At first this was not so much a sporting tradition as an assumption of a male-dominated society. But sport became increasingly stuck in the past as women took opportunities to prove their organisational and administrative skills in other areas of society. Even the majority of women's teams in association football and cricket were organised by men.

Women on the Huddersfield Supporters' Club Committees

The Huddersfield Cricket and Athletic Club (HC and AC) was no more or less enlightened than the rest of the sporting world. The Supporters' Club, founded by about 50 members of the HC and AC on 6 June 1921, became the first committee in rugby league to allow women members – in 1954!

The courageous pioneers, Nancy Beaumont and her friend, Elsie Shaw, were in their usual spot on the Fartown terraces when they were approached by a Supporters' Club committeeman, suggesting that they should be co-opted onto the Social Committee. Seven ladies were co-opted, of whom Nancy and Elsie were allowed to attend full committee meetings, with voting rights. At the next AGM all seven ladies were elected to the Supporters' Club Committee. The ladies did most of the digging as foundations were laid for a tea hut, from which they served refreshments for many years.

Nancy Beaumont took over as Supporters' Club treasurer in 1961 and was President in 1967 and 1968, the first lady President of any rugby league organisation. Among her many duties, she ran the club's lottery for 26 years.

Nancy Beaumont (second left) and the ladies who ran Fartown's terrace side tea hut

In 1996 Nancy founded the Senior Supporters' Association which has become an institution in the game. Their meetings on the first Wednesday afternoon of the month continue to attract high-quality speakers and 70 to 80 members. At one of these, in May 2013, Giants' Chief Executive Richard Thewlis announced that Nancy had been awarded the club's ultimate honour of life-membership.

One of the Senior Supporters' Association's more unusual meetings was to celebrate the 70th birthday and 50 years of supporting Huddersfield, of Nancy's friend, Joyce Rushforth. For the occasion, Nancy wrote and recited the following poem, cataloguing their rugby league experiences.

157

Joyce at Fartown
by
Nancy Beaumont

Joyce first arrived at Fartown
With her Uncle Fred,
"Give it go, you'll like it,
And come with me," he said.

It was a fish to water,
She was hooked in every way,
And fifty years along the line,
She still is there today.

It was a different game to now,
I'm sure you'll all agree,
For when the players scored a try,
The points were only three.

And then we had the drop goals,
Which were very, very few,
Which really was a pity,
Because the points were two.

We'd referees – George Phillips,
Matt Coates, Billy Thompson too,
Sartorially elegant,
In blazers navy blue.

And when the players scored a try,
They didn't draw a square,
They simply blew their whistles,
And pointed straight down there.

We always played on Saturdays,
Each team kicked off the same,
For there was no confusion,
Until Sky came to our game.

We'd Featherstone and Widnes,
And good old Barrow too,
For Bulls and Bears and Rhinos,
Were something in a zoo.

Oh what a hardy breed we were,
We stood in rain and snow,
At times we were so frozen,
We could hardly feel our toes.

But the football was exciting,
You soon forgot the pain,
When Cooper started scoring tries,
Who cared about the rain?

One day whilst on the terrace,
We had a conversation,
With a man from the Supporters' Club,
Who gave an invitation.

I think you girls are wasted,
It really is a pity,
Come to the annual meeting,
And stand for the committee.

There was a huge furore,
I tell you not a fib,
But we were in, we'd cracked it,
We were Fartown's women's lib.

So then we started working,
In the terrace side wood hut,
And we were like the Windmill,
For we never ever shut.

To keep the terrace-siders warm,
We never seemed to fail,
We served them piping cups of soup,
The flavour was oxtail.

And we had our little bus,
Which travels far and near,
And we are always on it,
The Fartowners to cheer.

I remember one occasion,
The driver had been squinting,
The team were playing Salford,
And we arrived at Swinton.

The bus was run by Norman,
A Fartowner sincere,
The only thing with Norman was,
He'd never tasted beer.

And when a cry came from the back,
Oh Norman hear my plea,
I am excruciated,
I am dying for a pee.

We always got the same reply,
"This bus I will not stop,
You lot sit there and suffer,
You should all keep off the pop."

In '92 we had a thought,
Our savings we would plunder,
So we could go on holiday,
And take a trip Down Under.

We travelled down to Melbourne,
To the Second Test,
The Pommies came out fighting,
Each man gave of his best.

We well and truly stuffed them,
Much to our delight,
If we live to be a hundred,
We won't forget that night.

Off we flew to Brisbane,
To a ground they call Lang Park,
It was an evening kick off,
And we played them in the dark.

But when the Aussies scored a try,
Supporters did not cheer,
They hurled their plastic glasses,
And showered us with beer.

We hurried from the stadium,
And didn't count the cost,
For we were very thankful,
That all we'd done was lost.

Arriving back in Huddersfield,
Some dreadful news we found,
Alas, we were all homeless,
We'd lost our Fartown ground.

They packed us off to Leeds Road,
To share a ground with Town,
It wasn't very nice there,
And we often wore a frown.

Off then to the stadium,
A Giant to become,
Which isn't very easy,
When you're only five feet one.

So that's it in a nutshell,
Fifty years gone in a flash,
Today we join together,
For Joyce's birthday bash.

At times we've been to heaven,
At others deep in pain,
But if we had our time to come,
We'd do it all again.

To be a good supporter,
You take the good with bad,
We've had our ups, we've had our downs,
But what a time we've had!

Alas, we're getting wrinkled,
And we are getting old,
But what a privilege to follow,
The claret and the gold.

So come and raise your glasses,
"To Joyce, so staunch and true",
I only wish dear Fartown,
Had ten thousand more like you.

The Pavilion, Fartown

Fartown Football Ground

Women's Sporting Liberation

Like Nancy, Elsie and their friends, after World War II female supporters across rugby league were elected to committees in greater numbers – albeit often in catering-related roles. Peter Crabtree, in a *Rugby League Magazine* article about Nancy in 1967, attempted to extol the virtues of women on club committees.

> It is certainly true that when it comes to fund raising, meal preparing and dish-washing, general enthusiasm and the hundred-and-one little jobs that crop up, the ladies will do a better job than the men.

The next major step for women was to play the game, a development which took off in earnest during the last two decades of the 20th century.

By 1980 society had come a long way since the *British Medical Journal*, a consistent 19th century opponent of rugby football, recommended in 1894 that women should not play any form of football as such 'reckless exposure to violence' was unsafe for their bodies.

Developments in women playing association football, and eventually rugby football, progressed in fits and starts, roughly in parallel with enlightenment about women's abilities, and with legislation granting more equal rights and freedoms. The first infrequent women's association football teams appeared in the 1880s, simultaneously with Acts of Parliament that improved women's rights in many areas of life. The first high-profile team, the British Ladies FC, was founded in 1894 and was possibly Suffragette-inspired. From about 1900, progress stalled until World War I, when women proved themselves more than capable of 'men's work' in a multitude of occupations. Numerous factories spawned association football teams whose charity matches attracted some huge crowds, notably one of 53,000 at Goodison Park to watch the outstanding Dick, Kerr Ladies of Preston play St Helens Ladies.

Huddersfield's first women's association club, Huddersfield Atalanta Ladies AFC, was founded in November 1920, and in their short existence raised over £2000 for local charities. On Good Friday 1921, 15,000 watched their first competitive match, a 1-0 win over Bath Ladies at Huddersfield Town's Leeds Road ground. Following a 3-1 defeat to St Helens Ladies at Thrum Hall, Atalanta hosted a French touring side drawn mainly from the Parisian club, Fémina, at Fartown on 18 May. It was the first major soccer occasion at the ground since the 1882 FA Cup semi-final. Atalanta lost 1-0, but the match raised £424 8s 6d for the Mayor's Distress Fund.

Huddersfield Atalanta AFC outside their clubhouse at Cowersley in 1921

Six members of the Huddersfield Ladies team which entered the English Ladies FA Cup in 1921-22

In 1921-22 Atalanta played a couple of prestigious matches against the all-conquering Dick, Kerr Ladies. They also entered the English Ladies FA Cup, beating a second local club, Huddersfield Ladies, in Round 1, and reaching the semi-finals before losing 4-0 to Doncaster and Bentley.

Women's football was rapidly growing beyond mere novelty value. In the eyes of a disconcerted FA, it had encroached too far onto their hitherto male-only preserve, and in December 1921 they banned women from playing on their grounds. Like most women's clubs, Atalanta ceased to exist in the 1920s. The FA ban was lifted in 1971 as women's football again took off, inspired by the women's liberation movement of the 1960s and by the England men's team winning the 1966 World Cup.

From the 1960s, there was no looking back for women in sport or in society. The England Women's FA was founded in 1969, the Women's FA Cup in 1971, the Women's World Cup and English League in 1992, and by 2002 association football was the most popular and fastest-growing sport for women in the UK.

Both codes of rugby began to follow in the association game's slipstream. By the mid-1960s, there had been numerous if isolated women's rugby league teams, including one at Thornhill near Dewsbury in 1964.

The Hellcats

In August 1979 a ladies' rugby league team was formed in Huddersfield. Coach Neil Whittaker and trainer Cyril Tunnacliffe led practice sessions on Graham's Field, Bradford Road, which had no changing rooms or washing facilities. The Supporters' Club took an interest in the team, the players enrolling as members and using the club's rooms for meetings and post-match hospitality.

Adopting the name 'Hellcats' – confirmed on a specially-made pin badge – the women took their competitive bow on 16 December 1979 against Beeston (Leeds) Ladies, the opposition augmented by five 15-year-old boys. The Hellcats lost 19-14, but features and photographs appeared in the *Huddersfield Examiner* and *Rugby Leaguer* magazine and the match generated considerable publicity for the club and the women's game.

It was followed by two fixtures against Pilkington Recs (St Helens). The Hellcats were dominant in the scrums but no match for the opposition in the open, losing 17-16 away and 16-3 at home. Local firm Ben Shaws then sponsored a trophy to be competed for by the Hellcats, Dewvance Tigers (Dewsbury) and Pilkington Recs. The Huddersfield women defeated Dewsbury home and away and drew 6-6 with Pilkington's at Leeds Road Playing Fields to win the trophy. Mick Rhodes, the Huddersfield Supporters' Club secretary explained:

> People start watching for a giggle, but they soon realise these girls are deadly serious. The coach doesn't make allowances for femininity; they want to play so they will learn to play properly. Once they are on the field in a competitive game it's no longer a novelty. They put that extra bit into every challenge.

The team played matches for charity and were totally self supporting, paying all their own expenses. They challenged the Huddersfield 'A' team, but the Huddersfield club would not promote it as a fixture so it was advertised as Hellcats v Huddersfield Reserves. International referee Billy Thompson took charge and, much to his disgust, was dumped in a large puddle after the match by some of the ladies. Undeterred, Thompson refereed a further game against a team of ex-Huddersfield and amateur men, which raised money for the Spina Bifida Association.

The women contacted several professional clubs about playing curtain-raisers and the first positive reply came from Bradford. Their game at Odsal on 13 April 1980, before Bradford Northern v Workington, was watched by a crowd of 6,000 and raised £119. Captained by Milly Garthwaite, Huddersfield beat opponents Dewsbury 21-3. Further games followed at Thrum Hall, Crown Flatt, Mount Pleasant and Watersheddings. An invitation was received from Blackpool Borough to play their ladies' team between the semi-final and final of the 1980 BARLA sevens' tournament at Borough Park. The Blackpool Supporters Club provided a cup for the match and presented the Huddersfield team with a gigantic stick of rock, which was later given to the children's ward at the Huddersfield Royal Infirmary.

In April 1980, an appeal was made in the *Rugby Leaguer* for anyone interested in forming a ladies team to contact the Huddersfield captain. At that time a team from Pontefract had been founded, increasing the number of 'serious' ladies' teams to four.

Not all were convinced that women's rugby would be much of a spectacle. In March 1981, the Huddersfield Rugby Club doctor, David Durie, responded to a feature in the *Yorkshire Post Magazine* about women's rugby union in Atlanta, USA. Despite its glib, sexist headline 'Happy Hookers of the Rugged Sex', the feature was broadly positive, but in the Huddersfield club's programme, Doctor Durie wrote:

> Women are only subtly aggressive, not usually openly so. And rugby is all about aggression; a male thing, a boastful, chest-thumping, bruising, herd dominating thing, an acceptable substitute for war. Ok for Tarzan, no good for Jane. There are not enough openly aggressive women to go around, and if there were, there would never be a serious possibility of there being enough strength and skill on display either. The girls back in Georgia are carrying out a life size male impersonation.

That afternoon the Huddersfield and Wigan players lived

Tony Johnson

The Hellcats, 1980

up to the male stereotype. After a first half of high and dangerous tackles, the match erupted into brawls and scuffles in the second. Tony Johnson, a strong-running back row forward of Jamaican descent, appeared to be a particular target and was floored four times by the Wigan players, assaults that can be viewed on an infamous You Tube video. Six players were sent off in the second half, three from either side, in a game described by Brian Batty in the *Daily Mail* as the 'Battle of Fartown.' Huddersfield won 9-7 and Tony Johnson withstood all provocation to be named man-of-the-match, his sporting reputation indelibly etched into the club's folklore.

Shortly afterwards, on Easter Tuesday 1981, the Hellcats played the Fartown Supporters' Old Crocks to raise funds for Holly Bank Special School. Sadly the Hellcats disbanded later in 1981 when a lack of fixtures and suitable training facilities proved too much, and the local women's game went into a four-year hibernation.

Huddersfield Sea Ossas and the First Women's League

During that time women's sport moved on, partly driven by the Sports Council's 'Sport for All' campaign, which promoted equal opportunities policies and practices. Consistent with these attempts to remove barriers to participation were the formations of the Women's Rugby Football Union in 1983 and, in 1985, the Women's Rugby Football League, which was affiliated to amateur rugby league's governing body, BARLA.

In March 1985 women's rugby league restarted in Huddersfield. Taking their lead from the marine-themed monikers bafflingly adopted by the Huddersfield club – 'Barracudas' for the first team and 'Piranhas' for the 'A' team – the re-formed women became the Huddersfield Sea Ossas. Neil Whittaker resumed his coaching duties, and they played one match before the season's end, beating Dudley Hill Ladies 28-4.

The women's first game of the 1985-86 season should have been at Thrum Hall against Halifax Ladies as a curtain-raiser to the first round Yorkshire Cup tie between the two senior clubs. Unfortunately only one Halifax girl turned up. Undeterred, the Sea Ossas split the team in half, one side putting on Halifax shirts. A touch judge from the main match refereed and the 'Halifax' side came out on top, much to the delight of the Thrum Hall faithful. A friendly match followed against Guiseley Angels on a bitterly cold afternoon that impeded ball handling but encouraged vigorous tackling. Several of the women were making their debuts, but 'stuck to their tasks and fitted in well', the Sea Ossas winning 18-10.

Michelle Wood, in the centre of the back row, with the England Women's 2005 World Cup squad

Tackling practice for Huddersfield women's team in 2012

Lacking the pattern of regular fixtures, playing numbers were not guaranteed and only twelve Huddersfield women travelled to play the Ossas' curtain-raiser against Keighley in December, prior to a Keighley v Wakefield Trinity fixture.

Later in the season there was a major development in the women's game when six teams, including Huddersfield, founded a new league. As this competition expanded year-on-year, Huddersfield was never one of the leading lights, but continued to operate at a time when the senior club in the town was struggling and interest in rugby league in Huddersfield was low. The women's team occasionally changed its name and headquarters, and for several seasons played as Huddersfield Ladies, based at Slaithwaite. Its best player, Michelle Wood, represented Great Britain in the 2005 World Cup in New Zealand. World Cups have been held in 2000, 2005, 2008 and 2013, organised by 'Women's and Girls' Rugby League', the international governing body which was established in 2000.

There is potential to develop women's rugby league further. In 2015 there were 34 women's teams across the country. A number of Huddersfield-based players represented Brighouse Rangers, the strongest local women's club, whose teams play in the Women's Amateur Rugby League Association League (WRLA) in the winter, and in the Women and Girls Rugby League in the summer. By 2015 plans were in place for the Huddersfield Ladies' team to be based at St Joseph's and to play in the WRLA in 2015-16.

Girls' Rugby League

Some of the women who play rugby league progressed from girls' rugby league, which operated very successfully from the late 1990s in Huddersfield, with girls' clubs at Huddersfield Sharks and St Joseph's. The revival of the senior men's club as Huddersfield Giants helped to stimulate interest, as did the 'Champion Schools' Competition. Some local secondary schools, notably Salendine Nook and All Saints, regularly entered girls' teams, giving many new players their first taste of rugby league. All Saints proved to be extremely competitive, reaching the national finals in three consecutive seasons, 2005-06 to 2007-08

A number of Huddersfield's women and girls have achieved representative honours. Emma Hodgson, a Giants supporter, played girls' rugby league for a number of years, took a break from the sport, then resumed her career at university where she was selected for England Students. A combative half back, Emma played for Brighouse on returning to Huddersfield, and was selected for Yorkshire after a trial match that she describes as the hardest she ever played in.

Yorkshire county rugby players: Lucy Eastwood (left), Emma Hodgson (centre) and Jenny Doughty (right), receiving the Yorkshire under-16s player-of-the-year award from Leeds Rhino's President Harry Jepson

Girls' rugby league: not for the faint-hearted! Determined tackles on St Joseph's players Brittany Webster (at Castleford's Wheldon Road ground, top) and Alys Senior (bottom).

In the early 21st century, St Joseph's emerged as the strongest local girls' club and was the Yorkshire girls' team-of-the-year in 2010. Their success owed much to the enthusiasm of coaches and organisers such as Steve Eastwood and Gail Doughty. Steve coached all the age groups from under-12 to under-16 and is very proud that some of the players moved on to play open age at Brighouse Rangers. Steve's daughter Lucy, a Yorkshire County stand-off, moved to Brighouse, her first open-age team, as a 16-year-old and more than holds her own in the women's game. Gail Doughty, one of the team managers at St Joseph's, was a driving force at the club, encouraging players to join and also ensuring that the teams were well organised. Her involvement was inspired by the enthusiasm for rugby league of her daughter, Jenny, who represented the club from the under-12 to under-16 age groups, for which she was also selected for Yorkshire, an honour that both Jenny and Gail regard as one of their proudest moments.

Playing at the old Fartown ground once graced by the Team of all Talents, the St Joseph's girls club has given opportunities for many girls to play the sport.

Top: Amy Plowman during and after a dive for the line at the Hunslet under-14s festival in 2010
Bottom, left to right: Patsy Briggs; Beth Swift; Emily Wilson in full flight at Fartown in 2013, and
Faye Hepworth in an under-14s match against Cramlington at Brighouse in 2011

Slaithwaite
Saracens
Under-10s,
an age group
in which
boys and
girls can play
on the same
teams.

Many of the women introduced to the sport through their involvement with the various schools', girls' and women's teams still make important contributions to rugby league. As this base of knowledge, experience and enthusiasm grows, the best days for women's rugby league in the town may lie in the future.

Chapter 13

Spiral of Decline

The bumper crowds enjoyed by spectator sports in the years immediately after the Second World War were a relatively short-lived phenomenon. Attendances began a long-term decline across association football, rugby league and cricket in the 1950s, affected by various social and technological developments. Television provided direct competition. The increase in motor car ownership considerably broadened the choice and geographical range of leisure activities, coinciding with and feeding the growing expectations among women about their quality of life, a long-overdue shift. For many non-sporting women there was a deepening belief that Saturday afternoon should be about more than looking after the home whilst their men went to watch and play sport. Between 1950 and 1960 the average attendance at professional rugby league matches halved from 9,600 to just over 4,800, the total figure plummeting by a further one and a half million between 1959 and 1964.

The clubs were in a financial trap between rising player payments and dwindling spectator income. Many of rugby league's own supporters thought the game was dying. Similar drops in spectator numbers were experienced by soccer and cricket. The end of the Entertainment Tax helped a little, but in all three sports the future increasingly lay in supplementing gate receipts with business sponsorship, merchandise and television broadcast income.

The spectacular fall of Bradford Northern sounded a loud warning across rugby league. From League Leaders in 1952, they declined to bottom (30th) ten years later, consigning them to Division 2 of the two division structure introduced in 1962-63. It was a self-feeding downward spiral ... poorer performances, leading to poorer crowds, therefore less money, leading to poorer players, leading to poorer performances ... that slid the club to the brink of oblivion. Just over ten years after Bradford's all-time record crowd of 69,429 watched their 3rd round Challenge Cup tie against Huddersfield in 1953, they hit their all-time record low when just 324 turned up to watch their defeat against Barrow in November 1963. A month later the money ran out. Bradford went into liquidation, resigned from the league and disbanded. Only an outstanding fundraising campaign led by former players Trevor Foster and New Zealander Joe Phillips, and the generosity of Bradford Council in keeping Odsal open, allowed the club to be readmitted to the League for the following season as Bradford Northern (1964).

Huddersfield was on a similar, if longer path, the initial impact of the decline in attendances cushioned by the good and then respectable performances of the team during the 1950s. After the club's last major success in 1961-62, the team and the club's finances mirrored the decline of the local textile industries whose factories had employed many of the club's supporters. The golden days of the Holliday family investment in the club were over. New sources of funding, such as the club's lottery, promoted energetically and successfully in local workplaces, and initiatives by the Supporters Club, provided only temporary respite. The shortage of funds and financial austerity was reflected in the steady deterioration of the Fartown ground, symbolic of the increasingly bleak state of the club.

Decline on the Field

For eleven seasons after winning the 1961-62 Championship, Huddersfield were, by and large, a mid-table team, and still attracted some highly talented players, if not so many as previously.

Two such were Dave Heppleston, signed from Shaw Cross Boys Club and Ken Senior from local club Moldgreen. Heppleston would be an unsung hero of the pack for the next 20 years, playing 374 matches for the club. Senior stayed until his retirement from first-team football in 1979 and was first choice on the left wing for most of that period. He represented Great Britain twice in 1965 and 1967, played for Yorkshire on two occasions and achieved the Huddersfield club record for a back of 474 appearances, scoring 212 tries. In 1999 he was among the 21 inductees to the Huddersfield Giants RLFC Hall of Fame. These two were joined at Fartown by Dave Valentine's younger brother, Robert, who signed from Hawick RUFC in December 1963. He played seven years at Fartown and won a Great Britain cap against the 1967 Australians.

Left: Ken Senior, a Great Britain international and Huddersfield's outstanding player for much of the 1960s and 70s. A one-club man, he signed for Huddersfield from Moldgreen in 1962 and played at Fartown until 1979. His 474 appearances for the first team are second only to Douglas Clark's 485.

Right: Dave Heppleston, who played 374 matches for Huddersfield from 1962 to 1981

In the first of several new initiatives intended to boost interest, attendances and finances, the RFL tinkered with the game's structure in 1962-63. The season began with a new competition, the Eastern Region Championship. Huddersfield won all eight group matches and beat Halifax in the semi-final before succumbing to Hull Kingston Rovers who were worthy winners of a close-fought Headingley final in November. In the following season, 1963-64, this competition was interspersed with League matches over several months. Huddersfield fell at the group stage, but hosted the final in which Halifax beat Castleford.

The Championship was also reorganised, the thirty clubs divided into a First Division of 16 and a Second Division of 14, based on their league positions in 1961-62. In 1962-63 Huddersfield never approached the heights of their championship season and even flirted with relegation before four successive home wins lifted them to ninth. The slide continued in 1963-64 when they were 14th, one place but a comfortable ten points above the two relegation places.

The two-division format did not improve the game's finances. Most clubs in Division 2, denied lucrative home matches against the leading teams and consigned to second-class status, were worse off, as Bradford's demise made only too clear. On 14 February 1964, only 18 months into the planned three-year experiment, the clubs voted 23-4 to scrap the third season and revert to one league.

Bradford re-built their team around the experience of Tommy Smales, who left Huddersfield in 1964. This brilliant strategist had made 295 appearances and scored 111 tries for Huddersfield, and earned the game's highest honours, including the captaincy of Great Britain, a position he regained in 1965. Huddersfield lost their other talisman, Peter Ramsden, at the same time. Granted a free transfer, he joined York. He had played for Huddersfield since 1951, making 246 appearances and scoring 54 tries.

The committee bolstered their ranks with Fijians Tomasi Naidole, Josefa Saukuru and John Ravitale, later joined by Tomasi Waqabaca, but the loss of Smales in particular was keenly felt and Huddersfield slipped to eighteenth in 1964-65.

A flimsy consolation was the RFL's latest innovation, a 'Bottom 14 Competition', designed to give the lower-placed clubs an end of season finale in parallel with the Top Sixteen Championship Play-Offs. Unsurprisingly, given its derogatory title, there was little enthusiasm for it. Four clubs – Bramley, Dewsbury, Liverpool City and Salford – conceded walkovers in the first round, and the competition was scrapped after just one season. Huddersfield beat Doncaster 13-3 in the final at Tattersfield to become its only winners.

Bob Hagan, an Australian international and more than competent centre, arrived in 1965 and stayed for three seasons, becoming club captain. But only fifteen local players were signed in the entire decade. Among the most successful of these were brothers Ian and Victor Van Bellen, Martin Calvert, Billy Pickup and Malcolm Branch.

Huddersfield improved to finish 11th in 1965-66. Brian Curry, who took over kicking duties from Frank Dyson in 1963, kicked 119 goals, second only to Len Killeen of St Helens. A month into the close season he joined Oldham, another significant loss. Curry would return to Fartown in 1971 as coach to the 'A' team, and briefly emerged from retirement during an October injury crisis. A substitute at Doncaster, he came on to kick two goals in a 12-4 win, taking his Huddersfield points tally from 999 to 1003 – 473 goals and 19 tries.

Brian Curry, Bob Hagan, Ken Senior, Martin Calvert and Mick Major

Billy Pickup   Ian Van Bellen

Television and Commercialisation

Not all of the RFL's experiments of the 1960s were unsuccessful and short-lived. In 1964-65 substitutes were allowed for the first time, following the example of soccer which first allowed substitutes in 1958. Two players, numbered 14 and 15, were nominated for each game, although at first they were only allowed to take to the field before the second half kicked off.

In October 1966 the four-tackle rule was introduced. An attempt to stop one team monopolizing possession for lengthy periods and frustrating the opposition – a key strength of Huddersfield's successful team of 1961-62 – this rule encouraged attacking play and speeded the game up considerably. It was increased to six tackles in 1972 to reduce the amount of kicking and to give teams a better chance of progressing into attacking areas of the pitch with each set, encouraging the game to flow.

Rugby league was not alone in its urgency to improve the spectacle. Professional cricket introduced three sponsored one-day limited overs competitions in ten years – the Gillette Cup in 1963, the John Player League in 1969 and the Benson and Hedges Cup in 1972. Many amateur cricket leagues followed suit and also became limited overs competitions. The Football League introduced a third competition, the League Cup, in 1960, as a midweek floodlit competition to help revitalise the game which had lost one million spectators in the previous twelve months. Boosted by England hosting and winning the 1966 World Cup, soccer's problems became less acute than those of rugby league and cricket.

In 1965, rugby league also introduced a new floodlit competition, in partnership with a new television channel, BBC2, which had been launched in 1964. The BBC2 Floodlit Trophy was the brainchild of the channel's director, naturalist David Attenborough, who perhaps discerned some endangered species in the world of rugby league. Televised sport was taking off. ITV's Saturday afternoon sport anthology *World of Sport* had recently begun its 20-year run as a rival to the BBC's *Grandstand*, which was first transmitted in 1958. This new rivalry helped the coffers of rugby league, as the BBC paid £31,423 for exclusive broadcast rights to the 1964-65 season. Even clubs that did not feature on television received £638, substantial and invaluable revenue at a time of falling gates.

The Floodlit Trophy matches were played on Tuesday evenings in the early part of the season, with the second half of one match broadcast live, invigorated by the infectious enthusiasm of commentator Eddie Waring. In the first season only eight clubs entered, seven of which had floodlights. In the second season more clubs entered. Several non-televised matches were played without floodlights, but the rush was on to install them. The RFL, encouraging support for the competition, offered loans to install floodlighting, and 21 clubs did so over the next four years,

One of these was Huddersfield. The Fartown floodlights were officially switched on by Robert Hanson, President of HC & AC, before the League game against Hull on 18 October 1967. Any dreams of a glorious televised launch had been scuppered a month earlier when Huddersfield's first Floodlit Trophy match resulted in comprehensive elimination, 16-0 at Halifax. The Floodlit Trophy ran annually until 1980 and proved to be a worthy venture, raising the profile of the game in addition to the direct benefits in finance and ground development.

Another new competition began in 1971, John Player extending their sponsorship to rugby league with the Player's No.6 Trophy, later known as the John Player Trophy, John Player Special Trophy and, from 1989, the Regal Trophy. Discontinued with the

Tommy Smales, captain of Bradford Northern and Great Britain, interviewed by Bill Fallowfield prior to *World of Sport*'s coverage of Hull KR v Bradford on 30 October 1965

advent of Super League in 1996, this competition coincided precisely with the least successful period of Huddersfield's history and the club made very little impression on it.

The first match at Fartown under floodlights, Huddersfield v Hull, Wednesday 18 October 1967

The First Sunday Matches

The encroachment of sport onto Sundays, another financially-motivated development, gathered momentum in the 1960s, made possible by declining church attendances and by more liberated attitudes to Victorian social constraints. Some amateur rugby league was played on Sundays from 1956, and in December 1967 the RFL sanctioned Sunday play by professional clubs. Cricket's John Player League was also a 'Sunday' League, and both sports were severely criticised from without and within. A few players refused to play on the Sabbath, some spectators refused to attend, and there were protests from the Lord's Day Observance Society. As it was illegal to sell tickets for Sunday matches, admission was officially 'free', but clubs exploited a loophole that allowed admission 'by programme only.' Supporters could only enter the grounds by purchasing a programme – which cost the usual admission price – at the turnstiles.

Unlike cricket, where gate receipts prove beyond doubt the difference that one-day cricket made to the game's finances, the financial impact of the various changes in rugby league is less quantifiable. The bottom line is that the vast majority of clubs survived professional sport's economic nosedive of the 1960s.

Huddersfield's first Sunday fixture was a 5-5 draw at York on 21 January 1968. Eight weeks later, on 17 March, Fartown made its Sunday bow for a Challenge Cup quarter-final tie against Featherstone Rovers. Huddersfield had reached the last eight with a shock 5-0 victory over St Helens in a classic first round tie at Knowsley Road, before overwhelming Halifax 23-5 in Round 2. A 9-7 victory over Featherstone set up a semi-final tie against old rivals Wakefield at Odsal. This ended scoreless, but Wakefield won the replay 15-10. Wakefield also knocked Huddersfield out of the League Championship play-offs en-route to the title. Unfortunately their season is best remembered for Don Fox's missed penalty with the last kick of the 'Water Splash' Final which handed the Challenge Cup to Leeds.

In seven seasons from 1966-67 to 1972-73 Huddersfield finished between 15th and 25th in the thirty-club League. Their mid-table obscurity was brightened in 1971 by another run to the Challenge Cup semi-final, but Huddersfield lost a try-less game 10-4 to Leigh.

This was the last major occasion for Don Close, one of the outstanding hookers in rugby league during the post-war era. He retired at the end of the 1970-71 season after 408 appearances for Huddersfield. He also represented Yorkshire seven times and Great Britain once, against France in 1967. A player who gave 100% for the Fartowners, he was quick and had the virtue of all the best hookers, the knack of nicking possession when it was most needed.

Don Close (left), playing for Great Britain, politely assisting a French opponent to his feet.

The Accelerating Downward Spiral

By 1970 Huddersfield's financial problems were acute. Refused a £10,000 loan by the RFL in November 1969, the club made a public appeal for £7000. In January 1970 coach Harry Street resigned to save the club £1000 – the last 18 months of his four-year contract. In December 1972 the club narrowly averted a strike by the players who demanded improvements on their pay of £17 for winning and £7 for losing. They settled for bonuses on selected matches, but were asked to take a pay cut. They agreed to play one match unpaid but, to raise funds, all 44 were transfer-listed.

Australians Greg Veivers and Wayne Bennett played four months of the 1972-73 season, but the team's improvement was marginal and temporary. Veivers returned to Australia and captained their national side, and Bennett would earn fame as coach to Premiership winners Brisbane Broncos, and to Queensland and Australia. Huddersfield finished 24th, which consigned them to Division 2 when the clubs again opted for two divisions in 1973-74. Unlike the previous short-lived experiments, the professional game's divisional structure was here to stay, albeit with various modifications that included the creation of Super League in 1996 and, eventually, a pyramid structure that provided a pathway from the amateur to semi-professional game.

To the dismay of Huddersfield's dwindling band of supporters, there was no immediate promotion challenge. In 1973-74 they were tenth in the Second Division, effectively the game's 26th best club, lower than at any point thus far in the club's history. On the pitch and financially, Huddersfield's accelerating downward spiral resembled that of Bradford a decade earlier. In 1974 the club launched its second 'survival' fundraising campaign in three years. Unfounded local rumours that the club was crying wolf undermined the credibility of future fundraising and requests for sponsorship. Huddersfield RLFC was hovering on the brink of extinction.

Huddersfield: Second Division Champions 1974-75
Back Row: T Davies, M Chamberlain, I Van Bellen, D Heppleston, M Branch, C Welsh, A Forster, T Bedford, A Wilson
Front Row: B Smith (Coach), J Hartley, L Shaw, D Hooson, T Miller (capt), T Leathley, T Doyle, B Curry (Asst Coach), Michael Kaye (Mascot)
Insets: D Weavill, G Knight, K Senior

The dire straits were most obvious in the dilapidated state of Fartown. Infamously and embarrassingly, one of the crossbars fell off mid-game. To great hilarity, two maintenance men walked the length of the pitch carrying a ladder to do the necessary, but it took the broad shoulders of Ian Van Bellen to lift one of them up to replace the woodwork.

Nancy Beaumont recalled another symptom of the malaise. Whilst the rest of the country had 'gone decimal' in 1971, the penny that women were required to spend in the Fartown toilets remained strictly imperial. The hut from which Nancy and her colleagues provided refreshments was en-route to the lavatories and the serving ladies kept a supply of 'old pennies', their hut doubling as Fartown's bureau de change. Loo-bound women were discreetly asked to confirm their destination and issued with the correct currency. The groundsman then recycled the pennies to the refreshments hut for the next game. It was a metaphor for a club and a ground that increasingly belonged to a previous generation.

A glimmer of hope for all the teams in Division 2 lay in the disproportionate number to be promoted and relegated each season – four out of 14 from Division 2 and four out of 16 from Division 1. Predictably, a yo-yo existence developed for clubs around the middle of the old table. Of 62 clubs promoted between 1973-74 and 1990-91, 44 came straight back down. Barrow were promoted and relegated six times in this period.

Huddersfield would need significant improvement to threaten promotion, but in 1974-75 coach Brian Smith transformed the Fartowners into a powerful Second Division outfit, lacking polish but brimming with endeavour and team spirit. Galvanised by new signings from Castleford, Glen Knight and Tony Miller, and by the reliable boot of John Hartley who kicked 110 goals, they won 13 of the last 14 matches to nick the Second Division title from under the noses of Hull Kingston Rovers.

From Committee Club to Limited Company

During the close season, the club underwent a seismic shift in management and organisation. The baton was passing from the old order to a more modern, professional and commercial world.

Since 1875 the club had operated under the control of the HC and AC, whose football committee had picked the team. The coach worked with the players through the week, then attended a meeting on Thursday evening to be told what his team was. As the game became more scientific, tactical and professional, the football committee's protection of this power became correspondingly regressive. Tensions between their iron grip and the effective coaching of the players grew, and erupted in a power struggle in 1975. Trevor Kaye, a long-time supporter who joined the committee in the 1970s explained:

> It came to a head around 1975. We'd won the Second Division Championship. Brian Smith was the first team coach. Brian Curry was the second team coach. They won everything they possibly could apart from the Challenge Cup, which was never going to happen because we were in the Second Division.
>
> The committee turned round and said they wanted to sack Brian Smith. I said, 'This just is not on! You won't let a man do his job yet you want to sack him when you think he's done it wrong ... How can you justifiably do that? The Chairman of ICI doesn't go down and tell his men how to mix chemicals. He expects that they know what to do.'
>
> Brian Smith was sacked, but a few days later he was re-instated, because my wife, in her wisdom, got a certain percentage of the members to agree to an Extraordinary General Meeting, which took place at Huddersfield Town Hall. The vast majority of the football committee resigned. We were left with myself, Richard Blandford and three or four more who came on at that particular time. From that point on we said: 'The football committee cannot pick the team. Employ the man and let him do his job. Then if he doesn't succeed you have got some justification to sack him.'

Newly promoted Huddersfield could not afford to significantly improve their squad and the gulf between the divisions was apparent when they were relegated after one season, their five wins all against clubs in the bottom seven.

Business sponsorship, which was becoming increasingly crucial to the clubs' survival, widened the gulf between the two divisions. David Oxley, appointed secretary of the RFL in 1974, was convinced that 'no club will ever again pay its way through the turnstiles alone.' Assisted by the RFL's first ever public relations officer, David Howes, he led an aggressive campaign to obtain sponsorship and related income for the clubs. By 1982-83 this had risen to £413,350, a hundred-fold increase since 1975. The downside to this new money was that businesses wanted to be associated with success. They were more reluctant to pay significant amounts to sponsor the players and the kit of losing teams, and Huddersfield was increasingly one of these.

Trevor Kaye recalled how lack of sponsorship and general finance caused acute embarrassment to the club in 1976. Against the odds, Huddersfield had defeated Division 1 clubs Wakefield (5-2) and St Helens (9-7) to reach the televised semi-final of the BBC2 Floodlit Trophy, away to Leigh on 30 November.

> We were in such a state that we had one set of tatty jerseys. The 'A' team played in them on the Saturday afternoon and we were sat in the bath washing them, then getting them dry for the first team to play in them on the Sunday ... The finance chairman said to me: 'You'd better get some new jerseys for this semi-final. We can't possibly play in these on television.' I said, 'Four days to get a set of jerseys?' There was no way. So we went out and bought a set of white jerseys. The players' wives, my wife, and anybody we could get, stitched a gold 'V' on the front.
>
> The problem came when they went out to play. Soon after the kick-off our scrum half was carried off in absolute pain. We didn't know if he was having a heart attack. We got him in the dressing room and there's a pin which hadn't been removed stuck in his chest. These are the things that kind of stick in your mind. You can see the funny side but it could have been serious.

Huddersfield lost 19-10. It would be their last cup semi-final appearance for many years.

Promotion to the top division was essential to attracting decent sponsorship, and was achieved under the astute guidance of player/coach, Neil Fox, in 1977-78, albeit in fourth place. On 2 January 1978 Fartown staged one the game's historic moments as Fox kicked the third of his four goals in a victory over Oldham. The two points took him past Jim Sullivan's career points-scoring record, which had stood since 1946. Fox's eventual tally of 6220 points remains the all-time career-record.

Four players signed by Huddersfield from Underbank Rangers:
Alan Redfearn (1959) Brian Blacker and Paul Dixon (1982) and Simon Kenworthy (1985)

Four players signed by Huddersfield from St Joseph's:
Dave Weavill (1970), Trevor Doyle (1972), Jimmy Johnson (1978) and Gary Senior (1982)

Five more players signed by Huddersfield from local clubs:
Ray Haywood (1955, Birkby Civic Youth Club), Leo Booth (1960, Flockton), Malcolm Branch
(1970, Deighton Civic Youth Club), Tony Johnson (1973, Paddock Civic Youth Club)
and Peter Cramp (1975, Bradley Civic Youth Club)

This promotion season coincided with further restructuring of the club, precipitated by the ongoing financial problems. The remaining antiquated committee structures and methods of the old guard, which had served the club well in their time, were swept away and HC and AC became a limited company. The first notification of this change came in the club's match-day programme of 19 February 1978 when the controlling group was, for the first time, listed as 'Huddersfield Cricket and Athletic Club Ltd, incorporating Huddersfield Rugby League Club.' The first two directors were Colin Wood, Managing Director of local firm Graham Gratrix, and Roy Brook, a builder. They became Chairman and Vice-Chairman respectively.

The first match-day programme for the 1978-79 season on 3 September, when St Helens were the visitors, included the following statement from the Chairman of the limited company:

> Only a year ago the Club's future seemed bleak, with a financial crisis of considerable proportions, and after a season of the most mediocre playing results. Today, we are back in the First Division and, whilst our financial problems still exist, the efforts put in last year have made an improvement and things look brighter with the introduction of our new £1,000 fortnightly lottery.

No amount of restructuring was going to turn the club's galleon-like problems round overnight. Despite the lottery, the financial situation continued to deteriorate. As was becoming routine for the fourth-placed promoted club, Huddersfield were immediately relegated, denying the club a share of the revenues from the revived attendances being enjoyed in the top division. Unlike most of the yo-yo clubs, this time Huddersfield did not bounce back. By the early 1980s, average crowds at Fartown had slipped below 1000, only their average age increasing. Supporters recalling the heady post-war successes were dismayed by the club's decline, but they had seen nothing yet. The barren years for Huddersfield Rugby League Football Club were now truly beginning.

Chapter 14

Keeping the Dream Alive

The Fartown Ground and Keith Burhouse

Supporters' clubs and volunteers played a vital role in the survival of many rugby league clubs during the 1960s, 70s and 80s. At Huddersfield the Supporters' Club raised more than £12,500 towards the purchase of 14 players in the first 25 years after the Second World War.

Many people contributed to the survival of the once-proud Huddersfield club, but during the club's very darkest days, 1983 to 1994, one man, with the considerable help of his family, effectively saved professional rugby league in the birthplace of the game. Epitomising the power of sheer dogged determination and individual unpaid commitment, Huddersfield RLFC was saved by Keith Burhouse.

It is no exaggeration to say that, without Keith, the Huddersfield club would not exist in its current form, would almost certainly not play in Super League, and might well not exist at all. Without Keith, the magnificent John Smith's Stadium, which the club shares with Huddersfield Town, might never have been built. When Huddersfield RLFC was at its weakest and most vulnerable, Keith and his family were its life-support machine.

Born in 1944, Keith first went to Fartown in his pushchair with his parents and Grandfather. Keith's Grandfather and Great Grandfather had attended the first Northern Union game at Fartown, Huddersfield v Wakefield Trinity on 14 September 1895, so their family dynasty spanned the entire history of the game. When Keith was a little older, in the late 1940s and early 1950s, he stood at the top of the large terrace side. From the mid-1950s onwards he went to most home and away games with his Dad and two friends. Keith's first idols were, like many of his contemporaries, the Australian trio Hunter, Cooper and Devery. Keith acknowledged the impact of such early involvement:

> It's in my blood ... and eventually it took over both myself and my family's life.

Huddersfield v Wigan 1953, viewed from the top of the terrace side

Keith's wife Carol must have known this from the outset. They eventually tied the knot in March 1969 after their wedding was rearranged twice because the dates clashed with Huddersfield fixtures. Keith believed that not many guests would have turned up on the two original dates as they were also Huddersfield supporters.

After leaving school Keith worked in the building trade as an electrical, heating and ventilation contractor. He went on to work for many years at the Polytechnic/University of Huddersfield in building and estates services.

Answering a Cry for Help

In August 1983 John Bailey, Chairman, and John Hillam, Vice Chairman, joined existing directors Roy Brook and Mel Bedford on the board at Huddersfield. Fartown was in a state of disrepair and John Hillam wanted to earn income by turning the track that surrounded the cricket ground into a stock car venue. However, planning permission was eventually refused owing to the potential noise levels in a largely residential area.

John Bailey, who also had stock car-racing links, was a local disc jockey and saw the potential to generate revenue by converting the pavilion into a party venue. He could not see how the rugby club, playing 17 home matches per season before low crowds, and a close season of four months, could be profitable. It appeared that there was a very real potential for conflict between the interests of the rugby league club and the other priorities of the new directors, John Bailey and John Hillam.

On 3 November 1983 the club placed a plea in the *Huddersfield Examiner* asking for volunteers to help with ground repairs, which were essential before the John Player Cup semi-final between Leigh and Leeds, scheduled for Saturday 10 December, could go ahead. Keith accepted the invitation and turned up at the ground on the next training night. He was on his own! Undeterred, Keith took a week's annual leave from his job to carry out the necessary work. He believed that his skills could slow the decline of the Fartown ground, and help in 'bringing back the glory days.' His contributions, however, soon developed well beyond his more obvious areas of expertise.

On the Saturday he started to fit a new roof on the West Stand and by Thursday the ground was passed fit for the semi-final. As Keith said later:

> I continued going to Fartown practically every night after work and every weekend, at first doing electrical, plumbing and joinery work on the ground and also in the pavilion. After only a few weeks of being involved with the club, the Board of Directors asked myself, my Dad Ron and Carol my wife if we would host the boardroom on a match day, and whether I would become a club official. Being a club official meant I could travel on the team bus to away games. This gesture was in appreciation of all the hard work my Dad and I were doing for the club.

> John Bailey and John Hillam convinced me, that if we could get the pavilion turned round as a party venue, it would provide revenue for the rugby club but unfortunately after a few years it never really worked out that way ...

> We refurbished the cricket hospitality room, installing a small bar and a shower room. The hospitality room had a dual purpose as the pavilion was often used for wedding receptions. The bride and groom would use the hospitality room to relax in and get changed before the reception in the main function room. On match days it could be used for boardroom hospitality and was also used by the cricketers for their teas. Unfortunately, the cricketers left Fartown a year or so later when they found another ground to play on.

I did all the plumbing, electrical work and some decorating, and pulled down the dilapidated box at the side of the pavilion that had been used by the cricket club's president. We then started work on the main bar area, firstly knocking down a chimney breast to make room to build a small stage. I did all the electrical work required, and fitted state of the art disco equipment. Along with John Bailey, we made a dance floor with glass panels incorporating lighting that pulsed with the music. I once again did the plumbing, heating and electrical work required fitting a new kitchen with up-to-date catering equipment.

When we had finished the work, the venue was a success, having functions more or less every weekend. Carol and I worked on a voluntary basis helping with the food for these functions.

A new entrance sign, erected in June 1984, welcomes supporters to 'Arena 84', home of the 'Barracudas'. The dilapidated state of the Fartown complex shows in the disrepair of the George Herbert Hirst Memorial to the right of the entrance.

Arena 84 and the Barracudas Era

In 1984, in an attempt to revive the club, John Bailey had Huddersfield RLFC adopt the appellation 'Barracudas' and Fartown was renamed *Arena 84*. Match day cheerleaders paraded large letters that spelled out not 'Huddersfield', but 'Barracudas'. In hindsight, these attempts to promote the club, whilst clumsy in execution, were the right idea but at the wrong time, failing to address the key problems of poor performances on the field and the alarming state of the ground.

Keighley showed how such marketing should be done in the early 1990s, effectively pioneering rugby league's change towards American NFL-style razzmatazz. Adopting the alliterative name 'Cougars', they blitzed their locality with community initiatives, dynamic cheerleaders and tub-thumping pre-match entertainment, all fronted by a *Top Cat*-style child-friendly mascot. In contrast to the Keighley Cougar, Huddersfield could hardly have chosen a less marketable creature than the barracuda, its exotic name at odds with the dour-looking,

180

snakelike appearance of this scavenger of the sea. The name of the 'A' team – Huddersfield Piranhas – had more commercial potential, but the entire makeover lacked the conviction of the full-on commercialisation of the game in 1996. 'Barracudas' lacked the macho aggression implied by creatures such as Bulls, Rhinos, Tigers and Wolves, and the local relevance of Hull Sharks, Dewsbury Rams or, from ice hockey, Sheffield Steelers. Barracudas and piranhas could hardly have been less relevant to a town situated 60 miles from the sea.

Despite the best intentions, Huddersfield failed to excite and attract new, younger supporters, whilst horrifying and alienating older, traditionalist fans who were suspicious of the motivation and priorities of the directors, and saw the changes for what they were, style over substance.

Left: The first Keighley Cougars' logo included a *Top Cat*-style cartoon cougar, the creature's expression combining fun, mischief and aggression.
Right: A barracuda.

Huddersfield Barracudas v Workington before a smattering of spectators in 1986

Trevor Leathley, a centre with excellent anticipation, whose 403 appearances for Huddersfield between 1973 and 1986 included 169 consecutive matches from 1977 to 1982.

Anthony Farrell, who made his debut for the Barracudas in 1985, shortly before his 17th birthday. He rarely missed a tackle or a match and went on to play for Leeds in the first Super League Grand Final in 1998, and in the Challenge Cup finals of 1999 and 2000.

Wally Gibson, a cavalier attacking full back from New South Wales who was a breath of fresh air in his three seasons at Huddersfield from 1989 to 1992

Continuing to patch up the ground, in 1984 Keith Burhouse took another few days' annual leave to do 'something about the floodlights.' About a third of the lamps had not worked for some time, making it difficult for spectators to see and for the *Huddersfield Examiner*'s photographer to take photographs. As the club could not afford to hire a cherry picker, Keith borrowed a safety harness so that he could climb the ladders that were incorporated into the pylons. Equipped with

Fartown's precarious-looking floodlight pylons, which Keith scaled regularly to change the bulbs.

lots of spare bulbs, he ascended the first pylon, but half way 'froze ... terrified.' Gritting his teeth, he continued to the top, eventually scaling all nine pylons. Many of the fittings were so corroded he could not replace the bulbs, but he did what he could and the result was a great improvement. From then on Keith replaced the bulbs on a regular, programmed basis.

Despite all Keith's work on ground improvements the crowds remained very low and he recalls there were often only 300 to 500 supporters, mainly older men, who stuck with the club through thick and thin. Keith suggested that many of the other supporters had deserted to watch more successful teams such as Halifax and Leeds.

In the late 1980s Keith investigated the hot water system, which was installed in the 1930s when the main stand was extended and new changing rooms were incorporated. He discovered that there wasn't any rise and fall in the circulation pipework, a gravity system from the boiler to the hot water cylinder. Inevitably, it had never worked efficiently.

Taking yet another week's holiday, Keith fitted a pump to the circulation pipes, cleaned out the tank and cylinder, separated the showers from the existing hot water system, and fitted an instant gas water heater in each dressing room with new shower units. For the first time in fifty years, players at Fartown had a reliable hot-water system for their showers and baths. As the modifications used less gas, Keith reduced ongoing running costs as well as the considerable installation costs.

The depth of the club's continued impoverishment was evident in the soap provided for the players. Keith remembered that on some match days and training nights there was no soap in the changing rooms.

> I would ask John Bailey for some more. He would get his penknife out and cut a bar of soap in half, one half for the away team and the other half for our lads. This used to be very embarrassing, so I would buy some or bring some from home. The Great Britain squad trained at Fartown in those days, but they still only got half a bar of soap, and in the end I supplied it.

Mixing with the Great Britain squad was one of the few perks for Keith. One filthy March night he was carrying their kit back into the changing rooms with mud all over his face and arms when Andy Gregory shouted to him to get in the bath with the players. Although Keith declined

SPORT

Gripping end to high-scoring draw but

Only 303 people turn up to watch Arena 84 game

By IAN LAYBOURN

Huddersfield Barracudas 32 Keighley 32

A CROWD of just 303—Huddersfield's lowest ever—saw a tremendous fightback and a gripping finish as the sides demonstrated why they have two of the worst defences in the league.

Huddersfield, who have now conceded more than 30 points in each of their last four matches, produced a woeful tackling display in the first half and they looked a well beaten side when they trailed 28-12 after 42 minutes.

But they staged a remarkable comeback, scoring 20 points in 12 bewildering minutes, and suddenly, and quite incredibly, they found themselves 32-28 in front with nine minutes left.

A win that at one stage seemed impossible had become a reality—until the ntful game took another ith only inut Kei

half chance to cross for an equalising try at the corner.

The match hinged on scrum-half Paul Moses's touchline goalkick but the emergency marksman had already surpassed most people's expectations by landing four goals from five attempts and his last-gasp effort was both low and wide.

The draw was a fair reflection of a game which both sides dominated in turn, usually with scrum possession. Huddersfield were badly beaten for the ball in the first half but the introduction of specialist hooker Billy Cook, immediately after Keighley had taken their 16-point lead, changed things dramatically.

The tricky surf ce made it awkward f fen rs br oo m

half, and then they went about the tackle in a half-hearted manner.

The danger signals went up as early as the second minute when second-rower Mick Hawksworth sailed through weak tackling to create a try for stand-off Ricky Winterbottom and full-back Jeff Butterfield and Moses added others inside 26 minutes to make it 16-2, Billy Platt having opened Huddersfield's account with a penalty.

Veteran centre Trevor Leathley marked his 400th senior game by scoring his 107th try after 32 minutes after a blockbusting run from 18st prop Paul Cockerham, but the celebrations were short-lived for slipshod defence enabled Keighley c h Pe r Roe t arve o ry cen B

Phil Johnson and Leathley resulted in winger Mark Cambell going over for a try just before half-time, and this, with Platt's goal, brought the score back to 22-12.

The visitors, however, appeared to be on their way to a comfortable victory within two minutes of the re-start when Roe touched down after kicking ahead.

It looked all over and the small band of supporters began to vent their understandable anger towards the Huddersfield players and officials.

But perhaps history ought to have forewarned them for, when Keighley last visited Huddersfield—on Boxing Day in 1984—the home side came back from 20-6 down to win 36-20.

It was Cook who spark off the revival wh forcer his v o solo

17 April 1986: Huddersfield's lowest-ever attendance of 303 witnessed an amazing 32-32 draw against Keighley. The average attendance in this thoroughly miserable season plummeted to 678, Huddersfield finishing fourth from bottom in Division 2.

the invitation he was soon pushed in with all his clothes on. Later he was able to say with pride: 'I've had a bath with all the Great Britain players and not many people can say that.'

Keith also loved being involved with the Huddersfield players and maintained close friendships with some of them long after their playing days. He would say: 'I did the work at Fartown and they played for Fartown.' Some of them played for nothing because they knew the club was in such dire financial straits. When offered their pay on a Thursday night they would tell him to put it back in the safe to help keep the club alive.

One Saturday night Keith and Carol were working as volunteers in the pavilion at a wedding reception. The weather had been very frosty for over a week and the ground was extremely hard. Everyone expected the game the following day would have to be postponed. However, at about one o'clock in the morning Keith went outside for some fresh air and noticed that it was warmer. The pitch had started to thaw and Keith decided that the game might go ahead after all.

The pipes, however, would still be frozen. When he turned the water on it was evident that there were lots of burst pipes in the changing rooms, the referee's room and under the stand. Without further thought Keith set about repairing the burst pipes. He recalled:

> It was about 4am. I was under the floorboards in the referee's room, the last of the burst pipes to be repaired and I started to cry. I thought: 'What am I doing with my life? We are at the bottom of the league, with a few hundred spectators. They won't know what's going on or what I am doing to get the match on. I don't think we will ever get to Wembley or even have any success at all. We might even fold up.'

Keith completed the repairs and, recovering from his moment of despair, got great satisfaction from knowing that he had made the ground playable.

As well as hosting the boardroom with his father and Carol, Keith had many other match day duties.

> I had to not just do the ground work but to act for the directors and help run match days with my wife Carol and my two sons Neil and Martin. My wife did the catering with the directors' wives for functions in the pavilion and on match days for the directors' lounge and the players. My two sons Neil and Martin helped me around the ground cleaning the seats in the stand and helping me to repair the fences so spectators couldn't get in for nothing. We also had to mark out the pitch for every home game and my sons operated the scoreboard.
>
> My father Ronnie went along most nights to help around the ground and he also organised the car park on match days.

Within 18 months of John Bailey taking over as Chairman all the other directors had left because of disagreements with him. The resignation of Vice-Chairman John Hillam left John Bailey as the sole director and, to Keith, he seemed 'more interested in the pavilion as a party venue than the rugby.' The departure of the directors resulted in even more responsibility falling on Keith and his family.

The club often did not have a groundsman or kit man so Keith carried out these duties. Between them, the family ran the Colts and second team matches. In addition, at this time Hunslet and Dewsbury played their second team games at Fartown. Sometimes, because of the shortage of money, Keith would even drive the team coach.

The introduction of new ground safety standards, following the Bradford City fire tragedy in 1985, piled further pressure on the finances. To pay for the essential ground improvements several talented and recently blooded local players had to be sold, stymying efforts to improve results on the field.

Despite all the financial problems at Fartown, the club decided to organise a fundraising event for the Bradford City victims and their families. The proposal was passed to the local authority, which responded by inspecting the ground, mainly because the main stand at Fartown was an all wood construction, similar to that at Bradford City. Ironically, Huddersfield was instructed to spend money on their ground before the fundraising event could take place.

Keith was given a list of essential work, and he and his family 'worked all hours' to make the ground safe. It included filling a skip with cigarette packets and sweet papers from underneath the stand – the initial fuel, via a lighted cigarette butt, that had kindled the Bradford fire. The game, a charity soccer match, TV All Stars v Soccer All Stars, was given the go-ahead. Veteran footballers such as John Charles, plus celebrities such as Cannon and Ball, David Hamilton and Jess Conrad attracted receipts of £11,500 for the Bradford City Fire Disaster Fund.

Since the earliest years, income at Fartown had been supplemented by a cricket section but by the mid-1980s no cricket had been played at the ground for several years. It seemed sensible to try to re-instate cricket and its associated revenue stream, so it was decided, after a meeting with the Yorkshire Cricket League, that the cricket changing rooms would be refurbished and the square and outfield would be brought up to the required standard for Yorkshire League cricket. Once again the burden of this work fell on Keith Burhouse:

> I fitted new toilets and showers, re-wired the changing rooms and tidied up round the ground. The Cricket League and the community of Huddersfield were very pleased that cricket had returned to Fartown. One important match that took place was India v Pakistan in which Imran Khan graced the turf; also at least two Yorkshire County second team games took place. Unfortunately, cricket continued for only one season, the cricketers leaving because of a dispute with John Bailey ... all the hard work I did refurbishing the changing rooms was in vain.

Keith simply could not be discouraged. Even major acts of vandalism did not deter him. An arson attack set the clubhouse ablaze after Keith had spent many weeks refurbishing it. Even people who thought of themselves as supporters committed acts of sabotage in misguided attempts to upset John Bailey and force his resignation.

On one such occasion, the team was travelling to play Fulham at Chiswick Polytechnic Sports Ground. Keith, in his role as kit-man, went to put the team's playing strip on the bus but was told twice by a club official that it was already on the bus and he should also get on. When they arrived in London there was no kit on the bus. Fulham had no spare kit but offered the use of their second team strip which had just been worn in a match preceding the first team game. Not surprisingly the players were not very happy, and afterwards the press was full of the story. Keith felt 'embarrassed and awful' and was duly reprimanded for his 'oversight.' Many years later he discovered that this shambles had been instigated by some club officials to upset John Bailey. Keith's feelings, the players' comfort and the club's reputation were merely collateral damage to people whose priority was the club's internal political shenanigans.

On another occasion Keith arrived as usual at 8am for a Sunday afternoon kick-off, to mark out the pitch and check the fences. He was horrified to find the fences significantly damaged and, at the scoreboard end, only one post standing and the other post and cross bar on the ground. The post had been snapped off at ground level. Fortunately the club had a spare post. He dug out the damaged post and whitewashed the spare one. One of the directors and a few players helped him to hoist it into position and to fit the cross bar. Keith only completed his usual duties just in time for the kick off.

Damage to the fences was a regular occurrence so that a few spectators could get in for nothing, but in 2011, over 20 years later, Keith learned that the goalposts were also broken by so-called supporters. They were trying to get the game postponed and the club reported to the RFL, in the hope that John Bailey would be embarrassed into resigning.

New Owners

From 1987 onwards John Bailey began to seriously doubt that he could stop the decline at Fartown. Huddersfield RLFC was close to collapse, propped up by profits from the pavilion which was thriving as a party venue. Aware of his unpopularity, he told Keith and his Dad that he had had enough. The rugby was a drain on his finances. He intended to 'fold up' as a professional rugby league club at the end of the 1987-88 season. The lease did not state whether professional or amateur rugby should be played at Fartown, so he intended to join the amateur district league.

It would have marked the end of professional rugby league in the birthplace of the game, a wrench that would probably have extinguished the club. Keith and his Dad pleaded with John. 'This is one of the founder members of the Rugby League. The club was once one of the greatest in the game, you can't fold it up.' John replied that the club had a lot of debt, and 'if it hadn't have been for us we would have been in even more debt.'

After discussions, John Bailey was persuaded to carry on, his main reason being a sense of loyalty to Keith and his family, and his respect for all of their tireless work. He saw that it would be unfair of him to fold up the club with little notice, but warned:

> I know you will work hard to save the club from going out of existence, but if we don't find anyone to take over before the start of next season, it will be the end.

Keith and his dad agreed to do their best to keep the club going, and act, along with John Bailey, as caretakers until someone was found to take over. John said he would advertise the club, which 'will be given away debt free', absorbing the debts himself and bequeathing the club to a new owner, providing that they could offer new investment. He interviewed several applicants, including the Huddersfield ex-Players' Association, but he thought none of them suitable, and the prospect of amateur rugby league at Fartown loomed ever larger.

Meanwhile, Keith and his family continued to work unstintingly, keeping professional rugby league alive during the increasingly desperate search for a new investment consortium.

At the eleventh hour, investors were found. In 1988 a new board of directors took over, under the leadership of Mick Murphy, and injected some much needed capital into the club. A new limited company, HRLFC Ltd, was formed, with Mick Murphy as Chairman, Jim Collins, a local builder, as club President and Neil Shuttleworth, a lifelong supporter, as Managing Director. Together they formed a new Board of Directors.

Keith was very generous in his assessment of John Bailey's time as Chairman of the club. He credits him with sustaining the club through very dark days and handing the club over to the new owners debt-free.

> John kept the debt the club had incurred and it took him 25 years to pay it off ... and he sadly died shortly after paying it off.

The failed attempts to commercialise the club's names – 'Barracudas' and 'Arena 84' – were dropped for the 1988-89 season. This was a popular start with the fans, but unfortunately there was embarrassment at the first home game. Kirklees MBC instructed Keith to close the main stand because of storm damage to the roof. Although the players and officials were allowed to use the changing rooms and the directors and the press were allowed into the Directors' Box, it was standing room only for spectators until the roof was repaired. No matter who the owners were, Fartown was a growing albatross round the club's neck.

John Bailey had retained the ground safety certificate and the lease, and whilst the repair work was carried out Keith liaised between the previous owner, the new owners and the council. Negotiations became very heated over Bailey's determination to retain control of the pavilion, and after several months the lease was split in two with a fence erected to separate the pavilion from the rest of the ground.

The agreement reached with John Bailey required separate gas, water and electricity supplies for the two sections of the ground, and new toilet facilities at the back of the main stand, all of which Keith installed.

The club was still just about functioning. Neil Shuttleworth ran it from a Portakabin under the stand with a staff of three, including a part-time clerical assistant. He bought some new shirts, but a deep 'V' on them provided a handhold for opposing tacklers and they were frequently torn, requiring the sewing skills of Neil's 85-year-old mother.

> She would sew two half jerseys together so that the team could go out in full kit.

The new owners appointed Nigel Stephenson as coach and, assisted by several clubs, notably Featherstone Rovers, Huddersfield assembled a reasonable squad. Even so, the club's winless run, already seven matches long from the previous season, was extended to 20, including ignominious defeats to Mansfield Marksmen, Fulham, Carlisle and Chorley Borough. Neil Shuttleworth remembers 4 December 1988, an away trip to play Hunslet at Elland Road, as a red-letter day.

> We had this feeling that 'today's the day' ... we took a lot of supporters 400 to 500. I was sick twice before the game in sheer anticipation ... it was only by three points, 21-18, but we won, and every Fartown fan in that stand stood up, turned towards the Directors' Box and gave us a fantastic cheer. It was the first win of the new club that led to the Giants.

Eight more matches were won in 1988-89, including, encouragingly, all of the last four, as Huddersfield finished 18th in the 20-team Second Division.

Meanwhile, professional contractors worked alongside Keith to improve the stadium. Progress on and off the pitch was reflected in support for the club, and in 1989-90 average crowds topped 1500 for the first time in a decade.

Hillsborough and the Taylor Report

Just as the club appeared to be turning the corner, another football ground disaster impacted on Fartown. The deaths of 96 Liverpool supporters at Hillsborough in 1989, coming only four years after the Bradford City and Heysel Stadium disasters, persuaded the Government to commission Lord Taylor of Gosforth to lead an inquiry into ground safety. Published in January 1990, the Taylor Report had profound repercussions for Fartown and, eventually, for sport in Huddersfield.

The resulting legislation required the club to close Fartown's wooden main stand until essential work was completed. For practical and financial reasons, this could only be done piecemeal, beginning with rewiring the changing rooms, then plasterboarding the roofs of the changing rooms, the seating above the changing rooms and the Directors' Box. Next came further repairs to the stand roof. All the while, the rest of the stand had to remain shut, as did the back half of the West Stand and parts of the main terracing that was crumbling away. After months of hard work and expense, the local authority allowed seating for about 300 people in a stand that originally held about 4,000.

Kirklees MBC was now closely involved, inspecting the ground regularly and specifying the work which had to be done. They also insisted on a match day Safety Officer, a role which Keith accepted in addition to his other duties, recalling ...

> ... I was responsible for ensuring the safety of supporters and the stewarding of the ground. We got 16 volunteers to steward on match days. I had to make sure they were adequately trained to local authority standards. I had to do pre and post-match inspections of the ground, making sure it was safe for public entry. Mick Murphy held the Safety Certificate and was ultimately responsible.

Eventually, after more hard work, permission was granted to raise the capacity of Fartown – which had once held 35,136 spectators – from 2000 to 6500.

The steady progress at the club continued with new directors Dave Parker and Trevor Park coming on board. Joe Bramley became Chairman and in 1991 Alex Murphy and Terry Flanagan were appointed to the coaching staff for the club's first season in the newly formed Division 3. They were successful, winning promotion as Champions in 1991-92. One of Keith's treasured mementoes was a photograph of himself with Alex Murphy and Terry Flanagan on the balcony of Huddersfield Town Hall with the Third Division Championship Trophy.

Success, however, had come at a price. The club's finances were once more in dire straits and, to meet Division 2 standards, Fartown required a further £50,000 in safety improvements that the club did not have. This figure would rise to between £300,000 and £2 million should Huddersfield win promotion to the top division. Kirklees MBC had already assisted, buying the Fartown lease for £50,000 in 1992. The final straw was a fire that partially destroyed the changing rooms later that year. Fartown, the club's ground since 1878, had become untenable.

Third Division Champions 1991-92

Huddersfield 1991-92: first-ever winners of the Third Division Championship.
Running in a remarkable 173 tries, and with Simon Kenworthy and Jason Gilbert kicking 70 goals each, the Fartowners were just 13 points short of 1000 in league and cup matches.
Back Row: Huck, Sewell, Kenworthy, Scholes, Naidole
Middle Row: Ronnie Burhouse, Karen Hellawell and Sue Ford (Physiotherapists), Louise Hamer,
Keith Burhouse, Jack Balmforth, Dr. David Hooper, Oates, Maskery, Jowett, Boothroyd, Walker,
Lomax, Terry Flanagan (coach), Alex Murphy (team manager), David Parr, Les Coulter,
Frank Doyle, David Parker
Front Row: Brian Henley, Mick Murphy, Gilbert, Thomas, Edwards, Gibson, Jim Collins, Chapman,
Shuttleworth, Cocker, Senior, Joe Bramley, Neil Whittaker

From Fartown to Leeds Road

Scenes from the last match at once-mighty Fartown

In 1992 Huddersfield RLFC entered a ground-sharing agreement with Huddersfield Town to play at Leeds Road for a 'rent' of £1000 per match. As a stop-gap, it made economic sense. Keith Burhouse recalled that:

> The last first team game was played at Fartown on 23 August 1992 against Ryedale-York in a Yorkshire Cup preliminary round. There was a sad feeling round the ground. Fans were taking photos for sentimental reasons. The club officials and players were sad. My wife Carol and Elizabeth Parker washed all the cups and plates up in the board room, my sons Neil and Martin put away the numbers and locked up the scoreboard. I then checked over the ground and locked everything up.

The loss of Fartown for first team matches was a cruel disappointment for Keith and the small group of dedicated fans who had stuck with the club through seasons which had been not so much thick and thin, as thin and thinner.

For a short time Fartown still hosted Academy matches and training sessions, and the club offices were still in a Portakabin at the back of the main stand. Everything required for first team match days had to be transported from Fartown to Leeds Road, where Keith recalled that the Huddersfield Town officials were very helpful and welcoming.

Under the guidance of Alex Murphy, Huddersfield began the 1993-94 season, their second at Leeds Road, with a ten-match winning streak that took them to the top of Division 2. But off the pitch the survival of the club was once again at stake.

The ground-sharing arrangements were designed to sustain the fragile rugby club as a partner in the new Kirklees Stadium project. Adjacent to the Leeds Road soccer ground, the new stadium was funded through Kirklees Stadium Development Ltd (KSDL), whose shareholders were Kirklees MBC (40%), Huddersfield Town FC (40%) and Huddersfield RLFC (20%). Construction of the new stadium had already begun when, in October 1993, the rugby club received a winding-up petition from the Inland Revenue. The £38,000 that the club owed in tax came on top of debts of over £500,000 that had been revealed by club Chairman Mick Murphy. It was the straw that broke the camel's back.

Keith Burhouse was now on an associate board appointed by Mick Murphy to help with the day-to-day running of the club. At one of their board meetings Mick Murphy asked the members if they would be willing to give bank guarantees, as the club had no assets. Keith recalled:

> I was the only person to offer. After the meeting some of the members of the associate board said to me: 'Let the club go down, and then we can take over.' I was bitterly disappointed.

The rugby club's impending liquidation threatened the development of the new stadium, for although it had the smallest share it had attracted other sources of funding, such as a million pounds from the Foundation for Sport and the Arts. This funding would be lost if the club was liquidated. To sidestep this eventuality and thereby safeguard the funding secured for the stadium, Huddersfield RLFC went into administration.

During this most difficult of seasons, the curtain finally came down for Huddersfield Rugby League at the grand old Fartown ground. As Keith remembered …

> In 1993 the last Academy match took place at Fartown and the ground as we know it came to an end. My Dad and I did what we normally did – washed out the baths and showers, and tidied everything away. Carol and Elizabeth Parker did the washing up in the boardroom. I turned off the lights and gave my Dad the keys to lock up for the last time in its present state. My Dad had supported Huddersfield since the 1920s, so I gave him this honour.

Fartown – the sign says it all as the stand is demolished

Eventually, the lease of the ground was handed over to the local authority for £85 and the JCBs came to demolish the Fartown infrastructure. Keith recalled:

> The day the machines came to Fartown and ripped out the terracing was one of the saddest times of my life. They also knocked down the main stand and the west stand. This brought tears to my eyes, to think of all the famous players that played on this great ground and of course all the fans that came through the turnstiles. It was terrible seeing over 100 years of history and all the hundreds of hours of voluntary work gone just like that. While it was being demolished they uncovered an old mine shaft between the west stand and the terrace side, and it had been covered over with railway sleepers and ash. You never know what might have happened if it had collapsed whilst people were walking over it.

Keith ensured that the contractors left untouched the Dave Valentine Memorial Stone that was incorporated into the scoreboard. The stone was moved by the Players' Association, with the approval of the Valentine family and the local authority, to a new location in front of the Supporters' Club. Later, it was moved to face the entrance of the new stadium.

Operating the scoreboard towards the end was Graham Wittrick. His job included collecting the minute hand of the clock from the office, setting the clock going at the start of each half, and returning the hand afterwards, a task which almost landed him in hot water.

The Fartown scoreboard, incorporating, bottom centre, the Dave Valentine Memorial Stone

> After one night match I'd finished the scoring, put all the numbers away, taken the hand off the clock and was taking it back to the office. It was two to three feet long and I carried it like a soldier on my arm. This policeman grabbed me by my shirt collar and threw me against a wall. A sergeant was looking at him and asked 'What's happening?' The officer replied, 'I thought he'd got a gun.'

Needing temporary offices, the club erected two Portakabins on the site of the old main stand, a final footprint on the ghost of Fartown.

For years after Fartown was demolished, it remained the club's spiritual home for hundreds of older supporters. Nancy Beaumont was one of many who were too upset to visit the old ground for quite a while. Eventually, she summoned up the strength.

> We were all heartbroken. It was like I was losing my second home ... I didn't work very far away from the ground and one day – it was a nice day – I thought: 'Well, you're going to have to go sometime Nancy, you might as well go.' So I walked up in my lunchtime. As I was walking up the drive somebody was coming down and they said, 'Have you seen it Nancy?' I said 'No.' He said 'You're not going to like it.' I stood in the middle of the field. I could imagine it all with the ground full and the Lockwood Band playing *Hurrah for the Claret and Gold* when they came out. Two big tears ran down my face. And that was it.

The Administrator's Story

In October 1993 Andrew Wilkinson, a partner in Revell Ward chartered accountants which dealt in insolvency work, received the call to arms as the club's administrator. He assumed control of the club and became a director of Kirklees Stadium Development Ltd, roles that attracted a full page feature in the *Yorkshire Post* and a documentary on Yorkshire Television.

Andrew's first task was to secure funding to kick-start the administration process. Kirklees MBC, protecting both its vested interest in the new stadium and rugby league in the town, provided an initial £40,000 (later supplemented by a further £30,000), enabling him to obtain an administration order from the High Court at Manchester. This meant that the creditors, such as the Inland Revenue, had to stand back and wait, allowing Andrew to prioritise the players' wages which at least kept the club in business.

The funds from Kirklees sustained the club in the short term and Andrew's plan was to keep the successful team intact, to minimise debts and to find a buyer by December, a logical handover time because of the way the fixtures had fallen.

From the start, the administration process was fraught with problems. Andrew's legal advisors, the Leeds-based Brook North Solicitors, who accompanied him to the High Court, were already engaged by Huddersfield Town and withdrew to avoid a conflict of interest. Andrew replaced them with RC Moorhouse Solicitors, all of which took time and energy.

Andrew recalled that the club was not only virtually penniless, but had hardly any assets. There had been no club sponsor for two years.

> They were operating from a cabin at Fartown which they didn't even own and they had literally nothing at all. They owned nothing down at Leeds Road other than the players' contracts.

To get an idea of the players' worth, Andrew sought the help of agent Jeff Wine, a chartered accountant, life-long rugby league fan and Chairman of Bramley. Once valued, the players were offered for sale. There was little interest and none were sold, but at least the club was able to show them as notional assets.

Another possible source of funds was the RFL. At that time the governing body was providing financial support for London Crusaders in the latest attempt to expand the game beyond its traditional geographical heartland. Andrew was therefore optimistic that they would help Huddersfield, one of the game's founder members and the birthplace of the game, at least on the principle that 'charity begins at home.' Meeting RFL Chairman Maurice Lindsay, he was dismayed to be told that funds had been earmarked for developing clubs, not for established ones that had fallen on hard times. It was a philosophy that also frustrated and enraged other established clubs. Keighley Cougars, for example, was twice denied promotion because of re-organisation and restructuring, whilst the London club was fast-tracked into the top division.

Exploring other avenues, Andrew followed up a rumour that some spectators were getting in without paying. He organised the club's staff to physically count the crowds and crosscheck their numbers with gate receipts, but nothing was proved and little extra cash was realised. Andrew also tried to attract Ken Davy to the club, but the timing was wrong as Ken was fully occupied floating his own business. Ken Davy's involvement with rugby league was still three years away.

All these frustrations left Andrew with no alternative but to cut costs, which included the high-profile sacking of first team coach Alex Murphy, entirely for financial reasons as the team was top of Division 2. Andrew Wilkinson recalled the events:

> I began to run out of cash quite seriously late in the autumn and that's when Alex Murphy had to go. I just couldn't support his salary which was not substantial. He was

a bit stunned. That's one of the things with sporting clubs isn't it – 'You can't do that,' he said. 'We'll start losing games!' Obviously there is an imperative to win and the balance between that and the cash side of the business is often not properly understood. Most clubs limp along trying to match the two sides, the playing bit with the finance bit.

With no new substantial sources of funding, Andrew's December deadline for selling the club came and went. He was reluctantly persuaded to continue in the role by his legal advisors, working to an even stricter budget. The players stuck together and saw out the season, but following the loss of the coach, results deteriorated. Having won their first ten matches, Huddersfield lost ten and won ten of the next twenty to finish fifth in the league. They then lost to Batley in the play offs.

Incongruously, during this period of almost unmitigated gloom, the club became European Cup Holders. In 1993 six teams were invited to play in an inaugural European Clubs Championship. They were Batley, Huddersfield, two from the then USSR, and French clubs XIII Catalan and Carcassonne. Only weeks before the tournament was due to start the grand plans collapsed as both Soviet clubs pulled out owing to financial difficulties, closely followed by Carcassonne because of a players' strike, and then Batley. Improbably, this left Huddersfield and XIII Catalan to meet in the 'final' in Barcelona, which Huddersfield won 23-22.

A nine-day tour of France followed. Keith Burhouse and his family missed this rare moment of glory. He stayed at Fartown to look after the ground along with club secretary, Margaret Caldwell, who was responsible for the office. The directors were very grateful, as they could go to Spain and France knowing there was somebody minding the shop back home.

More importantly, the club survived the season, no mean feat for all involved. May 1994 marked a watershed. With no matches and therefore no money through the gates for the following three months, there was little more that Andrew Wilkinson could do to find a buyer and he stepped down as administrator. Reflecting on his time at the club, he concluded:

Keith Burhouse at the
Gillette Rugby League Heritage Centre
in Huddersfield's George Hotel

> I didn't see it as my role to run the company longer term. I was merely a stopgap, to stop the creditors piling in and ruining the club after it went into liquidation and get the club in a state where I could offer it for sale to another party. That's what I was there for. I succeeded on the first point because it's a matter of law that once you are appointed the creditors have to stand back, but I failed on the second in that I didn't find anybody to take the club over and buy it.

The close season was a breathing space to determine a longer-term solution. The club went into liquidation, wiping out its debts, in the knowledge that it would be replaced immediately by a new limited company, Huddersfield Rugby League 1994. Kirklees MBC took over the short-term funding of the club, once again ensuring the survival of both the club and Kirklees Stadium Development Ltd.

Both the football and rugby league clubs knew that the arrangements at Leeds Road were temporary for two years whilst the new stadium was built.

New Owners, New Ground

Whilst the club was in administration, Keith Burhouse and his family continued to assist the day-to-day running of the club. In the summer of 1994 a new consortium took control, and a new Board of Directors was formed with Bob Scott as the Chairman. Keith recalled with regret that he could not become a director as he did not have enough money of his own to put into the club. However, at their first board meeting the new directors unanimously agreed to appoint Keith as an Associate Director in gratitude for all his hard work. With self-deprecating humour, he remarked, 'I was now saddled with the grandiose title of Ground Director with no ground.' Keith had the privileges of a director but with no voting rights or financial ties. He proudly accepted and remained in office for the rest of his life.

Keith's breadth of knowledge and vast practical experience about the workings of a rugby stadium, combined with his technical background, was recognised when he was invited to be the club's client representative in the new stadium project, a role he accepted, working as part of KSDL. With the support of his line manager Colin Blair, Director of Estates at the University of Huddersfield, he was able to devote some of his time to working on this major project.

Involved from the initial planning stages of the stadium, Keith recommended that a building management system be installed to optimise efficiency in controlling the heating, ventilation and air conditioning. So that the rugby players would not be dazzled when catching high kicks, he advised that the floodlights should be higher, safe in the knowledge that he would not have to climb them to change the bulbs.

Paul Sykes and Brian Buckley later increased the rugby club's representation on KSDL to three. Incorporating Keith's ideas, the new McAlpine Stadium was sufficiently completed for Huddersfield's first game against Barrow on Sunday 28 August 1994. Keith was among the 4300 present.

28 August 1994: Huddersfield 50 Barrow 12
A grand start to life in the new stadium as flying wingman Brimah Kebbie touches down.

It was very strange for us, after all the work we had done at Fartown. We only had the referee's tea to make before the game and at half time, and meet and greet the directors from both clubs, plus sponsors in the boardroom. We decided to sponsor a member of the backroom staff, so we didn't feel guilty at not contributing so much to the club as before.

The operators of the stadium's electronic scoreboard were unfamiliar with rugby league scoring, so the old Fartown operative Graham Wittrick sat with them for the first match to pass on his experience. They had a busy afternoon as Huddersfield beat Barrow 50-12.

Keith continued his work for the club at the new stadium for many years. He and Carol were 'the face of Huddersfield', looking after the away team's directors and the sponsors.

The construction of the new stadium, without any delays, was a minor miracle given the tribulations of the rugby club. One of the best stadiums of its size and one of the best in rugby league, it remains a monument to the co-operation between the two professional clubs and Kirklees MBC, and to the individuals whose skill, perseverance and graft kept the most vulnerable of the parties, the rugby league club, afloat. As administrator Andrew Wilkinson commented, 'I held the fort whilst the stadium was built.'

For Huddersfield's rugby league supporters, The McAlpine Stadium was infinitely preferable to Leeds Road and its soccer heritage, and grand indeed compared to decaying Fartown. Yet many supporters yearned for the old Fartown atmosphere that they were unable to recreate from the seats of their much larger new home.

In 1996 Ken Davy took over as chairman of the club that was still convalescing from the dark days of administration. It coincided with a restructuring of the professional game, with a 'summer' season and Super League. Only a year later the club, re-named Huddersfield Giants, beat Hull 18–0 in the Divisional Championship at Old Trafford to return to the top division. The new stadium was an essential requirement in order for the club to enter the new Super League. At last, Keith was able to experience some top-level success. No fan deserved success more.

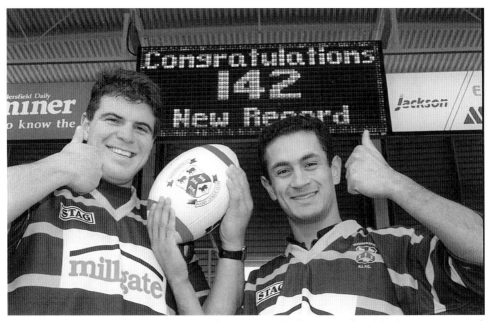

26 November 1994: The McAlpine Stadium was only three months old when it witnessed a record score as Huddersfield hammered Blackpool Gladiators 142-4 the first round of the Regal Trophy. Dave King and Laurent Lucchese celebrate.

In 2007 Keith became seriously ill and was diagnosed with leukaemia. He spent many months in hospital undergoing treatment and chemotherapy and, in remission, underwent a stem cell bone marrow transplant to reduce the risk of the leukaemia returning. This entailed a further nine weeks in an isolation ward to avoid infections as his immune system was compromised. Only his wife, Carol, was allowed to visit him. Unfortunately during this difficult period, Keith's father died and he was unable to attend the funeral.

The Rugby League Heritage Centre in the George Hotel, 9 October 2010: Keith Burhouse, David Gronow, Tom Van Vollenhoven, Ken Senior and Maurice Oldroyd

Awards and Tributes

Keith received a number of awards and tributes for his devotion to the game and outstanding work for Huddersfield Rugby League Club. In April 1989 in a surprise ceremony at Headingley, in front of RFL dignitaries, regional television, local radio, and national and local newspapers, he was awarded the Traveleads Rugby League Top Fan award. This came with an all-expenses-paid trip for two to America to watch an exhibition match between Wigan and Warrington. It was followed by a week's holiday in Florida. John Bailey and the new directors, Mick Murphy, Jim Collins and Neil Shuttleworth attended the ceremony, Bailey telling the *Huddersfield Examiner*:

> No praise is high enough for Keith and his family. They have stuck with the club through thick and thin and the fact there is still a club is down to them.

In addition to his work with the town's professional rugby league club, Keith was involved for a long time with amateur teams and eventually became an independent member of the Huddersfield and District Amateur Rugby League. After he retired from his full time job in 2005 Keith heard that Mike Stephenson, the ex-Dewsbury and Great Britain forward, and Sky Sports pundit was to open the Gillette Rugby League Heritage Centre at the George Hotel in Huddersfield. Keith offered his services and worked alongside Sam Morton and Simon Foster as a volunteer curator, eventually becoming manager of the centre.

Recovering from leukaemia and its debilitating treatments, Keith resumed his work for the club, and at the Rugby League Heritage Centre in 2008. When the George Hotel went bankrupt and closed in 2013, Keith oversaw the removal of all the artefacts into temporary storage at the now renamed John Smith's Stadium. Later that year Keith's leukaemia returned. More chemotherapy followed. His immune system weakened, Keith caught and died of pneumonia at the age of 68 on 8 March 2014.

On 19 March the entire Huddersfield Giants squad formed a guard of honour at Keith's funeral. They joined many famous rugby league faces in a packed St John's Parish Church, Newsome. As the game joined Keith's family and friends in mourning his passing and celebrating his life, Mike Stephenson paid the following tribute:

> Keith was a wonderful gentleman who gave so much to our game, and his loyalty and service to my heritage museum at the George Hotel can never be underestimated. I will miss him and his passing away is a sad loss. The Australians have a great saying that a true friend is a 'brick', solid, dependable, trustworthy and the first bloke you would invite to your barbecue, a mate. It sums up my friend Keith in one sentence.

Mike Stephenson, Simon Foster and Keith Burhouse at the
Gillette Rugby League Heritage Centre in the George Hotel

Keith worked closely for almost twenty years with the Giants' Chairman Ken Davy who also paid fulsome tribute to him after the funeral.

> Throughout his life Keith was a tower of strength for Huddersfield Rugby League Club, his beloved 'Fartown.' There is probably no job he hasn't done or task he wouldn't undertake to help Huddersfield's professional rugby league club survive and prosper. Keith, ably and loyally supported by his wife Carol and all his family, was always ready to lend a hand whatever the task and even in Huddersfield's darkest days he was there to freely give whatever help and support was needed to keep the club going. Never seeking personal reward or recognition, Keith's personal support to Jennifer and I during my past eighteen years at the helm of the Huddersfield Giants, both as the ever-welcoming host to visiting directors of other clubs (again always ably supported by Carol) and as an Associate Director of the Giants, has been as constant as it has been outstanding. I am pleased that last year the success of the Claret and Gold of Huddersfield Giants in winning the League Leaders Shield was something that Keith

was able to share despite his continuing illness. It was also a pleasure for everyone connected with the Club that last year we were able to bestow the first ever 'Lifetime Achievement Award' on Keith and the Burhouse family ... All of us at the Huddersfield Giants and everyone involved in the Game of Rugby League in general are the poorer for the passing of Keith Burhouse.

Keith spent the final two years of his life working, as a volunteer of course, on Huddersfield Rugby League: A Lasting Legacy, the heritage project which has published this book. At the project steering group's request, he gave a detailed interview and provided written memories about his time at the club, which have informed much of this chapter. This remarkable, kind, modest and selfless man died 'in office' as a project volunteer and as the club's longest serving director.

On 22 May 2014, the *Huddersfield Examiner* presented a Special Recognition Community Award posthumously to Carol and to his son Martin. It was Keith's second award of the year. Just over a month before he died, Keith was inducted into the Rugby League Roll of Honour. It was, in the words of Ken Davy, 'an honour which Keith not only deserved but one he was absolutely delighted to receive ... He was a rugby league Giant.'

Keith (right), inducted to the Rugby League Roll of Honour
alongside Ron Girvin and Natalie Gilmour on 27 January 2014

Chapter 15

Ken Davy and the Super League Era

The launch of Super League, the new, top-tier competition to replace rugby league's old First Division, marked the beginning of a new era for the game. A result of negotiations with Rupert Murdoch's BSkyB company which had offered £87 million to televise the game for the next five years, Super League was comprised entirely of full-time clubs and players and revolutionised the sport. The most far-reaching change was a switch from the traditional August to April season to a 'summer' season running from February to September.

Influenced by Murdoch and by the successful, trailblazing 'Cougarmania' marketing campaign at Keighley, the sport as a whole was rebranded during this period. Many clubs chose to adopt American-style 'nicknames' and marketing gimmicks to coincide with the sweeping changes in the sport. While many other clubs introduced suitably macho and aggressive animals to their name and market brand, Huddersfield became the 'Giants'. For Huddersfield, where financial problems and the very survival of the famous club remained serious concerns, the family-friendly potential of summer rugby offered a lifeline, as did the riches of Super League – if they could get there.

The introduction of the 'Giants' moniker saw the club represented by a new mascot, 'Big G'. There were teething problems with the branding, Big G's appearance somewhat at odds with his jovial, child-friendly role. A hairy beast with an unnerving, psychotic expression and sinister, staring eyes, Big G was a fearsome sight, and his short-lived partnership with the even more hideous and menacing Ma G terrified some young supporters, reducing them to tears on occasions. Despite this, the brand grew to be successful. Ma G was quietly retired, malevolent beyond redemption, and Big G was re-designed as a smiling caricature, a favourite at home matches and a popular, instantly recognisable gimmick when fronting the club's many activities in the community.

The club's vigorous and enterprising commercialisation included the reintroduction of its own cheerleaders. This has since expanded into a thriving cheerleaders' school which fields competition teams in several age groups, in addition to providing match day entertainment. Their intricate synchronised routines are a far cry from the well-rehearsed but more gentile performances of the club's early cheerleaders, often featuring gymnastic agilities and spectacular lifts. Progression to the senior squad requires several years' commitment.

The ogre that was the original Big G (left), and, his child-friendly successor (right)

The Giants' Cheerleaders, 2014

The Giants' Senior Squad Cheerleaders 2015
Back: Lauren Wright; Maisie Armelli; Charli English
Centre: Katie Boyle; Robyn Evans; Charlotte Higginson
Front: Lucy Fox; Olivia Rhodes

An Unlikely Chairman

Along with Big G and the cheerleaders, a lifeline arrived in new club chairman, Ken Davy. Ken's appointment, coinciding with the Super League revolution in 1996, proved to be the most positive development at the club for decades and, arguably, since the club was founded.

Dave Thomas, who supported the club from the late 1940s, reflected on the task facing Ken Davy and his directors.

> From the early 1960s to the mid-1990s we'd nearly 40 years of nothing. Leeds, St Helens, Wigan, they've all had their ups and downs, but none that lasted 40 years. That's why Ken Davy has such a job to get the crowd, because we've lost generations. We went nowhere for such a long time.

Ken was an unlikely rugby league benefactor. His father was from London and had settled in Yorkshire after the war. His family had no knowledge, interest or connection with rugby league and Ken freely admits that, as a youngster, he had no involvement or interest in sport. Always 'last pick' for playground matches, he recalls 'having a go' at a game of football at school but, after being hit on the head by a 'very hard, wet and heavy object with laces in it', decided that it really wasn't for him.

Ken was brought up on the east coast at Filey, where there were no local sports teams of any consequence. The only sport discussed at school (outside of the cricket season, which he did follow) was football. His peers seemed to support the likes of Leeds or Manchester United, so to be different Ken picked Arsenal, although he freely admits that he could 'no more tell anyone the feats of Arsenal than he could fly to the moon.' Years later, Ken would became Chairman of Huddersfield Town Football Club and learn about Herbert Chapman's unique achievement of winning the League Championship three times with two different clubs – Huddersfield in the 1920s and Arsenal in the 1930s, a coincidence which rekindled Ken's affinity with the north London club. Ironically, to mark Huddersfield Town's centenary season in 2008-09, Arsenal visited for a pre-season friendly and presented Ken, on behalf of the club, with a bust of Herbert Chapman. A photograph of the presentation subsequently appeared in the Arsenal programme so, by the most improbable route, Ken would one day appear in the programme of his childhood 'favourites.'

That aside, Ken's main interest as a youngster was photography, beginning after he swapped a pair of roller-skates for a camera. He took photographs 'of anything that moved' providing he 'could get it to stand still for a while', spending hours processing and enlarging the prints in his bathroom and making a reasonable amount of pocket money by selling them. It wasn't Ken's first entrepreneurial activity, but it was the one that provided a platform for future business success – and led to his accidental introduction to rugby league.

First contact with Rugby League

Ken's introduction to the sport came on the maiden voyage of the *Oriana*. At the time one of the largest cruise ships in the world, the *Oriana* left the UK in December 1960 with 19-year-old Ken working aboard as the ship's photographer. Three months into the voyage, the ship was somewhere off the Australian coast between Perth and Sydney when a lady approached him and introduced herself as Russ Pepperell's mother-in-law. Ken looked at her in confusion – what on earth did that mean? She said: 'Russ Pepperell, Fartown.' Ken was no wiser, and the conversation went on for several minutes until, exasperated, she asked, 'You are from Huddersfield aren't you?' Ken explained that his family had moved to the town the previous autumn but he had only lived there for two or three weeks before taking his job aboard the *Oriana*.

The woman then explained that she was travelling out to Australia to join her daughter, Barbara, and son-in-law Russ in their new home in Manly. She added that Russ Pepperell was the Huddersfield captain who had lifted the Challenge Cup in 1953. This didn't mean much to Ken at the time, but the *Oriana*'s three-day mooring in Sydney was a big event for the city and Ken arranged to show the whole family – Russ Pepperell, Barbara and their children – round the ship. It was the beginning of a firm friendship, which initially had nothing to do with rugby league.

Invited back to their home, Ken was shown photographs of Russ with the Challenge Cup trophy. 'They are pictures that I am now incredibly familiar with,' reflects Ken, 'but at the time I did not fully appreciate the significance of a victory like that to the club, to the individuals involved in the team, or to the town as a whole.' It was only much later that Ken came to fully appreciate what a momentous event it was.

The friendship blossomed. Every few months Ken would arrive for his three days in Sydney, buy some steaks, take them up to the Pepperell family in Manly and they would spend a convivial evening round the barbecue. On a subsequent trip Russ introduced Ken to Pat Devery and Johnny Hunter. Ken had the pleasure of showing them around the *Oriana*, finishing off with a few beers in one of the lounges and listening to the reminiscences of the former Huddersfield stars.

Ken left the sea in 1963, but the friendships endured. Years later, in 1998, Russ and Barbara accepted his invitation to return to Huddersfield to watch the Giants' first Super League match, while Pat Devery would also make a sentimental return visit to Huddersfield in 2013. Despite these connections though, Ken continued to be relatively apathetic towards sport in general, instead devoting his time to growing and developing a string of successful businesses that saw him become a self-made millionaire.

Financial Involvement with the Giants

So how did a man with no real interest in sport and very little understanding of rugby league become a major financial benefactor of Huddersfield Giants and eventually Chairman of the club? Ken admits that for much of the time between 1960 and 1996 rugby league 'was not even in the back of his mind', although he did take a passing interest in the 1962 Challenge Cup Final. His fiancé Jennifer was a regular on the Fartown terraces and the couple watched the match together on a television bought in preparation for married life.

> I remember the frustration when, I think it was Fox, kicked a drop goal, and whether that was the winning margin I can't quite recall, but it was felt that kicking field goals like that was not really the done thing and we lost that one.

Jennifer, a Huddersfield girl, was to be a catalyst for Ken's later involvement. Her father's enthusiasm was for football and her love of rugby league came from her uncle's influence. She first attended Fartown at the age of nine and continued to support the club regularly until she married Ken and family responsibilities took over. It was from this early start, and after a break of many years, that the interest in rugby league in the Davy household was eventually rekindled.

In 1995, Ken was running the very successful DBS Management Plc, a business which employed 400 to 500 local people, when he was approached by Huddersfield's then-Chairman Bob Scott and the club's commercial manager. They asked him whether he would be interested in sponsoring the team's shirt. Ken knew nothing about sponsorship and his business had no real need to develop a local profile because its customers were nationwide, but his London advisors recommended that it was 'a good deal' and he should 'go for it.' Along with the sponsorship came match tickets and Ken attended regularly along with Jennifer, who enjoyed returning to the sport and team she had grown up with. Ken, meanwhile, was impressed by the potential of the new McAlpine Stadium, which at the time had only two completed sides, and by the intensity and the integrity of the sport.

> If a player stayed on the ground you knew he was injured. There was none of this pussyfooting around and falling over, grabbing your leg, and then thirty seconds later getting up having got a free kick and stuff like that, and it seemed to me – and it's a phrase that I quite like – that it's a man's game for all the family. There is occasionally a bit of fisticuffs on the pitch, obviously, but the tough stuff does take place on the pitch, not amongst the supporters. When you go around to matches, you will often see groups of Huddersfield supporters mixed in with the supporters of the other team and the camaraderie is wonderful. It's perhaps not quite unique, but almost unique in that sense, so it really is a man's game, a tough game, but it's for all the family to enjoy.

Despite Ken's and Jennifer's initial positivity, it was obvious that the club was struggling. Attendances were poor, perhaps not helped by the abbreviated 1995 season which was improvised to handle the transition between winter and summer rugby. In what he now describes as 'a careless moment', Ken invited the club's Chairman to call him should he need any additional help.

> ... very soon after that I got a call ... basically, the club was under ... serious financial pressure. Indeed, they had not long been out of administration and they were in serious danger of either going bust again or being taken over ... by the council. I didn't think that would be a great idea for the club, its history, or its supporters, or indeed the community at large.

So Jennifer and I started to, essentially, give money to the club, and support them, on the absolute understanding that it was anonymous. We wanted no involvement with the club as such. We were happy to come down and see the games. We didn't want to be on the Board. We didn't want to be Chairman, anything like that. We just wanted to help the club financially. We took the decision to do that literally in a half hour conversation with the Chief Executive at the time, and the Chairman, and they walked out with a cheque that evening for almost six figures to clear their debts, and we gave them additional moneys over the next two or three months which took the amount to significantly over ... £100,000. That was all on the principle that it was anonymous.

However, a crunch point was reached when the council, who were essentially being paid the money for rent – KSDL [the management company for the McAlpine Stadium] would probably be more accurate, but I wasn't to know at the time – said that they were not in a position to accept any more money unless they knew where it was coming from, because clearly they knew that it wasn't coming from the people who were running the club. So the Chairman approached me and said: 'Either we've got to stop accepting it or we've got to tell them,' and to be absolutely fair to Les Coulter, who was the Chief Executive, and to Bob Scott, who was the Chairman, they had revealed to no one where the money was coming from. They had respected our confidence completely.

Eventually, Jennifer and Ken talked it over and decided that the club could reveal where the money was coming from. The consequences were immediate and unexpected. A meeting took place and KSDL and the council agreed to accept the money, providing that Ken became Chairman of the rugby club and also became a member of the Board of the stadium. Very reluctantly, Ken agreed. Once the news broke, Ken went from anonymity to the front page of the *Huddersfield Examiner* overnight.

Ken agreed with Bob Scott to take over as Chairman prior to the last game of the season, away at Batley, in January 1996. For Ken, who had only ever been to home games at the new state-of-the-art McAlpine Stadium, Batley's Mount Pleasant ground was an eye-opener to the realities of rugby league's second division.

It was a bitterly cold day. It was absolutely freezing. I was taken down to sit in the seats which were old cinema seats. They had probably seen better days when they were in the cinema. They were bereft of anything that you would call comfort and we sat there in the freezing cold, watching this away game with probably another 600 hardy souls ... it got colder as the game went on. I hadn't been as cold as that since delivering newspapers at Filey in the midst of winter. I just kept looking at my watch and thinking, 'Oh, 20 minutes to half time, ten minutes to half time, three minutes to half time, thank goodness it's half time.' The hooter went and I thought, 'Well at least now we can go and get warm.' More fool me! We literally walked about 20 yards to the side of the stand and stood on a piece of concrete, probably 15 feet square, stamping our feet up and down trying to keep warm ... the lady member of the Board obviously recognised my plight and took pity on me and brought me a cup of coffee from the little caravan that they had selling snacks and stuff – at least I believe it was coffee ... It was definitely intended to be coffee, in a little plastic cup. I'm not a coffee drinker, but I literally stood there for the next five minutes or so with my hands shaking, holding this cup and warming my hands on it. Then, lo and behold, the break was over and we were back into the cinema seats for another gruelling 40 minutes of rugby league on the coldest day that I can recall. Whilst I had a coat on and gloves, I certainly wasn't dressed for the weather.

Now, when I go to an away match, when I think we're going to be in those types of conditions, I wrap up properly for it and find it quite stimulating and enjoyable. So that was my first introduction to rugby league at an away match, and my first match as Chairman. That was a pretty grim day.

Finishing in 9th position in Division 1 after the last match of 1995-96 at Batley, Huddersfield improved to finish 5th in the first summer season of 1996 and then to 2nd behind Hull Sharks in 1997, which saw the Giants narrowly miss out on promotion to Super League but earn a place in the Divisional Championship Final at Old Trafford. The contrast with Mount Pleasant could hardly have been greater and Huddersfield clinched their first trophy under Ken Davy's direction, sweeping Hull aside 18-0. However, after this promising start there were to be several very difficult years for Ken and the club.

1997 Divisional Championship Final winners at Old Trafford
Above: Ali Davys flies over to score.
Below: The celebrations begin.
Back: Craig Weston, Nick Fozzard, Danny Russell, James Bunyan, Matt Sturm, Dave King, Steve Booth, Andy Cheetham, Joe Berry, Ian Fairhurst (Asst Coach), Steve Ferres (Coach)
Front: Paul Dixon, Basil Richards, Paul Cook, Ali Davys, Tony Bowes, Neil Harmon
On ground: Phil Veivers

Huddersfield Giants' Squad 1998
Back: Harold Box (Alliance Coach), Danny Arnold, Basil Richards, Tony Bowes, Neil Harmon,
Dave King, Jeff Wittenberg, Jamie Field, Paul Loughlin, Trevor Commons (Fitness Conditioner)
Middle: Craig Weston, Chris Orr, Danny Russell, Phil Veivers (Asst Coach), Ken Davy (Chairman),
Garry Schofield (Head Coach), Paul Cook, Andy Cheetham, Paul Jackson
Front: Joe Berry, Steve Booth, Guy Adams, Matt Sturm, James Bunyan, Ben Barton, Dean Hanger

Super League Struggles

In 1997, the fledgling Super League competition had problems. Plagued by overzealous administration and flights-of-fancy from both the clubs and the League itself, many Super League clubs were struggling to stay afloat. Following the second Super League season in 1997, the competition's French club, Paris St Germain, collapsed. To replace them, the League promoted Huddersfield, as First Division runners-up. So, at short notice the Giants joined First Division Champions, Hull, in Super League for the 1998 season.

Considering the club's recent rapid progress from a modest base, a mere three months' preparation time to bridge the chasm between the First Division and Super League was woefully inadequate. Unsurprisingly, the club was hopelessly ill-equipped for the realities of competing at the top level amongst the sport's elite.

An enthusiastic crowd of over 12,000 packed into the McAlpine Stadium for the club's first ever Super League match, but it was a disappointing affair. In a sign of things to come, the Giants were brushed aside by defending champions Bradford Bulls. Far from the glory days that had been envisaged at the competition's inception, Super League proved to be a grim reality for the Giants, at least initially. Struggling to compete, Huddersfield won just two games in the 1998 season. As the club attempted to stablise there were some high-profile casualties, including head coach Garry Schofield, who was dismissed after just 12 matches because he lacked the necessary coaching qualifications. He was replaced by Mal Reilly.

The club predictably finished bottom of Super League III, but avoided relegation as the league was expanded from 12 to 14 teams for the following season. Despite this reprieve, the club didn't fare much better in 1999. Another disappointing campaign saw the Giants win only five of 30 games and finish bottom of the league once again. Mal Reilly left the club at the end of the season as the coaching merry-go-round continued.

At the end of the 1999 season, as part of Super League's sweeping proposals, the Giants accepted the financial incentive to 'merge' with another struggling club, Sheffield Eagles, to the almost universal dismay of the supporters at both clubs and throughout the game. In practice this meant that the playing squads and staff of both clubs were to be amalgamated, with home matches taking place in both Huddersfield and Sheffield. As later revealed by Ken Davy, the original proposals would have seen both Huddersfield and Sheffield remain as individual entities in a lower division while the 'merged' club would effectively be a new entity in Super League, a model that has been used effectively in Australian rugby league. However, this did not eventuate and the entire concept was widely rejected and derided by fans. A similar merger between Hull and Gateshead was equally unsuccessful. While the merger concept was intended to 'save' faltering clubs from extinction and allow wider exposure for Super League, it had virtually the opposite effect and is now widely condemned as an embarrassing chapter in the sport's history.

Despite finishing bottom of the league in 1999, Huddersfield, as a merged club, once again avoided relegation, albeit continuing with its amended identity. For the 2000 season, the squads and staff of Sheffield and Huddersfield were combined and Sheffield coach John Kear took over as head coach of the merged side, which was officially known as Huddersfield-Sheffield Giants but was referred to mockingly by many rival supporters as 'Shuddersfield'.

As the club broke with history and tradition by merging with Sheffield, the Huddersfield Rugby League Players' Association celebrated history by opening its Hall of Fame at the McAlpine Stadium. An initial 21 Fartown greats were chosen, of whom five survivors attended the ceremony on 22 April 1999 – Ken Senior, Peter Ramsden, Tommy Smales, Jeff Bawden and Russ Pepperell.

The plan for the initial season was to play three home games at Bramall Lane in Sheffield with the rest taking place in Huddersfield. However, owing to its universal unpopularity, the concept was effectively abandoned before the end of the 2000 season and the second and third Sheffield games were moved back to Huddersfield. As revealed later, the death knell for the merger for Ken Davy came when the Association of Premiership Clubs blocked proposals for a separate Huddersfield team in the Northern Ford Premiership.

> ... the concept behind the merger with Sheffield was that each club, Sheffield and Huddersfield, would continue in the second division, the division below Super League. The intention was to create a completely new club and, in fact, to test the concept of Super League, because we were going to create a new club which wouldn't be

called Huddersfield, it wouldn't be called Sheffield, and it certainly wouldn't be called "Shuddersfield" ... whether it would have been the "Pennine Something" or the "Yorkshire Something" or whatever, but it was to test the concept of Super League as bringing something new to sport which, in essence, it would have done.

That was the plan that we were committed to, then unfortunately and, I think stupidly, for all the wrong reasons, the ... decision-making body voted to fire Huddersfield – Fartown – to eject it from the game. So the result was that Sheffield would have stayed in the lower division, "Shuddersfield" would have been a new club, but there wouldn't have been a Huddersfield. For me, for the name of Huddersfield to disappear from the annals of rugby league was unthinkable, because, the reality is Huddersfield gave birth to the great game of rugby league, 29th August 1895, in a meeting at the George Hotel. For me to be Chairman of a situation that saw the name of Huddersfield disappear was absolutely unthinkable. I hadn't worked as hard as I had, with colleagues, to save the club and to start building it, for that to happen.

So, I would have been very enthusiastic about Huddersfield and Sheffield continuing as clubs in the lower division, and for this new concept of a rugby league club to be tested. I think it was a great opportunity, but given that the original Huddersfield was ejected from the game – the licence was taken away – that became absolutely untenable.

So the only way then was to make a hotchpotch of a merger, and we called ourselves Huddersfield and Sheffield, and we genuinely tried to make a go of it, but it was self-evident that the game we played over in Sheffield was poorly supported. Equally, we gained a number of fans, but we didn't take massive support over from there either. So it became very quickly obvious that it was a doomed strategy and we reverted the following season to Huddersfield, and the Huddersfield Giants has moved forwards since then.

Obviously, quite a few people understandably protested. There was a march from the old Fartown ground past the George Hotel, and I came down and addressed the crowd and tried to answer their questions and assuage their concerns. But in the event, because of what happened at the RFL, the concept of what we wanted to create fell apart, and I was then determined to ensure that the name of Huddersfield Giants and of Huddersfield in rugby league was perpetuated because I could not in any way, shape or form have sanctioned the disappearance of the name of Huddersfield from rugby league.

On the field, John Kear strove manfully to blend two very different squads of players, most not of Super League quality, but the club struggled once again, winning only four matches in the 2000 season, three of them against Wakefield Trinity Wildcats, as Huddersfield-Sheffield finished bottom of Super League. To everyone's relief, the merger was then scrapped and the two clubs resumed as separate entities for the 2001 season, with Huddersfield Giants continuing in Super League and Sheffield Eagles being reformed in the Northern Ford Premiership.

Stanley Gene, the Papua New Guinea international who breathed life and enthusiasm into every team he played for

Following the disastrous 2000 season, John Kear was sacked as coach and, after a vigorous screening process, a little-known Australian named Tony Smith was appointed as his replacement, having paid his own air fare to attend the interview. The new appointment initially seemed to have little effect as Huddersfield lost the first 15 matches of the 2001 season, surely condemning the club to a long-overdue relegation. However, an embarrassing 78-point hammering by Bradford Bulls was a turning point. Led by lively new signings such as Brandon Costin and Stanley Gene, the club managed to win six and draw one of their remaining 13 games to register their best Super League points total, effectively doing so in half a season. What's more, this gave the team a real chance of not finishing bottom of the league for the first time. Ironically, Wakefield, the one Super League club against which Huddersfield had enjoyed relative success, had their appeal against a four-point deduction for salary cap breaches upheld, condemning the Giants to a fourth consecutive bottom-of-the-league finish. Mercifully, they were relegated, albeit after their best – although still very modest – season in Super League.

In the four Super League seasons between 1998 and 2001 the Giants lost 91 times in 109 matches, suffering some embarrassing, heavy defeats along the way. Furthermore, the club's continued avoidance of relegation, for a variety of technical reasons, while clearly being out of their depth, drew the ire and contempt of the wider rugby league community. This was particularly damaging to the club's reputation, which they set about rebuilding in the less pressured lower division.

The Giants in Super League 1998-2001

Season	Played	Won	Drawn	Lost	Points			Points	Position
					For	Against	Difference		
1998	23	2	0	21	288	825	−537	4	12th of 12
1999	30	5	0	25	463	1011	−548	10	14th of 14
2000	28	4	0	24	502	1026	−524	8	12th of 12
2001	28	6	1	21	613	926	−313	13	12th of 12
Totals	109	17	1	91	1866	3788	−1922	35	

Relegation and Promotion

Despite relegation to the semi-professional Northern Ford Premiership, Ken Davy continued his financial support, enabling the Giants to remain a full-time professional outfit with Tony Smith as coach. Retaining top stars such as Stanley Gene as well as promising young players like Eorl Crabtree, 2002 was a far cry from the struggles of the previous four seasons. The club was unbeaten for the entire league campaign, drawing only one match against Whitehaven and winning their last 29 games in all competitions. Along the way the Giants accumulated 1156 points, equalling Leigh's 1986 record for points in a league season. The team won the Buddies Cup, as it was then known, and also the Northern Ford Premiership Grand Final against Leigh in October 2002, thus securing promotion back to Super League for the 2003 season.

On reflection, Ken Davy regards the Giants' relegation from Super League in 2001 as a blessing in disguise.

> My objective when I took over the club was to get into Super League. Given that we were in the doldrums at the time that was a fairly bold objective. However, I've always felt it is important to have a clear objective, and the fact is that we did get into Super League within three years. The equal reality was that, for the club, it was too soon. We simply weren't ready, and we spent three years really performing very badly in Super League, and you would go to an away match or indeed a match at the stadium and you'd think, 'Well, if we're ahead at the end of the first half that'll be a moral victory.'

So we had some pretty tough times and I think on one occasion we had a sixteen game run of defeats and of course, eventually, we were relegated from Super League ... in fact that turned out to be the making of the club. What we were able to do was recognise the problems we'd had and take the time to resolve them ...

... Much as I can say with hand on heart that relegation was the making of us, at the time it didn't feel like it. It felt awful, and I was very close at that point to saying, 'Enough is enough. I've done my best. It's now for someone else to take on.' It was a very difficult decision to not walk away at that stage. I didn't, we got back into Super League, and we're doing so much better now. But to give you a straight answer to that question, I was very, very close to walking away at that stage, because I felt I had done everything, I'd put my heart and soul into it and the fact is we hadn't been able to stay in Super League.

The previous three years or so, we would not know whether we were going to stay in Super League the next season. When we got into Super League the first time we did it with about three months' notice and so we had no time to assemble a team. There was then, 'Are we going to be relegated?' ... and the fact is you didn't know so you couldn't really build and we were always struggling to attract the kind of players we really needed to prosper in Super League. But then, having been relegated, we were able to go back and re-build. The fact was that we kept a full-time squad and we went through the whole of the (league) season unbeaten.

Growing Success and Confidence

After the exploits of the 2002 season, the Giants were cautiously optimistic about their return to Super League in 2003. With a settled coach in Smith and the boost of a number of impressive signings, including the return of influential Australian Brandon Costin, fans were hopeful that the bleak days of the club's previous Super League tenure were behind them. Despite this optimism, the Giants remained overwhelming favourites with bookmakers and opposition fans to be relegated, which was unthinkable for Ken Davy who desperately hoped that the Giants had turned a corner.

The fixture planners were not kind and the 2003 season saw a difficult start to Huddersfield's second attempt at Super League life, with an opening-night defeat to Warrington followed by further losses away at Wigan and Leeds – albeit with much more credible performances than in the past - leaving the club winless and bottom of the league once again. The fourth fixture saw the daunting visit of defending Super League Champions St Helens, who were unbeaten and had looked unstoppable in the opening three rounds. In the build-up to the match, St Helens coach Ian Millward took the opportunity to publicly criticise Huddersfield's Costin for an incident in 2001 involving an injury to St Helens star Sean Long. Costin responded with a man-of-the-match performance as the Giants pulled off a stunning upset, defeating the defending champions 36-22.

This marked Huddersfield's coming of age in Super League, the start of a memorable run. The Giants turned the McAlpine Stadium into a fortress, producing several more fantastic upsets throughout the 2003 season, including home victories over Leeds and Wigan for the first time in many years. The club went on to secure 11 wins and a creditable 10th position, a massive improvement from their previous Super League tenure, exceeding all expectations.

At the end of the 2003 season, coach Tony Smith departed the club for Leeds Rhinos, where he would go on to achieve great success. His replacement was former St Helens assistant coach Jon Sharp, who had also previously worked as an assistant at Huddersfield under Smith. Once again being tipped for relegation, largely owing to the reputation built over previous years, the

Left: Paul Reilly, who began his career at local amateur club Moldgreen. An outstanding full-back, he played 206 matches for Huddersfield from 1996 to 2007, and was named in the Northern Ford Premiership 'All-Star Team' in Huddersfield's promotion season of 2002.

Right: Chris Thorman, winner of the Northern Ford Premiership top player award in 2002, and man-of-the-match in the 2002 Grand Final. He holds the Giants' records for most points (36), tries (4) and goals (10) in a Super League game, a 68-16 victory over Leigh Centurions in 2005. Chris returned to the Giants as a coach in 2011. Both of these players played twice for England.

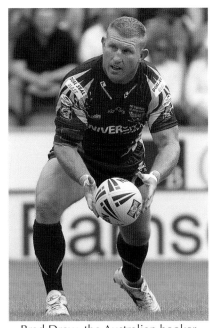

Brad Drew, the Australian hooker who was the supporters' player-of-the-year in each of his first three seasons at Huddersfield.

club continued to improve, briefly topping the table early in the season and eventually finishing 7th, just outside the play-off places. The Giants also made their first appearance in a Challenge Cup semi-final since 1971, their cup run ended by St Helens.

These successes, though moderate, were a far cry from the Super League struggles of 1998-2001, and the Giants were beginning to regain respect throughout the rugby league community. The 2005 season was one of further consolidation as the club added high-profile recruits, the dynamic Australian hooker Brad Drew and his compatriot, centre Michael De Vere. The first Australian international to join Huddersfield since Bob Hagan in 1965, De Vere was arguably the club's most high-profile signing in 40 years. Equalling their record of 12 wins in a Super League season, the Giants finished 8th in 2005, once again narrowly missing out on the play-offs.

The squad was further boosted by several significant signings in 2006, including New Zealand international scrum half Robbie Paul from Bradford Bulls. Now established in Super League, Huddersfield's 2006 season was dominated by their

Challenge Cup run. Following a convincing victory over Salford City Reds in the quarter final, the Giants went on to Odsal Stadium for their second semi-final in three years under Jon Sharp. This time the opponents were the mighty Leeds Rhinos, who were still coached by former Giants boss, and Sharp's former mentor, Tony Smith. Huddersfield were massive underdogs, and most fans limited their hopes to seeing a closer, more competitive semi-final than the Giants' one-sided defeat to St Helens in 2004. Instead, Huddersfield produced arguably their best performance for decades to record a 30–12 victory and qualify for their first Challenge Cup final since 1962.

The only disappointment was building delays at Wembley that denied Huddersfield the opportunity to play in the first rugby league match at the newly developed stadium.

Robbie Hunter-Paul, with Pat Devery's photograph behind him.
The great New Zealand scrum half later returned to Huddersfield in a promotional role.

Instead, the club from the birthplace of rugby league played their final at Twickenham, the home of rugby union. Although the Giants lost the match 42-12 to the all-conquering St Helens team, this first appearance in a major final for 44 years was another significant landmark in the club's progression.

The start of the 2007 season saw the Giants continue to strengthen their squad with a number of impressive additions, including three former NRL-winning Australians in John Skandalis, Jamahl Lolesi and Shane Elford. Expectation was high that the club would continue to progress, but the season got off to a terrible start. Seven consecutive Super League losses cast the Giants adrift at the bottom of the table. The familiar jeers from opposition fans returned and bookmakers quickly installed the Giants as relegation contenders. Many fans began to question coach Jon Sharp's ability, especially following that morale-sapping seventh defeat against fellow-strugglers Salford.

Sharp remained steadfast, pointing out that, although Huddersfield were bottom of the League, their matches had been close and they had, paradoxically, the second best defence in the league. On 1 April the Giants finally recorded their first win of the season, an emphatic 74-4 victory over National League 2 side York in the Challenge Cup. At the time, it seemed scant consolation for the club's poor start.

The next Super League match five days later saw the Good Friday visit of rivals Wakefield. In contrast to the Giants, Wakefield had enjoyed a great start to the season, riding high in the league despite pre-season predictions of a relegation battle. Pre-match, the Giants' players and supporters endured derision and mockery from Wakefield's large, boisterous and vocal travelling support. Their laughter turned to stunned silence however, as the Giants scored in the opening minutes of the match, and continued to score seemingly at will, eventually running out emphatic 56-12 winners.

This first league victory in eight attempts was backed up just days later on Easter Monday with an away win at Warrington. Another win the following Sunday against perennial title contenders Wigan lifted the club off the foot of the table. Unbelievably, this Giants' run extended to nine consecutive victories, including a comprehensive and elusive first Super League victory over Bradford Bulls in front of the Sky television cameras. Huddersfield had now beaten every other Super League club. Making a mockery of his early season criticism, Jon Sharp won the Super League Coach of the Month awards for April and May.

The Giants' winning run came to an unexpected end with a shock 14–12 away defeat by Salford, but in comfortably their best Super League season to date, the club went on to finish 5th, qualifying for the play-offs for the first time. Unfortunately, they fell at the first hurdle in a 22-16 defeat against Hull FC at the KC Stadium. Despite this, the season had certainly been a roller-coaster ride for everyone involved.

Buoyed by the improvements of 2007, a home Super League record crowd of 15,629 watched the club's opening day defeat of 2008 against Leeds, the biggest attendance at a Huddersfield home match for many years. A 64-12 victory over Castleford in February proved to be a false dawn. A season that started with great optimism was a rare step back as the Giants finished out of the play-off positions in 10th. On 2 June Jon Sharp was sacked after a poor run of results culminated in a 48-0 hammering away at Catalans. Chairman Ken Davy praised Sharp's contributions but felt that a new coach was needed to take the club forward.

The new coach for 2009 was experienced Australian Nathan Brown, who came with a strong pedigree having previously been successful as coach of NRL side St George-Illawarra Dragons. Brown's first season coincided with the arrival of another experienced Australian in former New South Wales State Of Origin full-back Brett Hodgson, who was immediately named team captain. The duo had an immediate impact and the resurgent Giants enjoyed their best Super League season yet, finishing third in the league and once again reaching the final of the Challenge Cup, now returned to the reconstructed Wembley. After a very competitive game they lost, somewhat unluckily, 25–16 to Warrington. Until 2013, Ken Davy remembered this as his proudest moment with the club.

Ken Davy and Nathan Brown lead out the Huddersfield Giants team
at Wembley v Warrington Wolves in 2009

I think that would have to be leading the team ... at Wembley for the Challenge Cup Final against Warrington ... we thought we had a really good chance of winning. However, as everyone knows, in the 19th minute we lost one of our key players at the time, Kevin Brown, and we narrowly lost the game.

... you go out from the tunnel and you have the welcome from the fans and the fireworks and so on, and then the game starts, and you have to come back through the tunnel, up the lift back to the stand. When I got back, which only takes a couple of minutes, Warrington had scored their first try and they showed the build-up to it and it was clear as a bell that it was a knock-on. Absolutely clear as a bell, and yet the try was given. I just got there as it was being awarded, and then, later in the game, there was another try – I think it went to the video ref – and there were very few people in the stadium who agreed with the video ref. The decision went against us to the astonishment of the majority of the people at the time.

The fact is, we lost, but that had to be the best – one of the proudest moments.

Similarly to 2007, a season of such great promise ended with a relative whimper as the Giants once again disappointed in the play-offs by losing twice, first to St Helens away and then at home to Catalan Dragons. Despite this, Brett Hodgson was voted Super League 'Man of Steel', Nathan Brown picked up the award for Coach of the Year and the Giants were voted Club of the Year. The fans could see the great progress being made on the playing field, and the Giants were now established as genuine contenders.

On 28 March 2010, Scotland international Danny Brough, recently signed from Wakefield, made his debut for the Giants. He would prove to be a key signing as the team became established as a real power in Super

Brett Hodgson, Super League Man-of-Steel 2009

League over the next few years. Despite finishing two places lower in 5th in 2010, for the first time the Giants continued their form into the play-offs. A narrow 18-12 home win over Crusaders was followed by a superb 22-34 victory away to bogey side Warrington, which saw Huddersfield progress to within 80 minutes of the Super League Grand Final. Unfortunately a 42-22 defeat at St Helens marked the end of the road for another season, but the club had broken new ground.

The Giants began 2011 at the Millennium Stadium against Warrington. Former captain and fan-favourite Brett Hodgson had, to the puzzlement of most fans, not been offered a sufficiently lengthy contract to keep him at the club, and thus ironically made his debut for Warrington in this match. Although the Giants won this game 28-18, it was the start of a run in which Warrington, predictably inspired by Hodgson, would often hold the whip hand over them. A 4th-placed finish represented another good season but the play-offs were a major disappointment, as two straight losses including an embarrassing 47-0 defeat by Warrington saw the Giants once again flatter to deceive at the business end of the season.

Further strengthening for 2012 raised expectations that the talented squad would finally be able to fulfil its undoubted potential. The Giants led the league in April and seemed like potential title contenders. However, the club suffered a calamitous mid-season collapse in form, as speculation over the future of coach Nathan Brown and other key personnel coincided with a run of injuries and the loss of the club's usual training pitch, a local show leaving it unplayable. Following the announcement that Nathan Brown would be leaving for St Helens at the end of the season, morale dropped away altogether. Some heavy defeats hastened the end of Brown's time at the club, and assistant coach Paul Anderson faced the difficult task of finishing the season as best he could. The team limped into the play-offs in seventh position, but the early season zest had deserted them. Predictably in the circumstances, the Giants failed to make an impact on the play-offs, losing heavily 46-10 away at Hull FC. Despite this, former Bradford Bulls and St Helens prop Anderson impressed enough to be appointed head coach on a permanent basis. He had served a long apprenticeship since joining the club as an assistant to Jon Sharp in 2007.

The turmoil and frustrations of 2012 undoubtedly made the task of expanding the fan-base, a continuing priority for Ken Davy, that much harder.

> I realised when I took over the chairmanship that the club had a great history. Yes, it was in the doldrums ... and if we had a 1500 crowd it was a good gate. But I did appreciate that the club had been very successful and well-supported between the wars and, of course, the Team of all Talents, 1914 etcetera, having swept all before them and won all four trophies and that sort of thing, so I did absorb that and take great pride in it and I still take great pride.
>
> What I hadn't realised was how difficult it would be to attract support back to the club, or indeed new support because, having lost so many supporters over those years and essentially two generations of support, I didn't fully appreciate what hard yards it would be getting people back.
>
> What we know now is that if we can get people to come to three games there is a very good chance they will become strong supporters of rugby league and ultimately season-ticket holders. When you think now that we have over three times as many season ticket holders as we used to have attendees for those early matches, it does show you how far we've come.
>
> From that 1500 we're now averaging certainly over 7000 and at times have been close to 8000 so that's a four to five-fold increase in the support, which is a massive increase. To ... break even, say about 12,000, we don't need to double again. It would be nice to – double would put us at 15,000.
>
> We are absolutely going the right way and it's exciting to think that ... and encouraging, but also we have to recognise that it has been a very hard and a very costly journey to get to where we are now. At one stage a couple of years ago an accountant friend of mine worked out that I could have given every attendee at every home match a £20 note and it would have been less expensive over the last 15 years.

'We Are Top of the League'

In the close-season prior to 2013, Paul Anderson made his intentions clear. Bemoaning a lack of toughness over the previous seasons, his signings significantly increased the size and strength of the Giants' forwards. Brett Ferres from Castleford, Craig Kopczak from Bradford, Stuart Fielden from Wigan and Tongan international Ukuma Ta'ai from New Zealand Warriors supplemented established stalwarts of the pack such as Eorl Crabtree. Talismanic half-back Danny Brough was made captain whilst the core of the backs, rampant in the first part of 2012, remained unchanged. A notable feature of the team was the high proportion of local, Yorkshire-born players, Yorkshire-born players such as home-grown duo Leroy Cudjoe and Jermaine McGillvary, who formed a devastating centre-wing partnership.

Great long-serving players of the 2013 League Leaders' team:
Top: Danny Brough. Centre: Luke Robinson, Michael Lawrence
Bottom: Leroy Cudjoe, Eorl Crabtree and Jermaine McGillvary

The season started well with four straight wins including the scalps of St Helens and Wigan. An unexpected home defeat at the hands of Bradford coincided with the absence of Danny Brough, although Paul Anderson refused to acknowledge this as an excuse.

Unlike the false dawns of previous seasons, the Giants continued their form and by early May Huddersfield, Wigan and Warrington had broken away at the top of the league. Each had spells of form when they looked the best team, but it was the Giants who peaked with a wonderful win at Wigan on 9 August taking them clear at the top of the table. The League Leaders' Shield was theirs to lose, and was sealed on 1 September with a majestic 40-0 victory over Wakefield in front of the Sky cameras. It was the first piece of major silverware that the club had won in the Super League era, and the first time the club had topped the table since 1933.

Left: Ken Davy awaits the presentation of the League Leaders' Shield
alongside RFL Chairman Nigel Wood.
Right: The players celebrate after their 40-0 victory over Wakefield clinched the Shield.

Andy Wilson of *The Guardian* wrote:

> Under Davy's generous stewardship, Huddersfield have become a model club for others who hope to launch a serious challenge to the established and better supported heavyweights such as Wigan and Leeds – finally becoming the sixth table-toppers in Super League's 18th season. They have invested heavily in youth development ... for Davy and the club's older supporters the sight of claret and gold ribbons on the underwhelming and previously little-loved League Leaders' Shield – the club's first major trophy of any form since they were crowned champions in 1962 having finished fourth in the table – represents a dream fulfilled.

Having triumphed during the regular season, the Giants entered the play-offs full of confidence, beginning against fourth placed Wigan at home. Despite a promising start, Wigan's magnificent defence was too good on the day, the visitors earning a 22-8 victory. This loss meant that despite such a fantastic season, Huddersfield were thrust into a sudden-death match at home to long-time play-off nemesis Hull FC. On this occasion the Giants were able to gain some measure of revenge, thrashing Hull 76-18 to move to within 80 minutes of the Super League Grand Final. Unfortunately, the Grand Final dream came to a predictable if hard-fought end at the hands of Warrington, the Giants going down 30-22 at the Halliwell Jones Stadium.

Despite the ultimate disappointment of once again missing out on a Grand Final place, it was refreshing for fans across the game to see Huddersfield challenging usual suspects Wigan, Warrington and Leeds for honours. In many respects, the Giants were the team of the season, and this was reflected in the honours that flowed their way:

Coach of the Year: Paul Anderson

Man of Steel: Danny Brough

Super League Dream Team: Danny Brough, Leroy Cudjoe, Eorl Crabtree, Brett Ferres, Shaun Lunt

Giants in the 2013 Super League Dream Team:
Brett Ferres, Eorl Crabtree, Leroy Cudjoe, Danny Brough and Shaun Lunt

The Giants in Super League 2003-2014

Season	Played	Won	Drawn	Lost	Points For	Against	Difference	Points	Position
2003	28	11	1	16	628	715	−87	23	10th of 12
2004	28	12	0	16	518	757	−239	24	7th of 12
2005	28	12	0	16	742	791	−49	24	8th of 12
2006	28	11	0	17	609	753	−144	22	9th of 12
2007	27	13	1	13	638	543	95	27	5th of 12
2008	27	10	1	16	638	681	−43	21	10th of 12
2009	27	18	0	9	690	416	274	36	3rd of 14
2010	27	16	1	10	758	439	319	33	5th of 14
2011	27	16	0	11	707	524	183	32	4th of 14
2012	27	14	0	13	699	664	35	28	7th of 14
2013	27	21	0	6	851	507	344	42	1st of 14
2014	27	17	3	7	785	626	159	37	3rd of 14
Totals	**328**	**171**	**7**	**150**	**8263**	**7416**	**847**	**349**	

The Giants' feat of topping the Super League table was the culmination of a decade of development and a just reward for the hard work not only of Paul Anderson and his squad, but also of coaches Tony Smith, Jon Sharp and Nathan Brown and the former players who had served the club with distinction. It was also testimony to the staff who served the club and helped to build it from the ground up, and of course to Ken Davy, who took over a club in the doldrums, witnessed a dark period in which it became a laughing stock and then oversaw its rise to the very top.

The 2013 World Cup saw Leroy Cudjoe and Brett Ferres help to take England to the brink of the World Cup Final with some excellent performances, not least in the trouncing of Ireland in front of a sell-out crowd in Huddersfield. Two other Giants players led their countries; Craig Kopzak captained Wales while Danny Brough enjoyed an outstanding tournament as captain of Scotland.

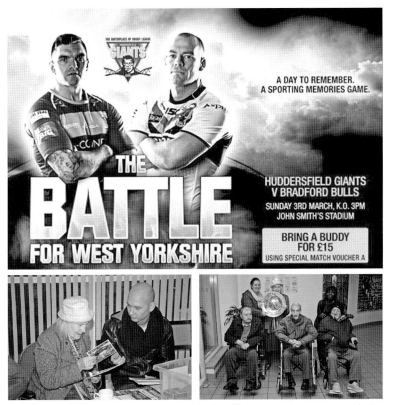

Top: The Giants' home match against Bradford Bulls in March 2013 was designated a 'Sporting Memories Match'. Partnered by the Sporting Memories Network, the club promoted sporting memories as an effective way of delaying the onset of Alzheimer's disease. Pre-match, children from Crosland Moor, Lindley and Scholes junior schools recorded almost 150 interviews with supporters about their memories of supporting the club.
Bottom: Residents of Abbey Place, a Larchwood Care Home, pictured with the 2013 League Leaders' Shield on their visit to the stadium, where they shared their sporting memories

Then and Now

In 2013, Giants fans old and new had something to celebrate after so many years of struggle. The team was re-established as a force in the world of rugby league. For those with long memories, it also opened up the delightful, if subjective, debate of comparing the merits of the modern team with the great Huddersfield teams of the past.

The Case for the Past

Of course the game has changed out of all recognition since the days of the Team of all Talents, since the glories of Len Bowkett's successful side of the inter-war years and even since the 1950s era of Valentine, Henderson, Hunter, Cooper and Devery.

Traditionalists look back fondly to muddy winter rugby played by part-time players at traditional grounds such as Fartown. Some are still not convinced that the modern game represents improvement with uncontested scrums the most frequently cited disparagement. How would modern players cope with the slog of defending unlimited numbers of tackles? Would their kicking, so crucial to turning the opposition, be so long and precise, or their catching be so secure, with the larger, heavier, muddier leather ball of a century ago? How would they cope with players dribbling such a ball at their feet, a regular route to the try-line for Albert Rosenfeld? Could the colossal 'hits' of the modern-day forwards as they contest the hard yards down the centre be so frequent or powerful if no substitutions were allowed? Would the risk of injury and the need to play a full eighty minutes see more attempts to run for the space and less running at the man?

Reports suggest that, in the days before cameras and after-match reviews, it was possible to get away with more foul play. Evidence of this is provided by 'Achates' in a letter to the *HDE* published on 5 November 1928 about a particularly unsavoury game between Huddersfield and Hull KR at Fartown:

- there were 58 scrums of which Huddersfield won 37

- these were fiercely contested scrums in which the hooker and prop forwards played a key role in winning possession, and players indulged in a considerable amount of, what was politely described as 'argy-bargy' on the blind side of the referee

- the referee awarded 32 free-kicks of which 23 were to Huddersfield; 9 were for offences under the play the ball rule; 5 for obstruction; 5 for dangerous kicking or tripping; 2 for offside; 1 for feet up in the scrum; and 1 for the now effectively obsolete offence of 'not putting the ball in straight' (these were, of course only the offences that the referee saw)

- the referee was considered to be 'somewhat lenient' even though one player from each side was sent off

- Huddersfield eventually won by 13 points to 4.

Modern coaches almost universally regard the Easter fixture schedule as 'demanding,' but how would their squads cope with the old Christmas programme of three matches in four days, with no substitutes allowed? Huddersfield's festive period usually included two keenly contested derbies against Halifax, home and away over Christmas Day and Boxing Day.

Until the modern era, nearly all rugby league players had another job outside the game. Many of these were physically demanding occupations. Their training sessions were usually limited to Tuesday and Thursday evening each week.

Any comparison between players of different eras should take into account the impact on performance of the many differences between then and now in:

- how the game was organised
- how the game was played
- the lifestyles of the players.

The Case for the Present

Traditionalists argue that great players would adapt to the training and demands of any era, and still be great players. The table below indicates the very significant physical differences between different eras, showing the heights and weights of three Huddersfield teams. They are:

- the first choice team of 1919-20, the season that would prove to be the last hurrah for the Team of all Talents, when they added three more trophies to the four they won in 1914-15
- the team that played against Hull in the Yorkshire Cup Final on 22 October 1938
- the Giants' first choice starting XIII in 2014.

Players Then and Now

	1919			1938			2014		
Position	**Name**	**Ht**	**Wt**	**Name**	**Ht**	**Wt**	**Name**	**Ht**	**Wt**
Full back	Holland M	5' 6½	12st 0	Taylor WJ	5'9	11st 2½	Grix, S	5' 10	13st 10
Wing	Rosenfeld A	5' 5½	12st 4	Johnson W	5' 9½	11st 0	McGillvary J	5' 10	15st 2
Centre	Habron R	5'9	12st 0	Madden D	5'7	11st 7½	Cudjoe L	6'3	16st 1
Centre	Wagstaff H	5'10½	12st 8	Fiddes AE	5'9	12st 1	Wardle J	5' 11	15st 2
Wing	Moorhouse S	5' 8½	13st 0	Markham R	5'9	12st 9	Murphy A	6'0	14st 11
Stand Off	Davies J	5'9	12st 4	Pepperell S	5'5	11st 0	Brough D	5'8	13st 1
Scrum Half	Rogers J	5'4	12st 0	Grahame T	5'6	10st 7	Robinson L	5'6	12st 8
Prop	Higson JW	5' 11	14st 2	Sherwood H	6'0	15st 6	Crabtree E	6'6	18st 6
Hooker	Lee A	5'9	14st 0	Whitehead H	6'0	13st 13	Lunt S	5' 10	14st 9
Prop	Swinden A	5' 10	13st 11	Evans DM	5'7	15st 3	Kopczak C	6'4	17st 0
Second Row	Sherwood A	6'0	14st 0	Hughes E	5' 11	14st 0	Ferres B	6'1	15st 13
Second Row	Gronow B	6'0	14st 2	Shaw JD	6'0	13st 5	Lawrence M	6'0	16st 0
Loose Forward	Clark D	5' 10	14st 4	Bailey R	5' 10	13st 1	Bailey C	6'2	15st 1
Average		**5'9**	**13st 2**		**5' 9¼**	**12st 9**		**5' 11¾**	**15st 2¾**

2014 team compared to 1919 team		2014 team compared to 1938 team	
Percentage increase in height	**Percentage increase in weight**	**Percentage increase in height**	**Percentage increase in weight**
4.0	15.9	3.6	20.2

On average the modern players are two and a half inches (6.5cm) taller than their 1938 counterparts, and two and three quarter inches (over 7cm) taller than the 1919 team. This is consistent with the incremental increase in average height of the general population.

The percentage increase in average weight of the modern team compared to the 1938 and 1919 teams is significantly greater than the percentage increase in average height, confirming the impact of more scientific training methods and diet, and the full-time professional status of the modern players compared to their earlier part-time counterparts. The average weight of the 2014 team is just over two and a half stones (15.9kg) heavier than the 1938 team and just over two stones (13.2kg) heavier than the 1919 team. Leroy Cudjoe, a centre in the modern team, is taller and heavier than any of the 1938 Huddersfield players. Eorl Crabtree, a modern giant in every sense of the word, is six inches taller and three stones heavier than his 1938 counterpart at prop, Herbert Sherwood.

The one anomaly in the trend for players to become taller and heavier over time is the average weight of the 1919 team, which is heavier than the 1938 team. Both were successful, but the 1919 Team of all Talents would appear to be powerful athletes for their time, perhaps one of the reasons for their phenomenal success.

There can be little doubt that players of previous eras would face a huge challenge against the physicality of the modern full-time professional players, but the argument that, presented with the challenges, opportunities and physical conditioning of a different era, good players would adapt and still be good players, is a powerful one.

A surprising comparison between the teams is the players' places of birth. Given the increased speed and frequency of international transport, the modern team might be expected to have the most overseas players, as in Premier League Football, but the reverse is true.

This maybe somewhat anomalous as Huddersfield's 2014 team had by far the lowest number of overseas players in Super League, and possibly the lowest number seen since the competition's inception.

Nationality	1919	1938	2014
American	1	0	0
Australian	1	3	1
New Zealander	0	0	0
Scottish	0	1	0
Welsh	3	4	0
English (born in Yorkshire)	7	2	11
English (born outside Yorkshire)	1	3	1

The exhibition, Huddersfield Rugby League: A Lasting Legacy which ran from October 2013 to April 2014 helped to attract 20,000 visitors to the Tolson Memorial Museum. It featured life-size statues of great international forwards Eorl Crabtree and Douglas Clark. Reflecting the 100 years between their respective eras, Eorl is taller by eight inches and heavier by 4 stones 2 pounds.

Above: Lindley Junior School Boys' choir, who opened the exhibition with a rousing rendition of *Hurrah for the Claret and Gold*, the song written to celebrate Huddersfield's 1890 Yorkshire Cup-winning team.

Below: Pictures from the Tolson Museum Exhibition

Just the Start of Something

The Huddersfield club has experienced the highest of highs through the Team of all Talents, and the lowest of lows, when Keith Burhouse and his family stood between it and extinction. It is overwhelmingly owing to Ken Davy's financial support that the club has progressed from the nadir of administration to achieve such success in Super League. All the fans fervently hope this is the dawn of a new golden era, with entertainers to match the greats of the past such as Wagstaff, Rosenfeld, Markham, Cooper and Smales, and for achievements to rival those of the 1930s, the 1950s and, of course, the Team of all Talents.

When interviewed by the *Huddersfield Examiner* after the Giants won the League Leaders' Shield, Ken Davy commented:

> This is a tremendous moment for this famous club, and as Chairman I couldn't be prouder. So many people have put in so much hard work over the years ... This was an occasion for everyone to savour. The fact it's 81 years since we last finished at the top of the table underlines what a magnificent achievement this is.

> But I want to make it clear that we see this success as the start of something rather than the end. I've always said success is a journey and not a destination, and the long, hard journey I've experienced since becoming chairman 17 years ago is far from over. I intend to do everything within my power to make sure that lifting the League Leaders' Shield is just the start of a new golden era for Huddersfield Giants.

Rugby league is the only sport that knows precisely when – 29 August 1895 – and where – the George Hotel, Huddersfield – it was born. As the only village, town or city in the world that is the known birthplace of a sport, Huddersfield has, now and forever, a unique sporting heritage. It is a heritage that demands and deserves a thriving rugby league club.

The old ground and the new

HUDDERSFIELD C. & A. C. FOOTBALL 1888-9.

FIRST TEAM.

DATE.	CLUB.	WHERE PLAYED.
1888		Home
Sept. 15	Birch	Away
,, 22	Cleckheaton	Home
,, 29	Halifax	Away
Oct. 6	Hull	Away
,, 13	Dewsbury	Away
,, 20	Lennox	Away
,, 22	Guy's Hospital	Leeds
,, 24	Cambridge University	Away
,, 24	County Trial	
,, 27	Leeds Parish Church	Leeds
,, 31	County Trial	Home
Nov. 3	Oldham	
,, 6	Smoking Concert	Away
,, 10	Wortley	Leeds
,, 10	Yorks. v. Northumberl'd	Away
,, 17	Mossley	Durham
,, 17	Yorkshire v. Durham	Home
,, 24	Castleford	Manchest'r
,, 24	Yorks. v. Lancashire	Away
Dec. 1	Rochdale Hornets	Away
,, 8	New Brighton	Home
,, 15	Batley	Away
,, 22	Manningham	Home
,, 26	Rochdale Hornets	Away
,, 29	Batley	Home
1889		Home
Jan. 5	Leeds St. John's	Away
,, 9	Maori Team	Home
,, 12	Wakefield Trinity	Away
,, 19	Manningham	Home
,, 26	Halifax	
Feb. 2	Dewsbury	Away
,, 2	Smoking Concert	Dewsbury
,, 9	Castleford	Home
,, 9	Yorkshire v. Cheshire	Bradford
,, 16	Mossley	Home
,, 16	Yorkshire v. Somerset	
,, 23	Birch	Home
Mar. 9	Selby (Yorks. Cup Tie)	

Mar. 5	Hull	Home
,, 9	Oldham	Away
,, 16	New Brighton	Home
,, 23	Birch	Away
,, 30	Leeds Parish Church	Home
April 13	Leeds St. John's	Away
,, 20	Wakefield Trinity	Home
,, 22	Cleckheaton	Home

SECOND TEAM.

DATE	CLUB.	WHERE PLAYED.
1888		
Sept. 15	Charity Cup—v. Trinity	Home
,, 22		
,, 29	Halifax	
Oct. 6		Away
,, 13	Dewsbury	
,, 20	Wortley	Home
Nov. 3	Leeds Parish Church	Away
,, 10	Oldham	Home
,, 17	Wortley	Away
,, 24	Castleford	Home
Dec. 1	Rochdale Hornets	Home
,, 8	Hill Side, Bradford.	Away
,, 15	Batley	Home
,, 22	Manningham	Home
,, 26	Rochdale Hornets	Away
,, 29	Batley	Home
1889		Away
Jan. 5	Leeds St. John's	
,, 12	Wakefield Trinity	Away
,, 19	Manningham	Home
,, 26	Halifax	Away
Feb. 2	Dewsbury	Home
,, 9	Castleford	Away
,, 16	Mossley	Home
Mar. 2		Away
,, 9	Oldham	
,, 16	Hill Side, Bradford.	Home
,, 23		Away
,, 30	Leeds Parish Church	
April 13	Leeds St. John's	Away
,, 20	Wakefield Trinity	Home
		Away

THIRD TEAM.

DATE.	CLUB.	WHERE PLAYED.
1888		Away
Sept. 29	Holmfirth 2nd	Away
Oct. 27	Paddock 2nd	Home
	Leeds Parish Church	Home
Nov. 3	Castleford Hornets 2nd.	Away
,, 10	Broughton Rangers	Away
,, 17	Kirkburton 2nd	Home
,, 24	Otley Clarendon 2nd	Away
Dec. 1	Kirkburton 2nd	Home
,, 8	Rochdale Hornets	Home
,, 15	Otley Clarendon 2nd	Home
,, 22	Paddock 2nd	Away
,, 26	Dewsbury Clarence 2nd..	
,, 29	Castleford Hornets 2nd..	Home
1889		Away
Jan. 5	Leeds St. John's	Away
,, 19	Castleford	Home
,, 26	Dewsbury Clarence 2nd.	Home
Feb. 2	Holmfirth 2nd	Home
,, 9	Castleford	Away
,, 16	Lockwood 2nd	Away
Mar. 9	Broughton Rangers	Home
,, 16	Rochdale Hornets	Home
,, 23	Lockwood 2nd	Home
,, 30	Leeds Parish Church	Away
April 13	Leeds St. John's	

Captains—1st Team, H. ARCHER.
2nd,   3rd, F. C. WATKINSON.

Hon. Secs.—1st, GEO. HARROP, North Villa.
2nd, A. E. CLAYTON, 63, Laburnum Terrace, Bradford Road.
3rd, F. C. WATKINSON, West Place.

Dressing Room—George Hotel.
Ground—The Club Ground, Fartown.
Club Colours—Claret and Gold.
An Omnibus will be provided to take the Players direct to the Ground on the occasion of a home match.

ALFRED JUBB, PRINTER, HUDDERSFIELD.

THE "HOLLIDAY" CHARITIES CUP.

FIRST ROUND, September 15th.
Played on the Grounds of First-named Clubs.
1. Longwood v. Grange Moor.
2. Paddock v. Primrose Hill.
3. Moldgreen Rangers v. Hall Bower.
4. Outlane v. Crosland Moor.
5. Golcar v. Hudd. Albion.
6. Honley v. Deighton.
7. Dalton v. Milnsbridge.
8. Shepley v. Lepton Highlanders.
9. Lascelles Hall v. Lockwood Rangers.
10. Huddersfield C. & A. C. 2nd v. Trinity.
11. Almondbury v. Paddock Congregational.
12. Kirkburton v. Lockwood
13. St. Thomas' v. Cowcliffe.
Byes—14 Lindley   15 Netherthong   16 Netherton

SECOND ROUND.
A   Golcar or Hudd. Albion v. Lindley
B   St. Thomas' or Cowcliffe v. Huddersfield C. & A. C. 2nd or Trinity.
C   Shepley or Lepton v. Netherton.
D   Almondbury or Paddock Congregational v. Lascelles Hall or Paddock Congregational.
E   Kirkburton or Lockwood v. Lockwood Rangers.
F   Netherthong v. Moldgreen Rangers or Hall Bower.
G   Outlane or Crosland Moor v. Dalton or Milnsbdge.
H   Longwood or Grange Moor v. Honley or Deighton.

THIRD ROUND.
I   J   K   The winner of round   A   v. winner of round   G
L   ,,   H   ,,   C
   ,,   E   ,,   B
   ,,   F   ,,   D

SEMI-FINAL.
M   The winner of round   K   v. winner of round   I
N   ,,   J   ,,   L

FINAL.
The winner of round   M   v. winner of round   N

Huddersfield Cricket and Athletic Club (Rugby) Football Fixtures Card 1888-89

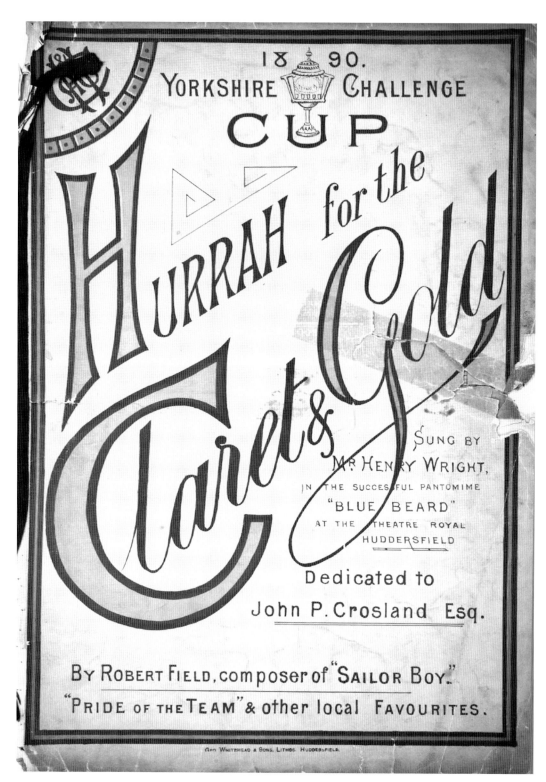

Title page of sheet music written to celebrate
Huddersfield winning the Yorkshire Cup in 1890

Huddersfield's first match against a Northern Union touring team, a 19-8 defeat to the All Blacks on 12 October 1907

Front cover of a menu for a Dinner, given to the 1947 New Zealand tourists

Huddersfield Giants' Shirt Amnesty 2013: supporters were invited to trade in their old Giants'
shirts for a £10 discount on the club's 2013 replica shirt. In partnership with former player
Stanley Gene and sponsors Bond It, the club shipped the old shirts out to Papua New Guinea
where they were donated to deprived families.

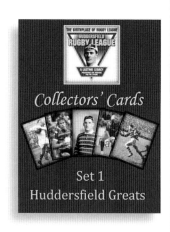
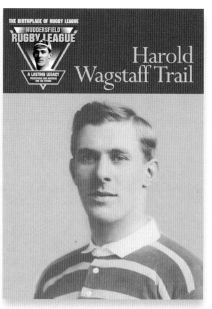

Title page of the Harold Wagstaff Trail,
a three-mile walk around Holmfirth and Underbank,
and original box designs of two sets of Collectors' Cards. The cards feature
Huddersfield players from Harry Huth in 1878 to modern day players such as
Danny Brough and Eorl Crabtree.

Bibliography

From the RFL Archives, University of Huddersfield:
RFL Yearbooks
RFL Management Committee minutes
Tom Webb Scrapbooks
David Raybould, Club and Competition Manager RFL: Women and Girls History

Huddersfield RLFC and Supporters' Club publications:
Fartown Yearbooks 1952 to 1970; 1981
Testimonial Books: Jeff Bawden; Ken Bowman; Douglas Clark; Lionel Cooper; Frank Dyson; Alex Fiddes;
Ben Gronow; Johnny Hunter; Bob Nicholson; Peter Ramsden; Russ Pepperell; Ted Slevin; Dave Valentine
Fartown Supporters 1921-1946
Fartown Supporters' Golden Jubilee 1921 to 1971
Sheet Music: *Hurrah for the Claret and Gold*

Books:

Chadwick, Stanley	*Claret and Gold: 1895-1945*	The Venturers Press, 1945
Collins, Tony	*Rugby League in Twentieth Century Britain: a social and cultural history*	Routledge, 2006
Collins, Tony	*Rugby's Great Split*	Routledge, 1998
Collins, Tony	*1895 and All That*	Scratching Shed Publications, 2009
Frost, Terry	*Huddersfield Town FC: Complete Record 1910-1990*	Breedon Books Publishing Co Ltd, 1990
Gronow, David	*100 Greats: Huddersfield Rugby League Club*	Stadia, 2008
Gronow, David	*Images of Huddersfield Rugby League Club*	London League Publications, 2010
Gronow, David	*Three Fartown Aussies: Hunter, Cooper, Devery*	London League Publications, 2012
Heywood, Brian	*Bradford Bulls RLFC: A Local History Scheme of Work for Primary Schools*	Sports Inspire Educational Publishing, 2010
Heywood, Brian	*Huddersfield Rugby League: A Local History Scheme of Work for Primary Schools*	Sports Inspire Educational Publishing, 2015
Heywood, Brian (Ed)	*Huddersfield in World War I*	Upper Calder Valley Publications in association with Huddersfield Rugby League: A Lasting Legacy, 2014
Heywood, Brian; Heywood, Freda Heywood, Malcolm	*Cloth Caps and Cricket Crazy: Todmorden and Cricket 1835 to 1896*	Upper Calder Valley Publications
Jacobs, Barbara	*The Dick, Kerr's Ladies: The factory girls who took on the world*	Constable & Robinson Ltd, 2004
Midwinter, Eric	*Parish to Planet: How Football Came to Rule the World*	Know the Score Books Ltd, 2007
Sanders, Richard	*Beastly Fury: The Strange Birth of English Football*	Bantam Books, 2009
Sheard, Stuart	*Making Up The Numbers*	Drop Kick Books, 2013
Sheard, Stuart	*Let Them Play By All Means*	Drop Kick Books, 2012
Williams, Graham; Lush, Peter; Farrar, David	*The British Rugby League Records Book*	London League Publications, 2009
Williams, Graham	*The Code War: English Football Under the Historical Spotlight*	Yore Publications, 1994

From the collection of David Thorpe:
HC and AC Minute Book, 20 August 1926 to 19 August 1932
HC and AC Press Cuttings Book, 25 November 1927 to 25 June 1932
HC and AC Gate Receipt Book, 11 October 1930 to 18 August 1938

Newspapers:
Huddersfield Chronicle
Huddersfield Daily Examiner
Huddersfield Examiner
Huddersfield Weekly Examiner

Oral Interviews with:

Roger Armitage
Nancy Beaumont
Bill Boak
Catherine Boak
Robert Boak
Leo Booth
Kevin Brook
Graham Buckley
Keith Burhouse
Jennifer Davy
Ken Davy

Brian Dobson
Lucy Eastwood
Steve Eastwood
Gerald Furness
Shirley Furness
Gail Doughty
Jenny Doughty
Emma Hodgson
Jean Horne
Harold Mitchell Jowett
Trevor Kaye

Maurice Oldroyd
Chris Roberts
Ken Senior
Neil Shuttleworth
Jeff Slevin
David Thomas
David Thorpe
Ian Van Bellen
Andrew Wilkinson
Alan Wimpenny
Graham Wittrick

Presentations by Professor Tony Collins:
Harold Wagstaff and the Birth of Rugby League in Huddersfield
Harold Wagstaff

Websites:
www.ckcricketheritage.org.uk
http://www.forgottenbooks.com/readbook_text/Football_1000003794/445
Great Britain Historical GIS Project, www.VisionofBritain.org.uk
www.huddersfieldrlheritage.co.uk
http://www.huddersfield1.co.uk
www.sportsinspire.co.uk
http://en.wikipedia.org/wiki/List_of_towns_and_cities_in_England_by_historical_population